I0799403

IMAGES
of America

REISTERSTOWN

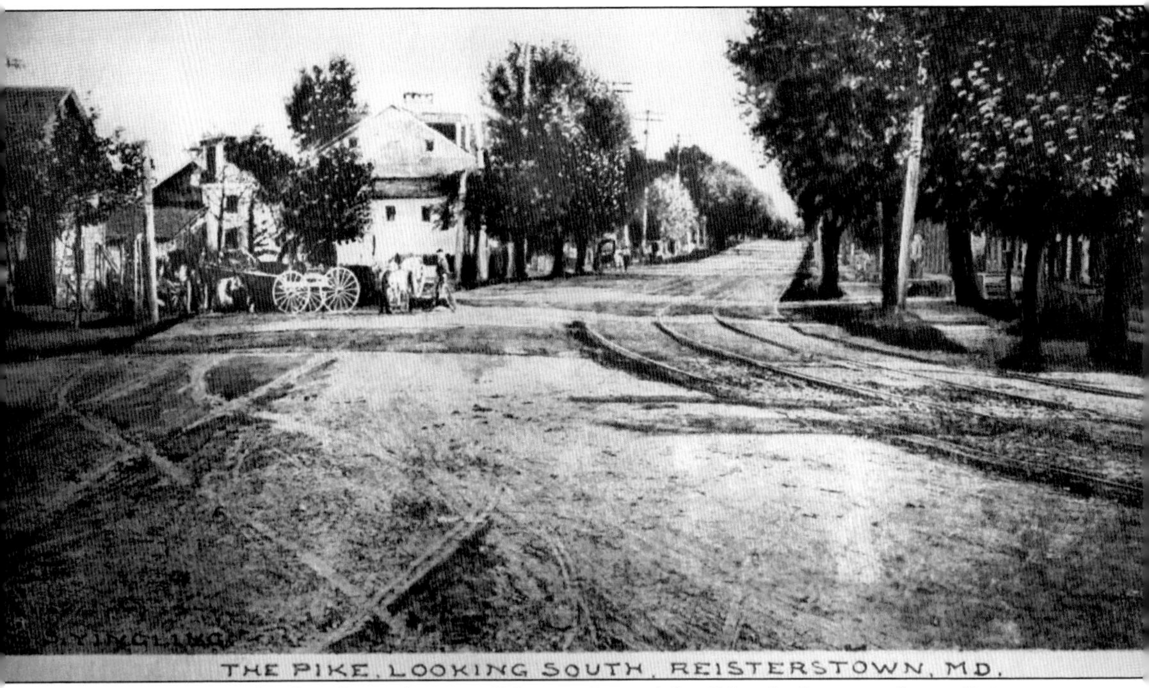

This view marks the place where it all began. It is of the Pike, looking south, on Reisterstown Road in the year 1901. John Reister, founder of Reisterstown, saw potential as he stood at this intersection where several Native American trails converged in 1758. He moved his wife, Margaret Sohn, and six children, Elizabeth, Catherine, Mollie, Peggy, John, and Philip, there. With fortitude and industry, he created a thriving town that catered to weary travelers heading to and from the Baltimore Harbor. The image appears on a postcard published by S. S. Yingling. (Courtesy of the Reisterstown Room.)

On the Cover: This photograph captures a moment in the aftermath of the Great Reisterstown Fire of February 11, 1928. The image shows a neighboring Glyndon fire truck, just one of 18 fire trucks called to put out the blaze that day. The photograph was provided by James Eline of the Eline Funeral Home in Reisterstown, whose father was one of the firefighters present that day.

IMAGES
of America

REISTERSTOWN

Gayle Neville Blum

ARCADIA
PUBLISHING

ISBN 978-0-7385-8635-9

Published by Arcadia Publishing
Charleston, South Carolina

Printed in the United States of America

Library of Congress Control Number: 2010924212

For all general information contact Arcadia Publishing at:
Telephone 843-853-2070
Fax 843-853-0044
E-mail sales@arcadiapublishing.com
For customer service and orders:
Toll-Free 1-888-313-2665

Visit us on the Internet at www.arcadiapublishing.com

This book is dedicated to my talented daughter,
Emerald, who shares my love of writing.

Contents

Acknowledgments

This book would not have been possible without the help of Doris Hoffman, curator of the local history collection of the Reisterstown Room, located at the Reisterstown Branch of the Baltimore County Public Library. Doris has almost encyclopedic knowledge of Reisterstown history and a talent for telling warm and engaging tales that should never be forgotten. Likewise, I would like to give recognition to Doris's predecessors who shared her love of history and did more than their share of preserving it. Without their efforts, it would not be as easy to peek into our past. I would also like to recognize the contributions of Jason Domasky and Richard Parsons, keepers of the Baltimore County Public Library photographic collection for their talents and dedication in creating this wonderful resource, which provided many of the photographs included herein. John Reddick Wright Jr. and the late James Brevard Eline, former president and chief, respectively, of the Reisterstown Volunteer Fire Company, lent their invaluable assistance giving clarification and insight into Reisterstown's past, of which they played an integral part. The author would also like to extend thanks and appreciation to photographer Charles L. Smith for his expert assistance, recommendations, and historical insights.

Unless otherwise noted, all images appear courtesy of the Baltimore County Public Library Photographic Collection.

Introduction

Reisterstown owes its name and beginnings to an industrious German immigrant by the name of John Reister. He was described as a man of great enterprise and sterling worth. He purchased 20 acres of land directly south of present-day Cockeys Mill Road and subsequently became Reisterstown's first resident after moving to the area with his family in 1758. At the time Reister first came upon the area known today as Reisterstown, it was thick with forests inhabited by fur-bearing animals; a wilderness with two families of Native Americans still around. Animal trails and Native American paths provided the only means to navigate the wilderness surrounding the Conewago Road, which had been cut through in 1737 from Hanover to Baltimore.

In 1758, the Conewago Road was little more than a trail widened for wagons to travel. Intersecting the Conewago Road was a Native American trail that went from the Patapsco Falls to the Native American settlement at Chestnut Ridge. The trail traversed the land on a path that roughly followed Academy Lane, presently called Cockeys Mill Road. There is no doubt that John Reister, an enterprising businessman, saw the potential of the site that featured intersecting roads originating in Westminster and Hanover and leading south to the harbor in Baltimore Town.

As a landowner in Frederick County, Reister had occasion to travel to Baltimore County to pay his quit rent. It was on one of these journeys that he must have noted that the intersection of the roads leading to Westminster (Pipe Creek Road) and Hanover (Conewago Road) was only 16 miles to Baltimore Town, a good day's journey, thus making it an ideal site for a settlement. John Reister recognized that the juncture of the roads would make an ideal location for an inn. He was quite familiar with inns, as his father-in-law, George Sohn, kept a public house in York Town. Reister took advantage of the opportunity and acquired a 20-acre grant on the Conewago Road (now Main Street), south of the trail leading to the Patapsco River, now known as Cockeys Mill Road. Reister called his patent "Reister's Desire." It was secured from the Sixth Lord Baltimore, Frederick Calvert, on March 2, 1758.

Before moving to Reisterstown, the patriarch was already a successful colonial farmer who was living in Frederick County with his wife and six children. His brother-in-law, Dr. Andrew Wiesenthal, was a doctor who lectured on anatomy at the first medical school in Maryland. It was not only that connection that drew John Reister to the area, but also his vision, which was illuminated by the opportunity he saw before him. Reister saw the area to be a perfect travel stop or destination for weary travelers to stop and refresh themselves and their horses from the long and dusty journey to and from Baltimore Town.

The Great Road to Baltimore Town (Conewago Road) ran diagonally through the Reister property. The road was what attracted Reister to the area in the first place. It was first known as the Conewago Road, and later it was referred to as the Packed Horse Road and later still the Wheelbarrow Road. By 1809, the road had been renamed Reister's Town Turnpike. Reister's Town flourished as Reister responded to the needs of the community and travelers and opened a blacksmith shop and a store. His son-in-law Henry Wiest opened a tannery on land south of his tavern.

Just north of Reister's patent was a piece of land that had passed through several owners or land speculators. In 1768, Daniel Bower purchased the land and erected a tavern on what is now the site of Franklin Middle School. Daniel Bower's father was Sir John Bauer, the burgomaster of Strasburg, Alsace-Lorraine. His widow fled to America when conditions in her country were unstable. She settled in Pennsylvania with her three young children. Daniel grew up and became a colonel in the Revolutionary War. George Washington is reputed to have slept at Bower's tavern on his way to Fort Pitt in Philadelphia.

More German settlers were attracted to the community of Reisterstown and settled here, calling it home. Daniel Bower became an innkeeper, and his brother-in-law Jacob Madairy, a merchant, also settled in the area. In 1784, Daniel Bower and an associate, James Morgan, anticipated an explosion of growth following the Revolutionary War. They acquired the Spring Garden tract and subdivided it into several hundred building lots located on both sides of Main Street. They called the development Washington Town. Legend says that Daniel asked George Washington to suggest a name for the town when he stopped at his inn, and Washington suggested he call the town "Washington." He did; however, the name did not stick.

In the beginning, Reister's Town accommodated travelers with a variety of taverns, smith shops, and saddleries. The town offered everything a traveler would need for their horses: a blacksmith, a feed store, a harness maker, a wagon builder, and a first-rate stables. Weary discriminating travelers could choose among the Yellow Tavern, Fisher's, Ducker's, Forney's, Dower's, or Reister's Inn and Tavern. Reisterstown flourished as a center of hospitality. The town's economy was built upon the road, just as John Reister had envisioned in 1758.

John Reister was a legendary successful businessman, but surprisingly he was not a wealthy man at the time of his death. His estate was valued at $3,400.69, a modest sum. During his lifetime, John Reister gave many of his assets away to his children. He gave the blacksmith shop to his son-in-law John Beckley. He gifted his son John his farm and his daughter Catherine his store. John Reister intended to give his son Philip the inn, but he died before receiving the title, so his son John Reister gave Philip's widow the bonds he received in payment for the sale of the inn. The successful patriarch was a family man first and foremost, providing both land and business opportunities for all of his children.

John Reister's generosity extended beyond his family. He was generous to his community too. He donated land for a cemetery, a church, and a school that helped build a strong foundation for the burgeoning colonial village. The church and school were simple log structures located next to the cemetery. The church was the precursor of present-day Trinity Lutheran, located at 109 Main Street, and the school was the precursor of the Franklin Academy that was eventually built in 1824 after the log school deteriorated. Although John Reister was a Lutheran, he made the church, school, and cemetery available to all denominations. At the time, the Church of England was declared the Church of Maryland, and every male over the age of 16 was obligated to pay a tax of 40 pounds of tobacco to have the privilege of using the cemeteries. By donating land for a cemetery, Reister cleverly helped his fellow men avoid the unreasonable tax burden.

Reisterstown is the only town in the United States with that name. It was carved out of a wilderness by sturdy pioneers whose resilience, hard work, and vision paved the way for it to become the historic and prosperous community it is today.

One

Gone But Not Forgotten

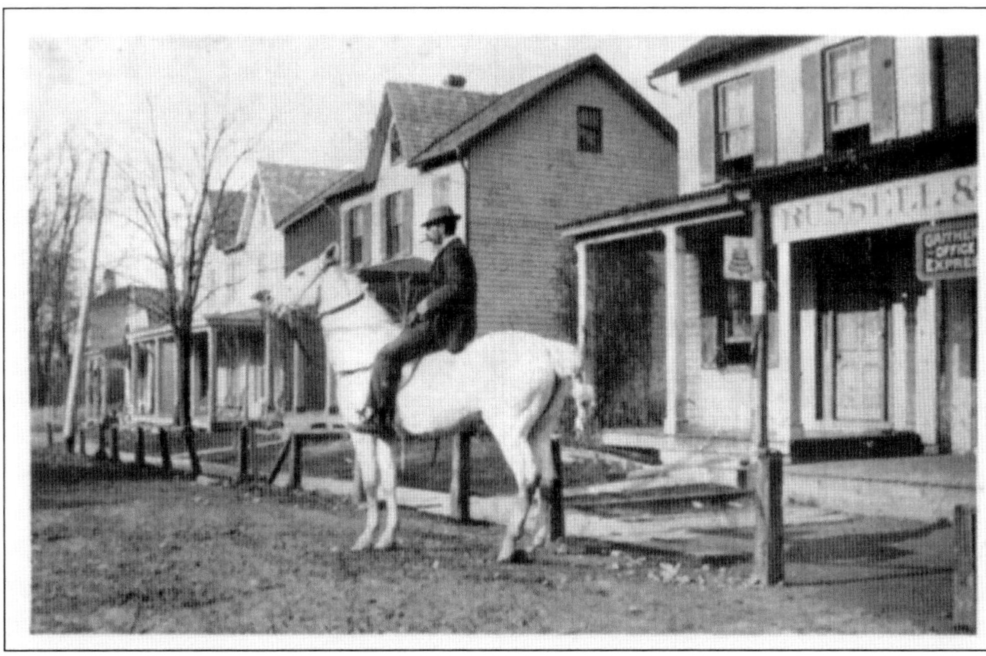

Arthur H. Uhler photographed George A. Jessop in the late 1800s sitting astride a beautiful white horse in front of the Russell Brother's Store at 23 Main Street. As homes and businesses were mixed, Main Street had no business district. The buildings had no front yards, as land was at a premium. Until the road was paved, citizens frequently put up with dust and mud. (Courtesy of the Reisterstown Room.)

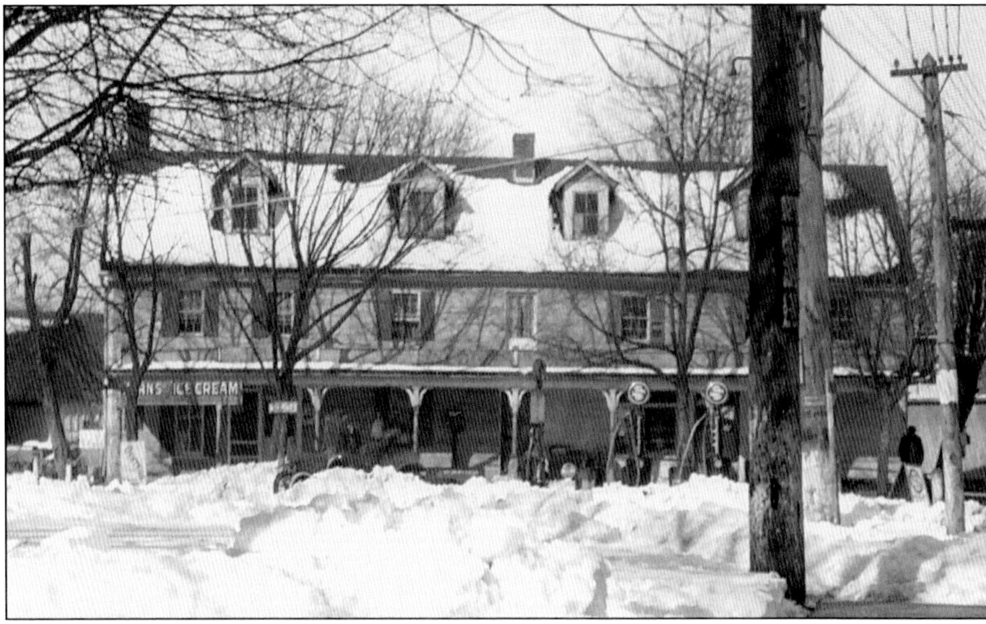

The Hitshue Hotel was built around 1818 by Capt. Jeremiah Ducker, one of the town's leading merchants. John Hitshue Sr. purchased it shortly thereafter and added additions to both ends. In the early years, elections were held there. In 1860, presidential candidate Abraham Lincoln received only one vote from a man in Boring, who was promptly run out of town on a fence rail. The hotel was almost completely destroyed by fire in 1930.

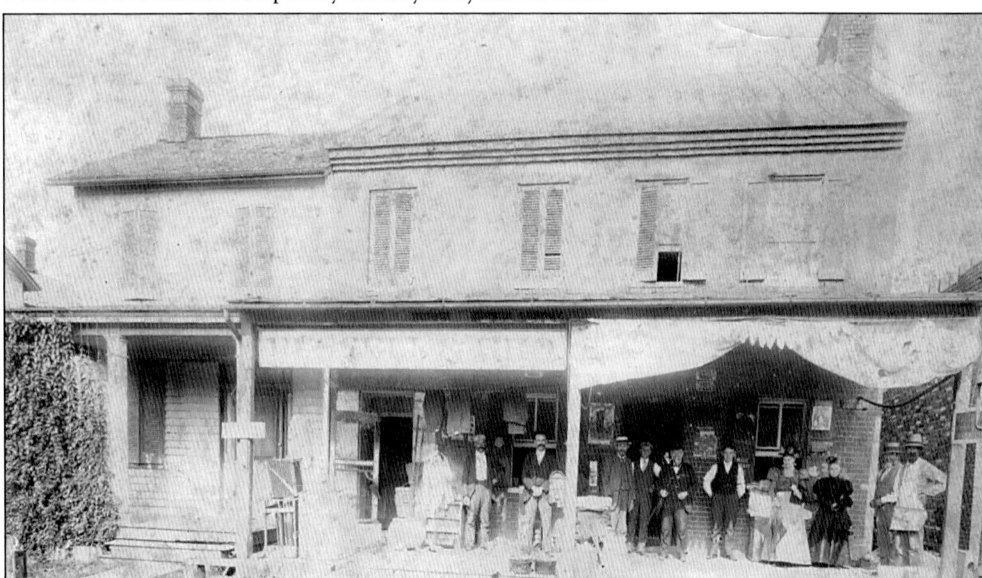

In 1867, Reister Russell and his younger brother William opened the Russell Brothers' Store, selling groceries and dry goods in the building that had previously housed Ducker's Store. A burglar shot and killed William on November 21, 1882. This 19th-century photograph of an group of unidentified folks shows posters on the brick advertising Magic Yeast, Eno's Fruit Salts, Lion Coffee, Horter's Powder, and baked beans. (Courtesy of the Reisterstown Room.)

An unidentified man poses on Main Street in Reisterstown with the Russell Brothers' Store at right in the photograph. Russell Brothers' Store was a long-standing landmark in the uptown section of town. In 1920, the Russell Brothers' Store changed ownership, and the business became known as Brook's Department Store. (Courtesy of the Reisterstown Room.)

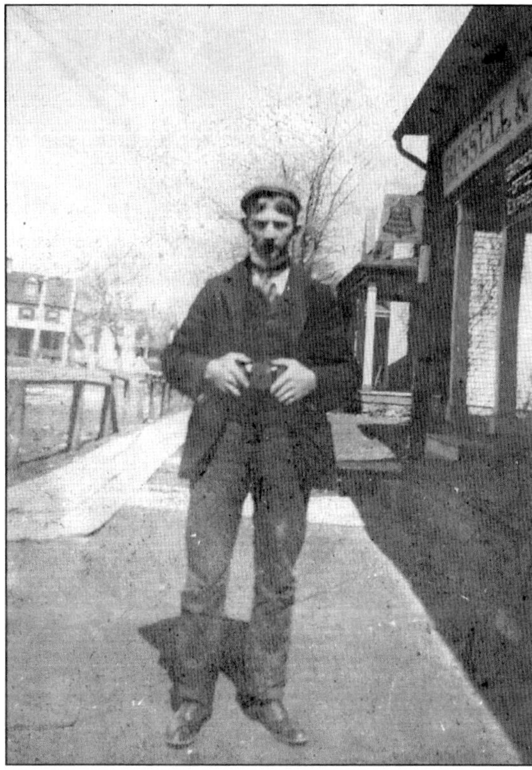

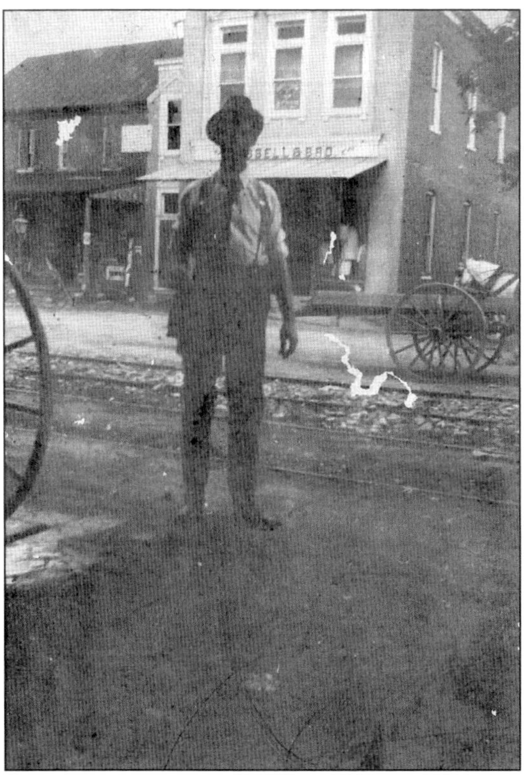

The quality of this photograph does not diminish its historical significance. An unidentified man poses for the camera while standing at Main Street in north Reisterstown. The Russell Brothers' Store served as a backdrop. Notice the rail tracks in the road frequented by horse-drawn wagons; one is shown at far right. (Courtesy of the Reisterstown Room.)

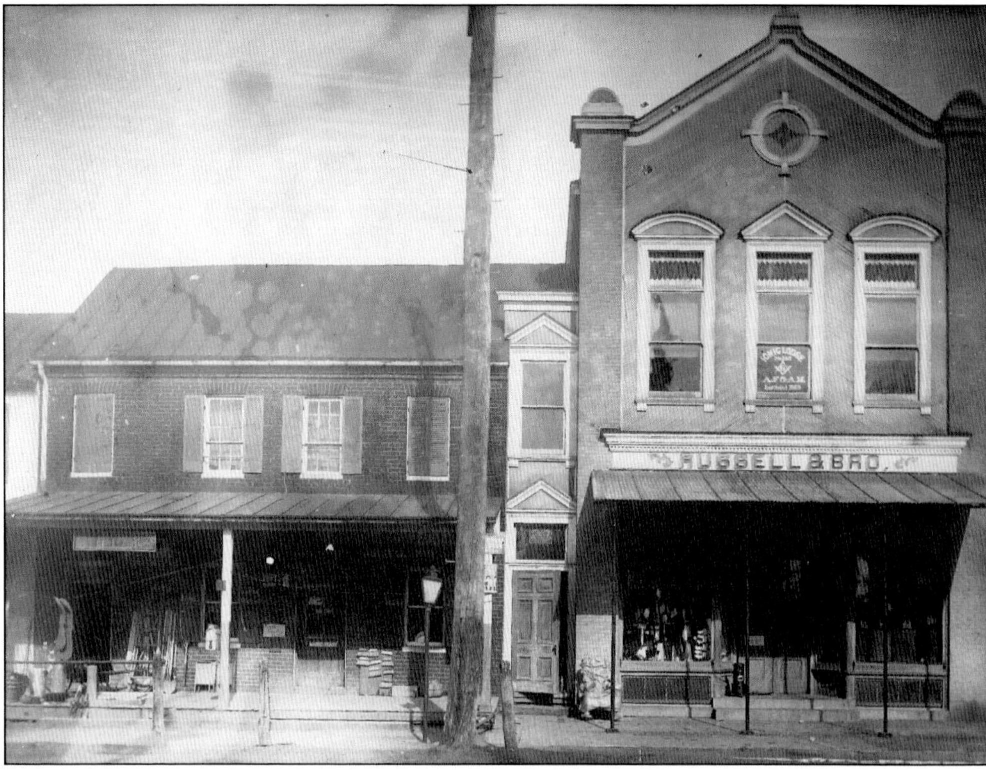

Maj. Harry H. Ducker, Capt. Jeremiah Ducker's brother, erected the original Russell Brothers' Store building around 1830. The photograph above shows how the structure looked in 1906. The Russell brothers purchased the building and ground from Ephraim Ducker, the major's son, in 1867. The addition (to the right of the pole) included space for the Masonic Lodge on the second floor. William Russell lived over the store at the left and was murdered by burglars around 1880. The store was sold in 1920 to a Mr. Sidle and eventually became Brook's Department Store.

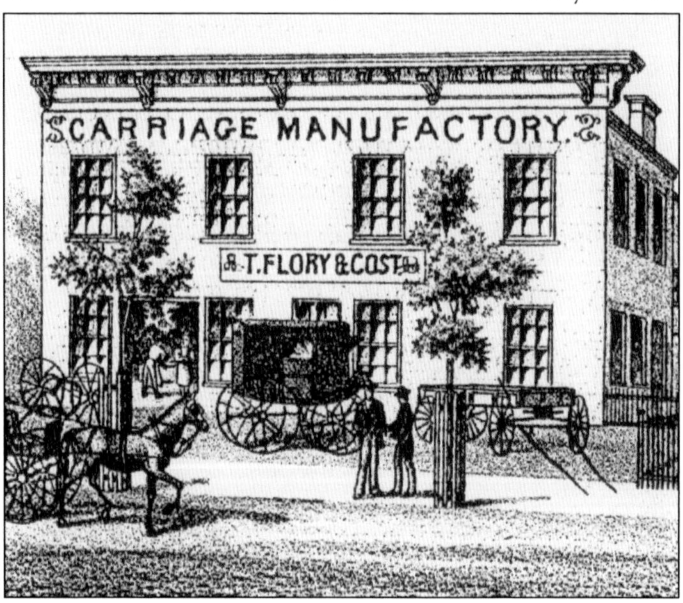

This 1880s engraving shows T. Flory and Cost's Carriage Manufactory, which was located at 37–39 Main Street. Horse-drawn vehicles were vital to transportation before railroads. Carriage manufactories provided carriage and wagon repair and custom manufacturing to a customer's specifications. The business was later the site of Uhler's Shoe Store and still later Caltrider's Hardware Store.

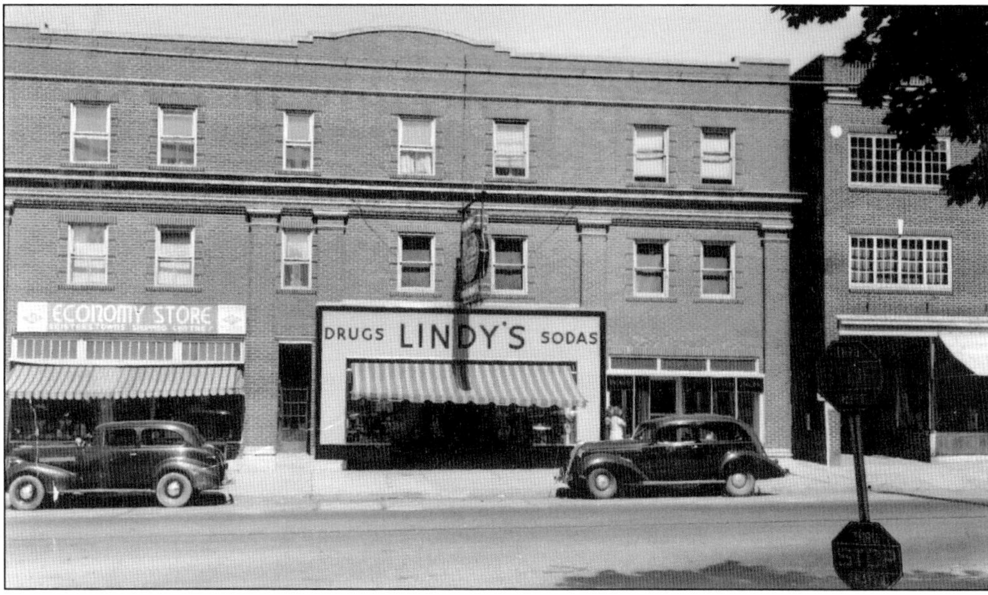

Lindy's Drug Store is shown at North Main Street. Louise Bland Goodwin took the photograph in 1941. The Economy Store stood just to the north of it. Lindy's Drug Store was burned out in 1972, but repairs were made, and the building still stands today on the east side of Main Street, across from Westminster Pike. The base of the structure now has a smooth stone facade.

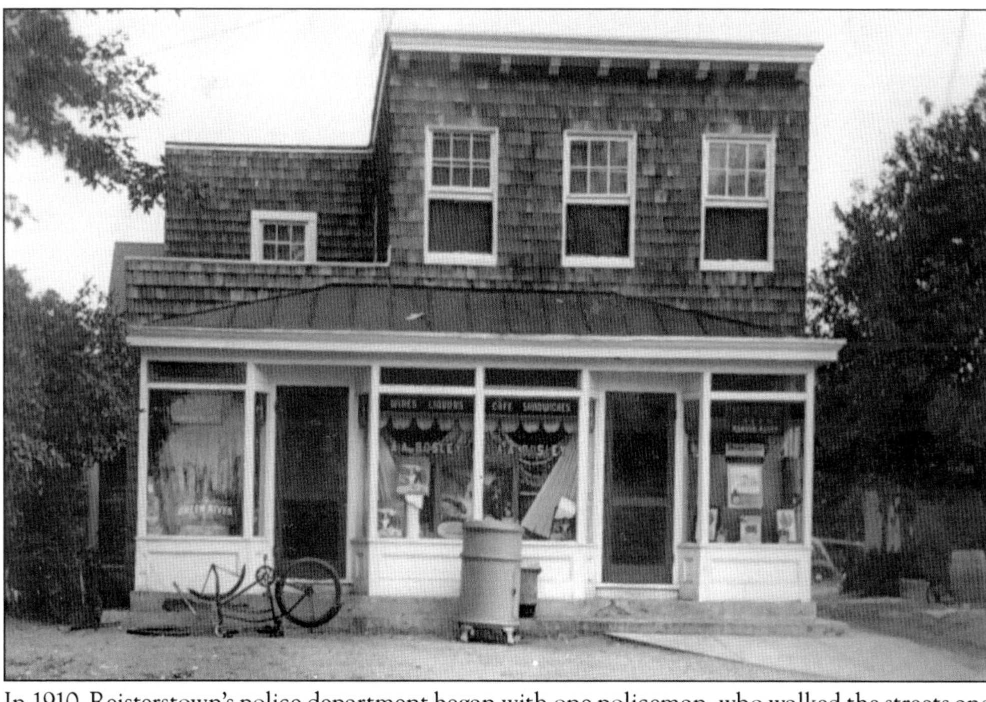

In 1910, Reisterstown's police department began with one policeman, who walked the streets and rode the streetcars in the town. The first police station, or lockup, was at Reuben Berryman's shingled store, known as the Bosley and Berryman Store (pictured above), which was located at 30 West Main Street. It was eventually moved across the street to the rear of the Hobbs Hotel and later moved again to Chatsworth Avenue. (Courtesy of the Reisterstown Room.)

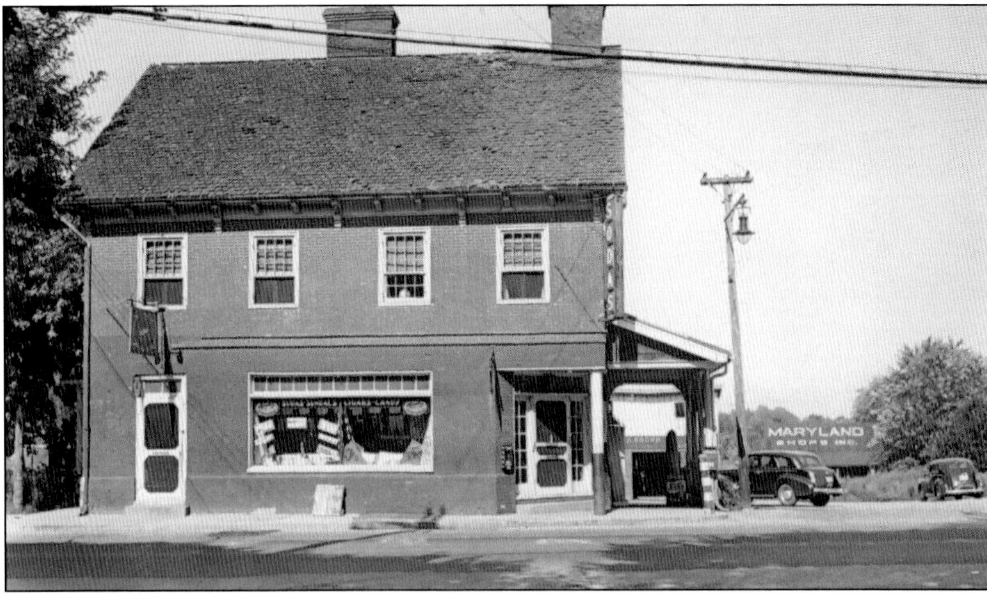

The Hobbs Hotel, located at 151 Main Street, is shown here in 1941. It is a frontal view showing the police station addition on the right side. The sign in the window advertised sodas, sundaes, cigars, and candy. The building was beginning to show signs of wear and neglect. It was razed in 1948.

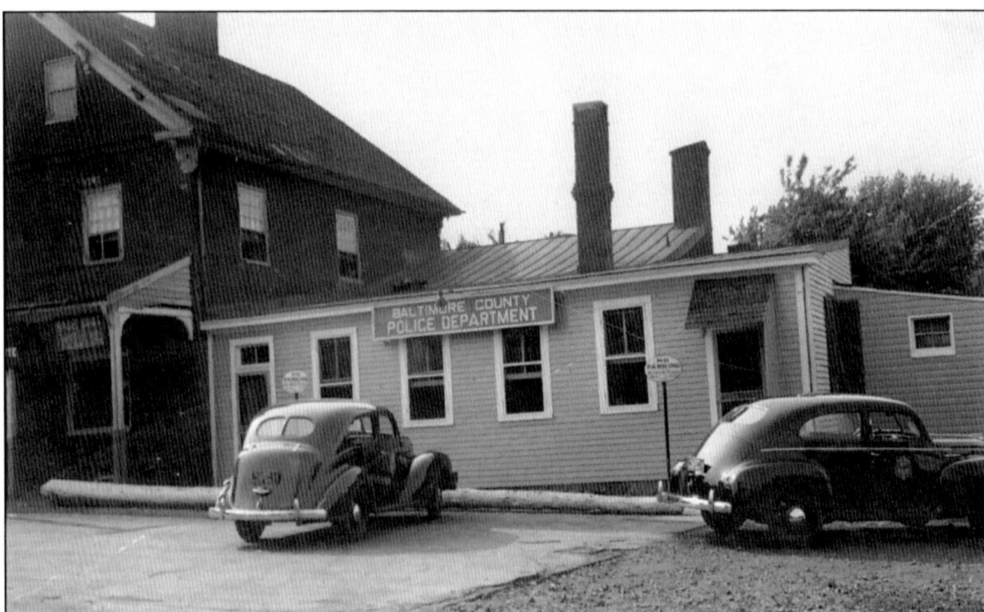

This image shows the rear addition to the historic Hobbs Hotel that housed the Reisterstown Police Station. Two period police cars are parked out front, one between the signs that say, "No Parking Between Signs." The sign on the Hobbs Hotel appears to say "luncheonette," and the handwritten sign says "Base Ball . . . West End . . . Sun . . . June? . . . 2 PM." Louise Bland Goodwin photographed the image in 1941. The building, located at 151 Main Street, was razed in 1948.

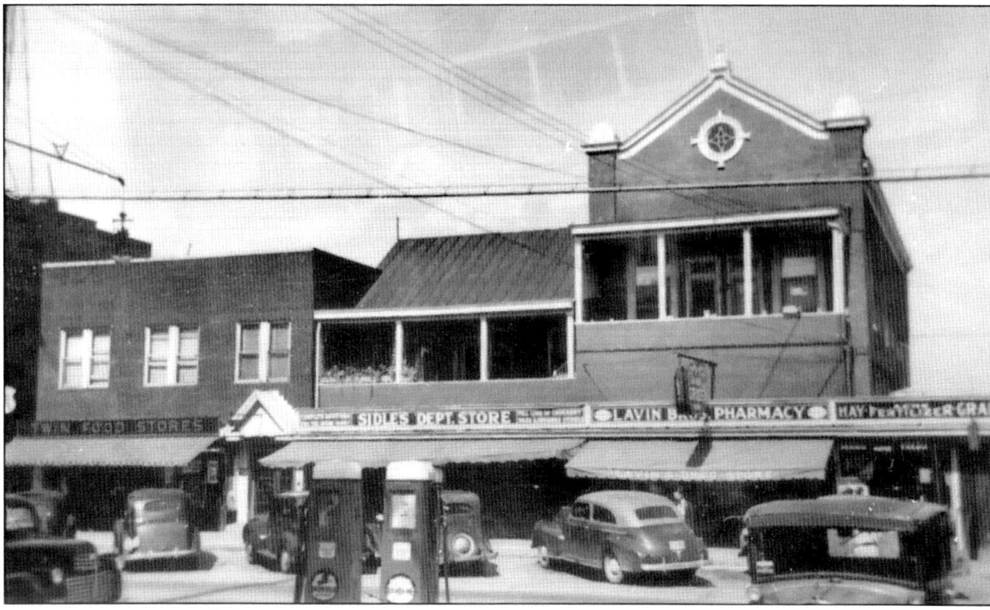

Standing near Goodwin's Hall and looking across Main Street in 1941, Louise Bland Goodwin photographed the Twin Food Store, Sidles Department Store, and Lavin Brothers Pharmacy. Lavin Brothers Pharmacy and Sidles Department Store are located in what was previously the Russell brothers' building. The structures have since been demolished to make way for a new shopping center in Reisterstown.

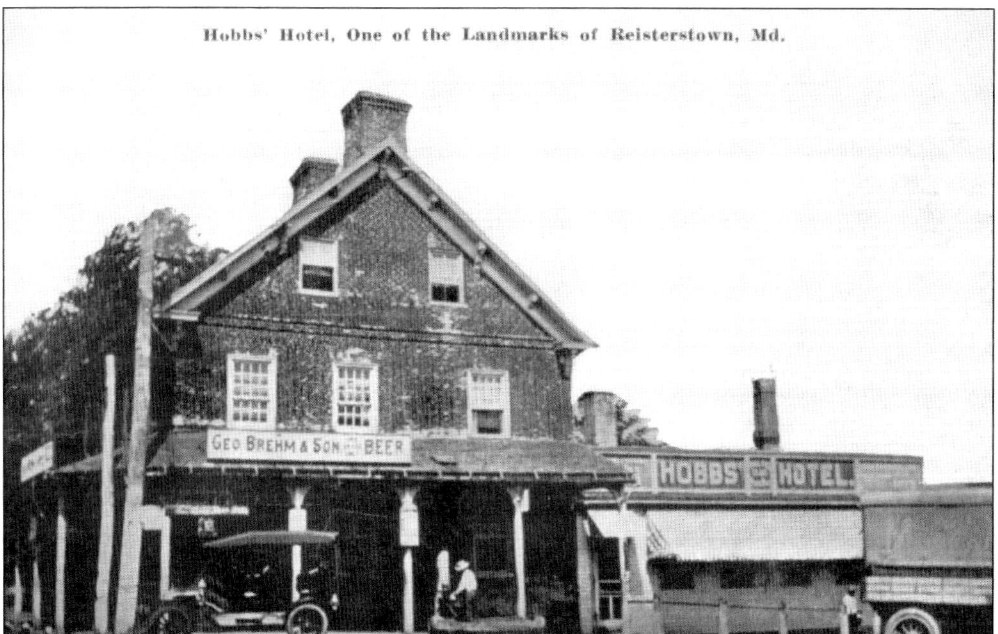

The c. 1914 postcard proclaims the Hobbs Hotel as one of Reisterstown's landmarks. The hotel had an old wooden pump that both horses and men depended upon to cool off. The building's history dates to 1779, when it was originally known as the Yellow Tavern. (Courtesy of the Reisterstown Room.)

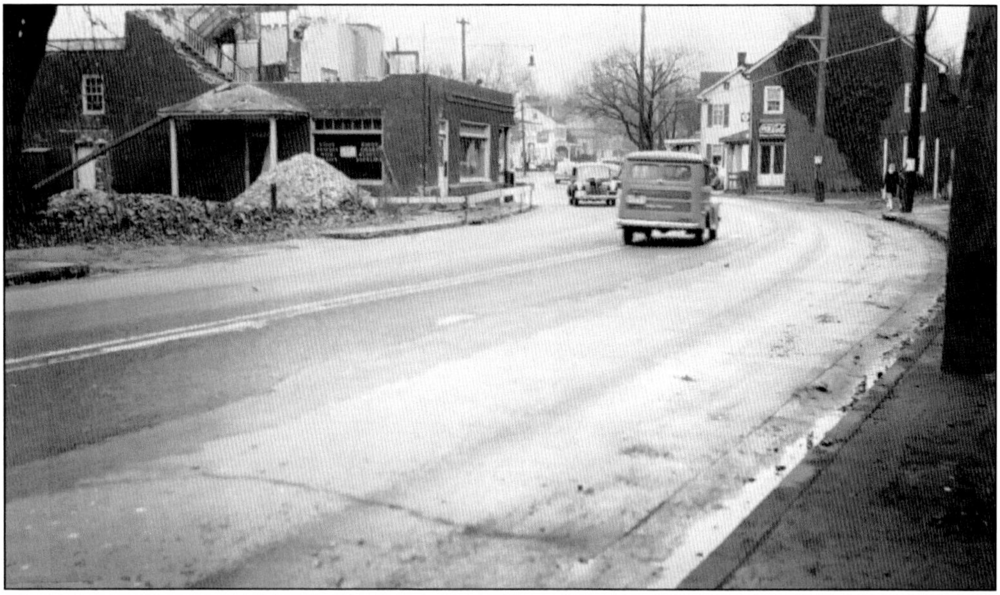

The forerunner of the Hobbs Hotel (shown) was the Yellow Tavern, built by John Medairy in 1779 and renowned for fine wines. Legend says he situated the hotel so the road had to go around it; others claim that Reister built his home to block the road entirely. Medairy wanted to prevent Pack Horse Road (now known as Reisterstown Road) from going through to Pennsylvania, thus preventing those in Pennsylvania from accessing the Baltimore Harbor. Today's "S" curve in the road is a reminder of Medairy's efforts. (Courtesy of the Reisterstown Room.)

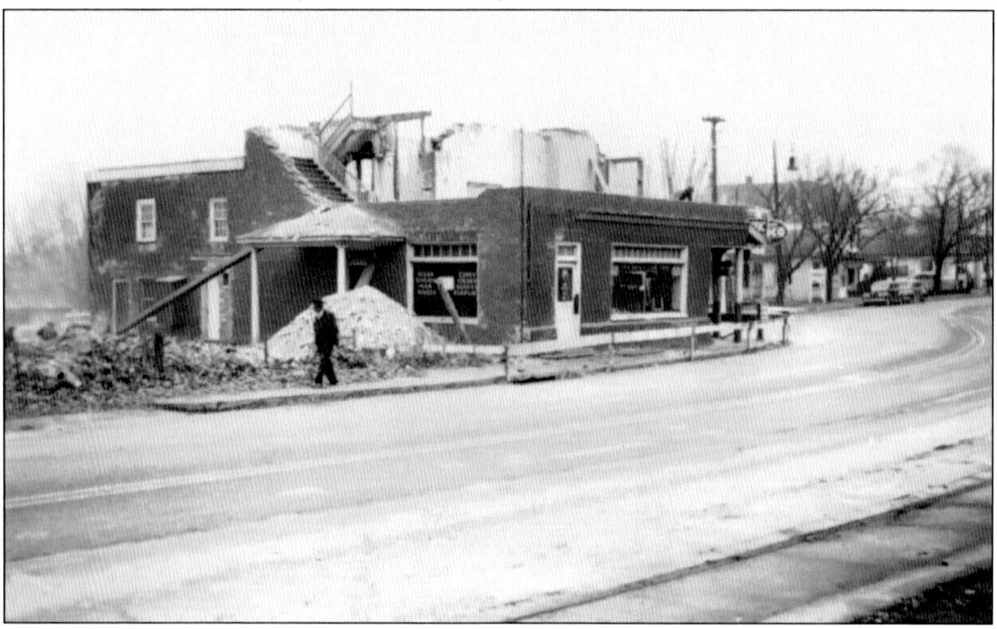

In 1948, the Hobbs Hotel was razed. It was the last of the hotels in Reisterstown. Louise Bland Goodwin recorded the remains of the Hobbs Hotel in this *c.* 1947 photograph. It was once regarded as the oldest structure remaining in Reisterstown. The photograph shows demolition of what remained of the structure after the 1928 "Great Fire." A filling station was later built on the property.

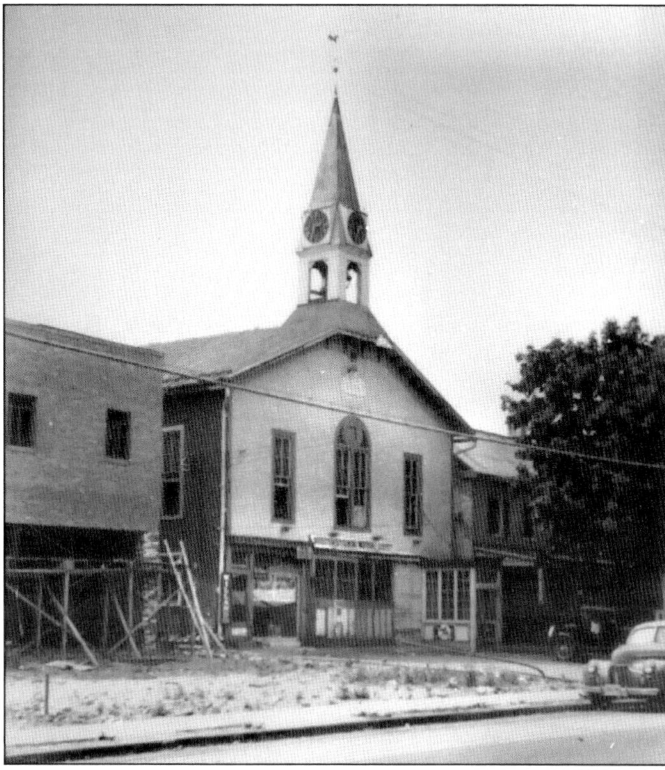

Louise Bland Goodwin took this picture of Koenig's Garage in 1941. Frank P. Goodwin built a livery stable there in 1887. It had a distinctive clock tower, and the second floor was used as a community hall, where Franklin High School held its commencements from 1890 to 1896. In 1940, E. R. Koenig replaced the Goodwin house next door with an Acme market. The livery stable became a filling station, and the community hall became apartments.

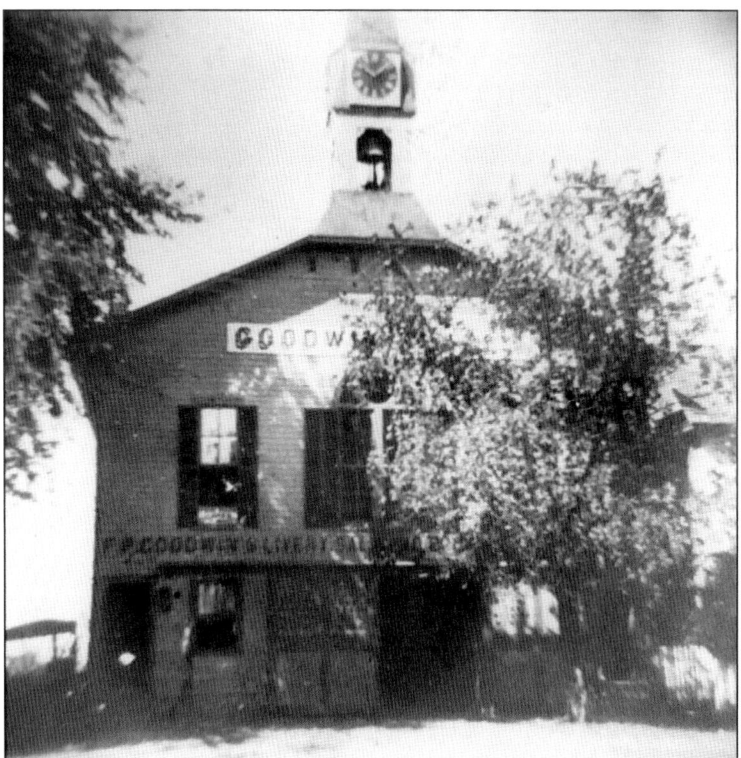

F. P. Goodwin's Livery Stable is shown here in the early 1900s, located at 20 North Main Street. This structure stood on the site of the old Fisher's Tavern, reputed to have been part of the Underground Railroad. The property became a Reisterstown landmark featuring the first town hall, a bell, a clock, and a weather vane, all acquired from public donations and erected in 1887.

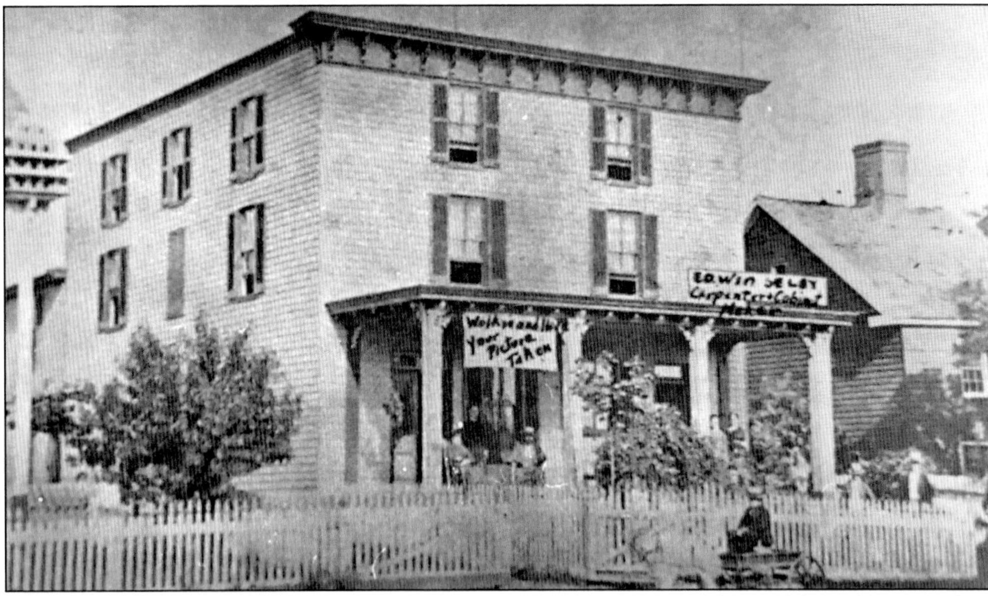

Shown in 1877 is Edwin Selby's funeral parlor, founded in 1863 and housed here for more than 100 years, until the building was demolished. The business was moved to 11824 Reisterstown Road. Today the business is known as Eline's, as Edwin Selby was grandfather to Edwin Eline, who took over the now fifth-generation business. Selby, a cabinetmaker, assumed the responsibilities as undertaker to help with the disposition of fallen soldiers during the Civil War.

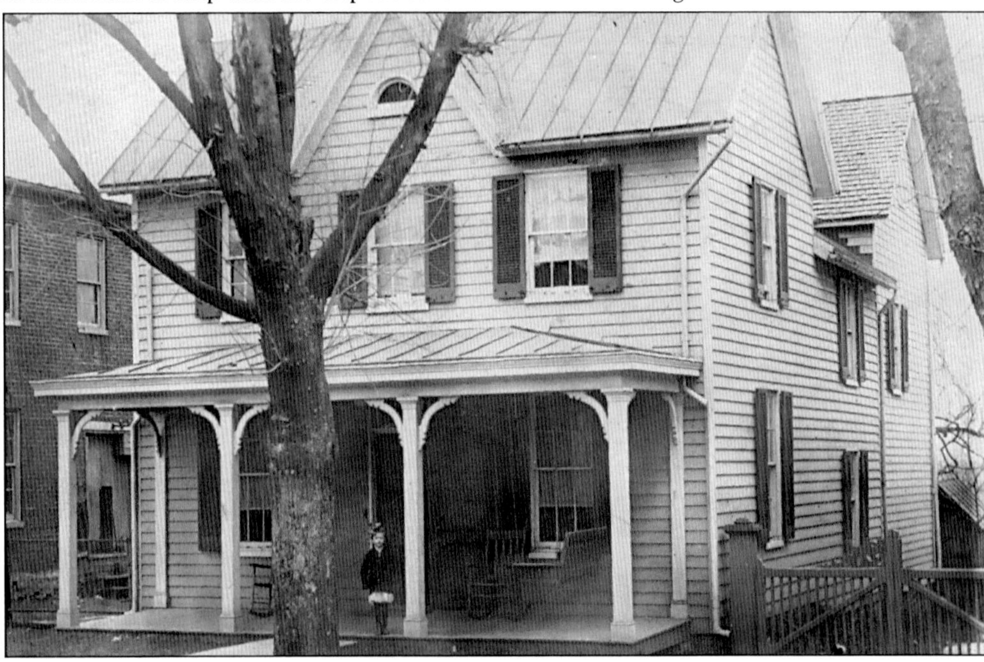

Nine-year-old Edna May "Feetie" Uhler stands on her porch at 303 Main Street. Her parents, Arthur and Abbie Russell Uhler, owned the feed and fertilizer store at 37–39 Main Street in the 1920s. Adam Debaugh of Appledale Farm operated a store under the name of Griffith-Turner at an earlier date in the same location. The house was torn down to create a parking lot. (Courtesy of the Reisterstown Room.)

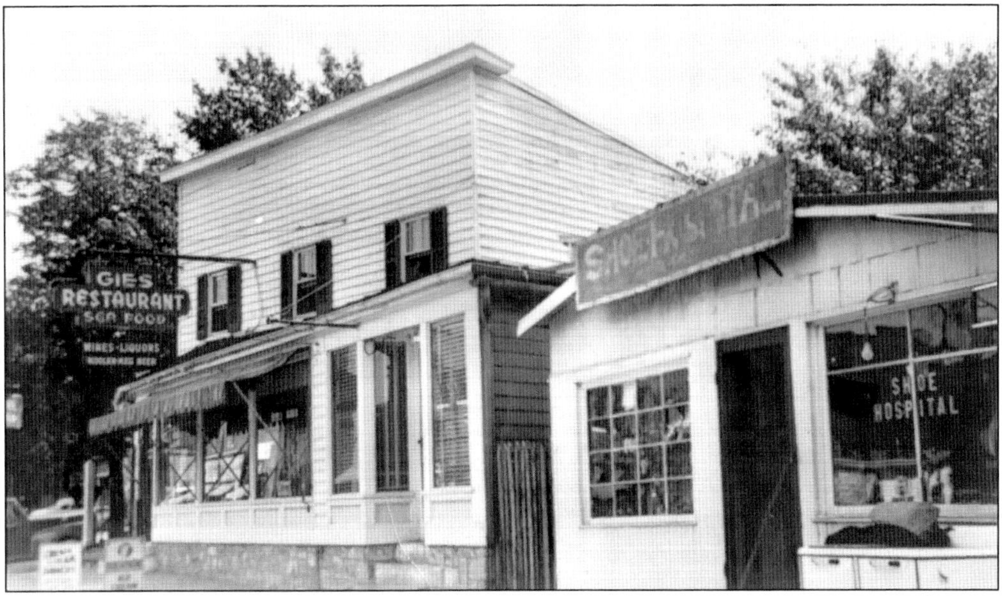

Gies Restaurant was a familiar sight in Reisterstown, providing the locals with wines, liquors, keg beer, and seafood. To the right of Gies Restaurant was Joshua Dett's Shoe Hospital. Kriete Osborn's Filling Station is not visible but was located to the left in this picture. The stores no longer exist, having been sacrificed for the widening of Westminster Pike. Louise Bland Goodwin photographed the stores in 1941.

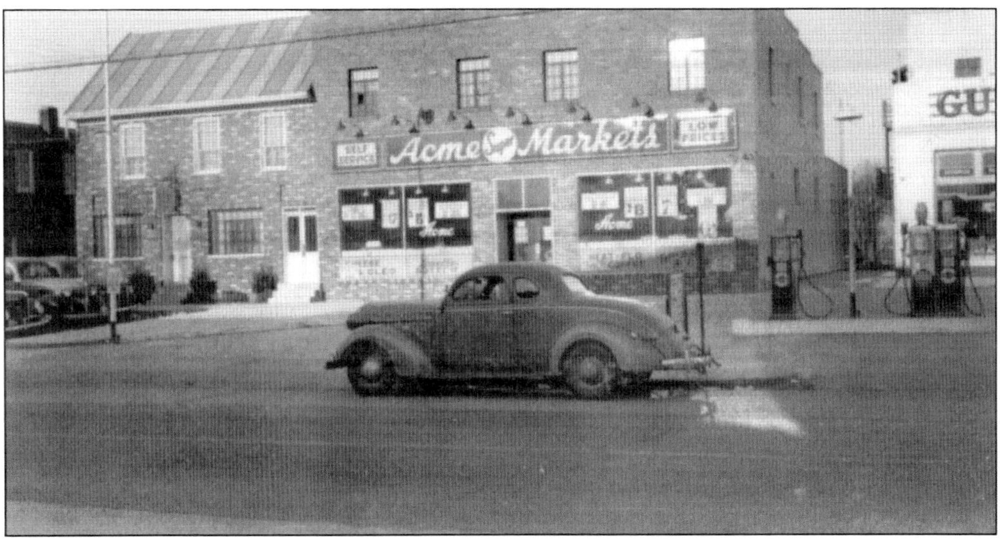

The Acme Markets store advertised low prices and self-service in this 1941 photograph. The building immediately to the left was the community health center, and the building at the far left, partially seen, was a two-story bar known as the Kit Kat Club. The structures were demolished to make way for the Food Lion Shopping Center off Main Street. (Courtesy of the Reisterstown Room.)

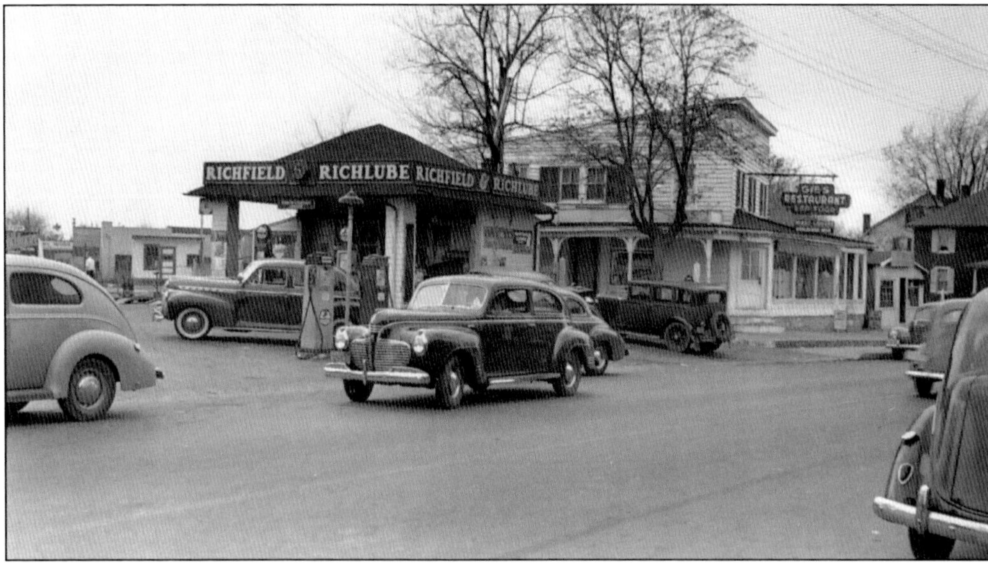

Kriete Osborn's Filling Station was located near the intersection of Westminster and Hanover Roads. It is not surprising that there is a large amount of traffic since the clock says 4:45 p.m. The Atlantic Richfield station stood next to Gies Restaurant. On the side of the building is a sign that advertises the original Zerex green antifreeze. The photograph dates to about 1941. (Courtesy of the Reisterstown Room.)

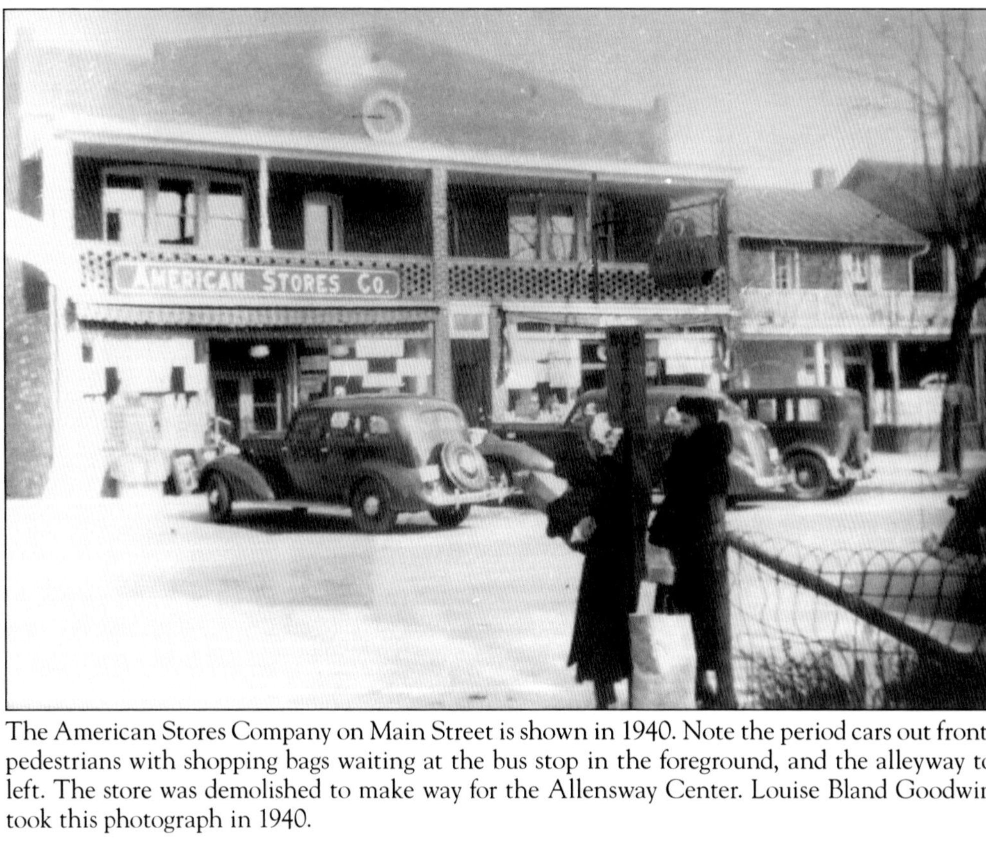

The American Stores Company on Main Street is shown in 1940. Note the period cars out front, pedestrians with shopping bags waiting at the bus stop in the foreground, and the alleyway to left. The store was demolished to make way for the Allensway Center. Louise Bland Goodwin took this photograph in 1940.

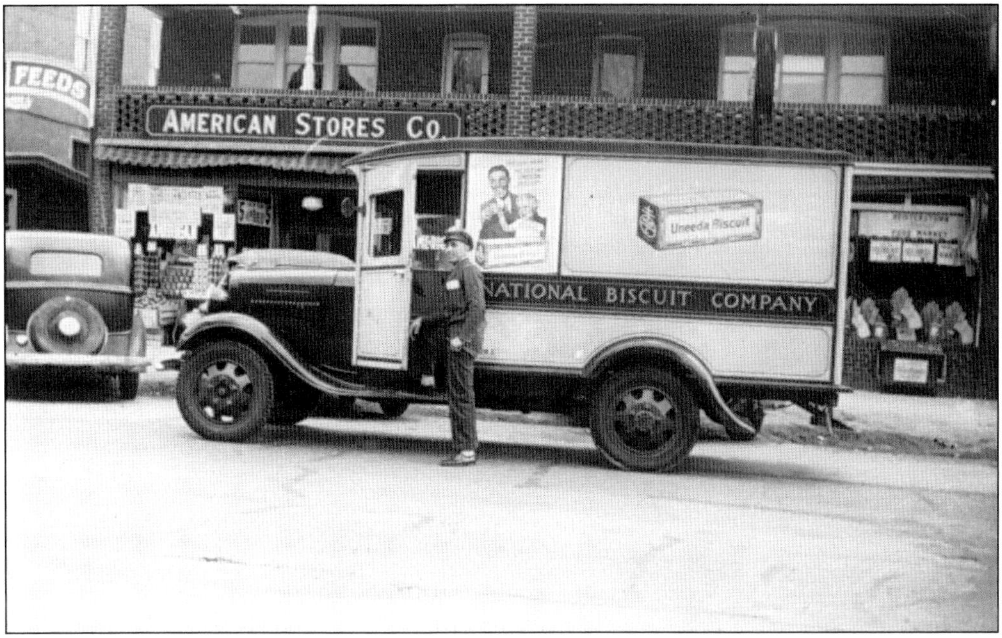

To the left of the American Stores Company is the partially visible Charles Geist Hardware and Feed Store. The shops were located on East Main Street at the north end of Reisterstown. In the foreground, the National Biscuit Company is seen making a delivery. The brick building was torn down in 1987 to make way for Allensway Center, occupying 21–25 Main Street. (Courtesy of the Reisterstown Room.)

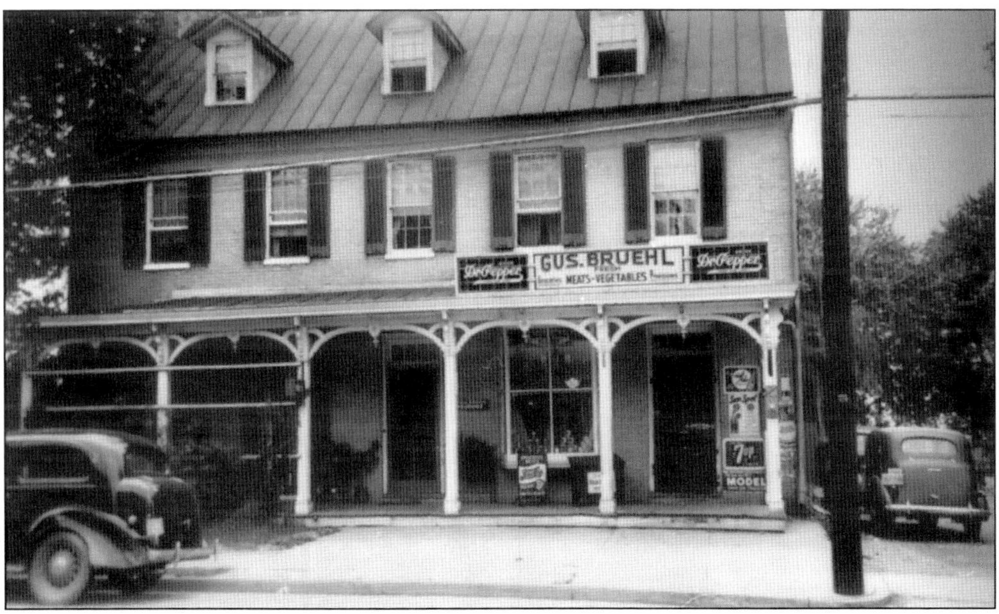

Originally the graceful house at 302 Main Street was home to the Larsh family. Dr. Silas Larsh later rented the building to James Thomas, who sold groceries, construction materials, farm implements, and manufactured bricks there. The last owners of this store were Mr. and Mrs. Gus Bruehl, who sold fresh meats, vegetables, and Dr. Pepper soft drinks. The property was razed after being sold in 1966 to the Reisterstown United Methodist Church.

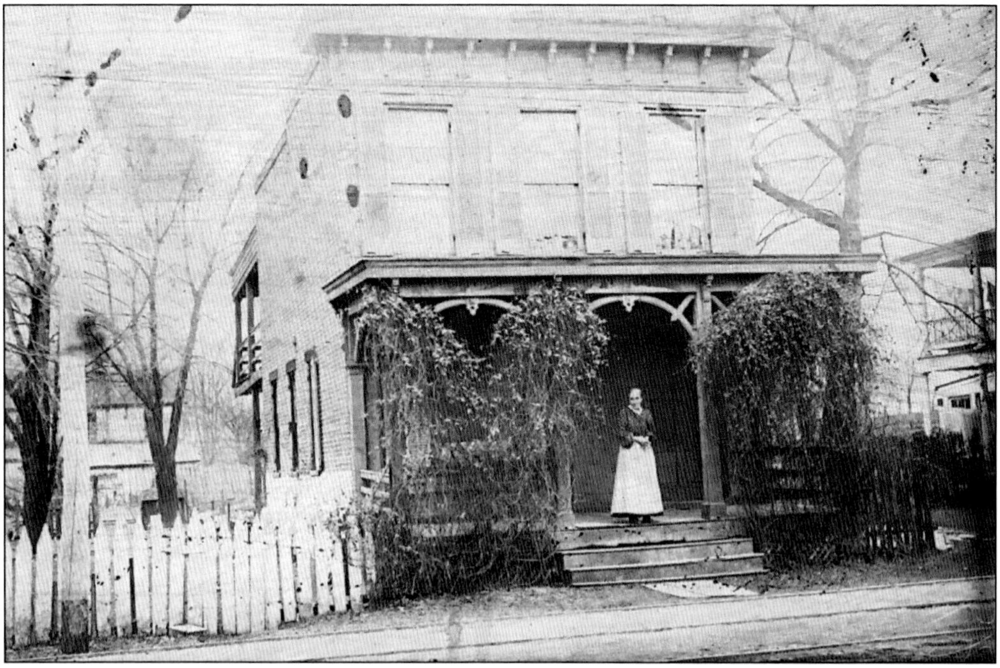

Elsie Burgess stands on the porch at 116 Main Street. The date of the photograph is unknown but presumed to be from the early 1900s. The building underwent substantial remodeling and later became the community health center in the 1950s. Eventually the structure was demolished. (Courtesy of the Reisterstown Room.)

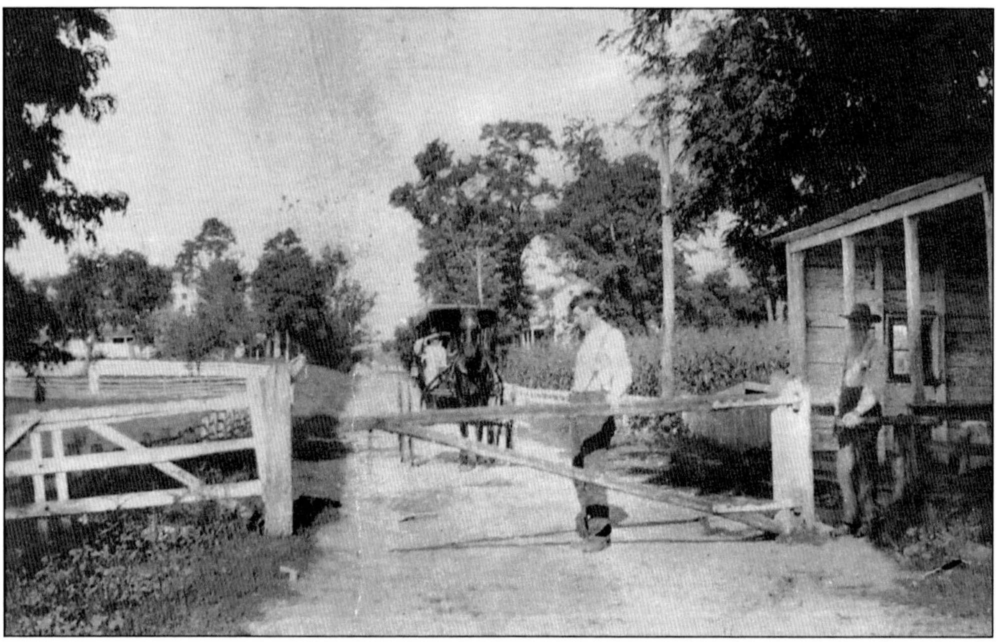

This tollgate was once situated along Reisterstown Road. Many believe it was the one at Owings Mills, built in 1856. The gate was taken down on May 25, 1915. Ten days later, a barbecue was held in celebration of the event. Celebrants enjoyed sandwiches and ice cream, and played baseball. An unknown photographer captured the image in 1900. (Courtesy of the Reisterstown Room.)

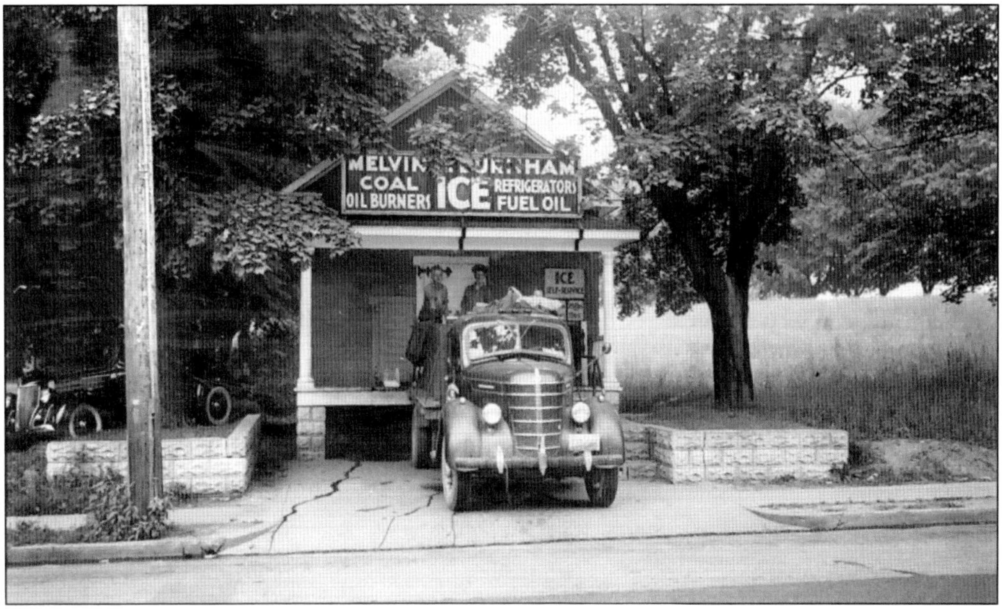

The Burnham Ice House was located on Reisterstown Road south of the firehouse. Everyone in town depended on Burnham's to keep their foods cool. Eventually the electric refrigerator made ice companies like this one obsolete. The property was subsequently purchased by the Reisterstown Volunteer Fire Company to build its first addition. Louise Bland Goodwin photographed the icehouse in 1941. (Courtesy of the Reisterstown Room.)

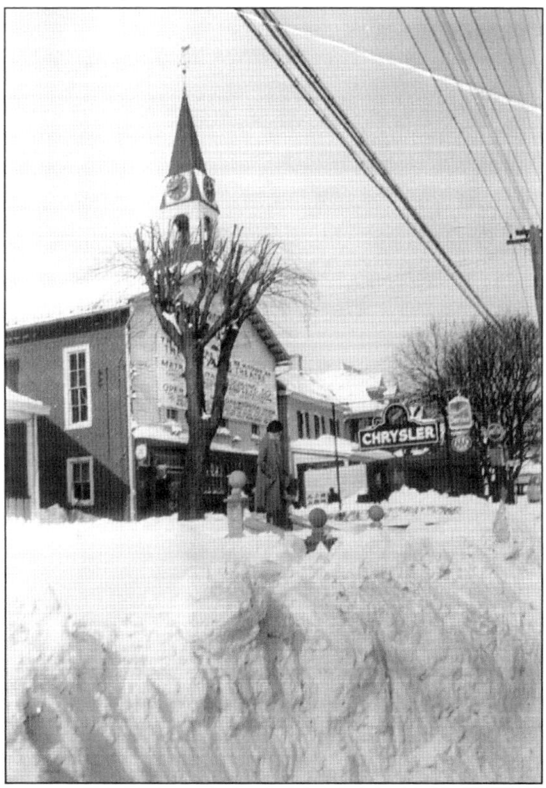

This treasured image of Goodwin Hall topped with the town clock and bell captures Reisterstown in January 1922, after it was hit with more than 25 inches of snow. According to the National Weather Service forecast office, the biggest unofficial snowstorm of January 1772 covered the Baltimore-Washington area with 36 inches of snow. It was called the "Washington-Jefferson Snowstorm," since the event was recorded in both of their diaries. (Courtesy of the Reisterstown Room.)

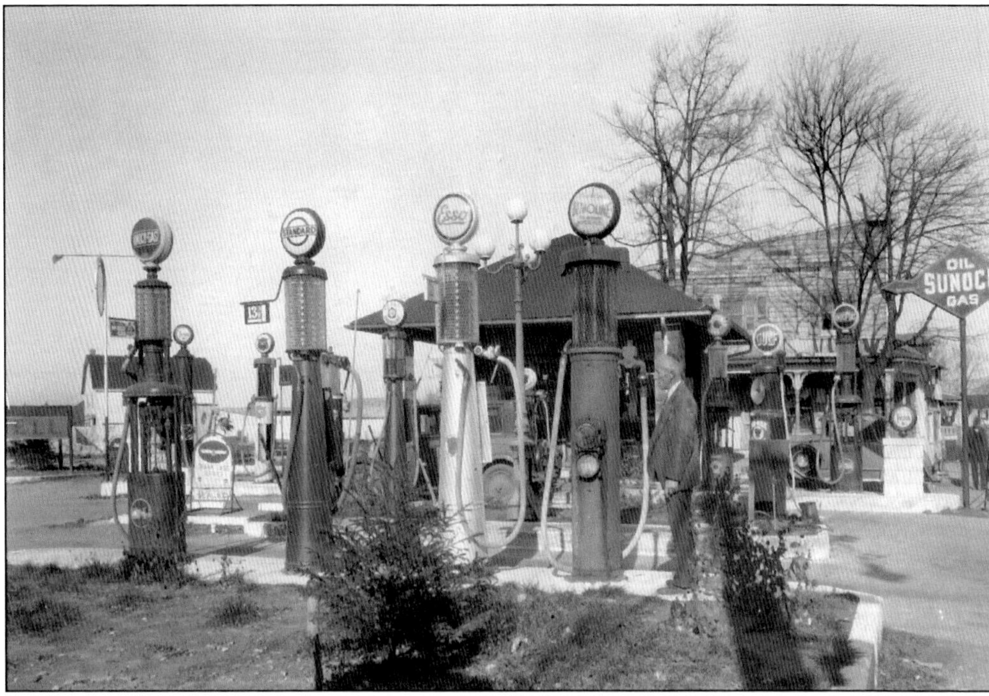

The Gies Station stood at the northwest corner of Main Street and Westminster Road. The split-pump station sold multiple brands of gasoline, including Amoco, Standard, Esso, and Betholine. At the time of this photograph, gasoline cost 13.9¢ per gallon. The man standing near the pumps is J. Leonidas Gies, the owner of the station. The gentleman at far right is possibly Louis Jefferson, who is likely coming from Joshua Dett's Shoe Hospital behind the station. (Courtesy of the Reisterstown Room.)

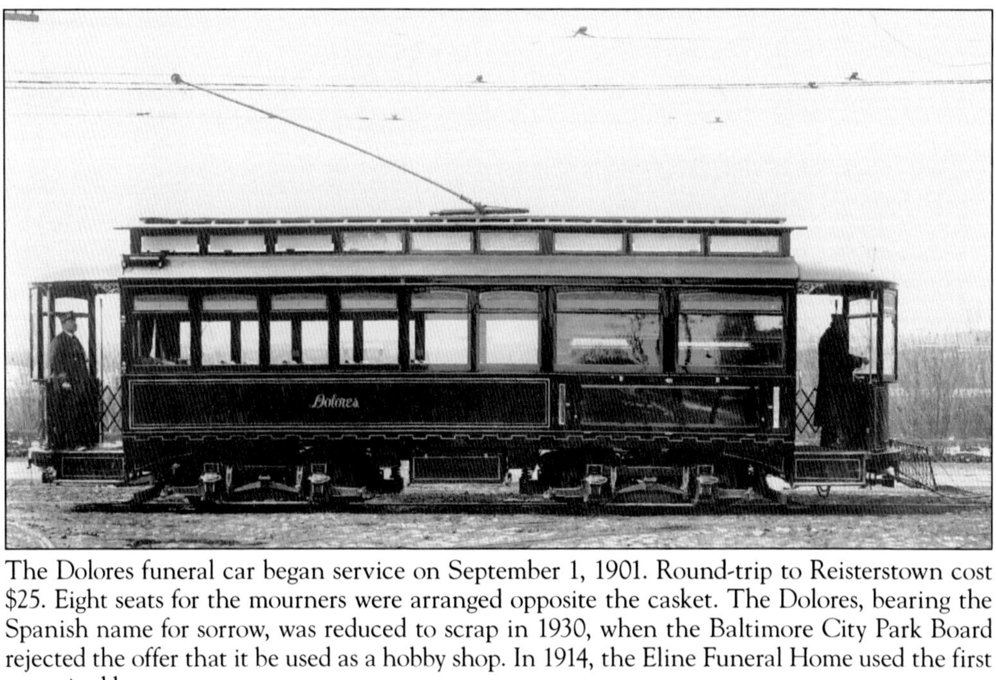

The Dolores funeral car began service on September 1, 1901. Round-trip to Reisterstown cost $25. Eight seats for the mourners were arranged opposite the casket. The Dolores, bearing the Spanish name for sorrow, was reduced to scrap in 1930, when the Baltimore City Park Board rejected the offer that it be used as a hobby shop. In 1914, the Eline Funeral Home used the first motorized hearse.

Two

MAIN STREET

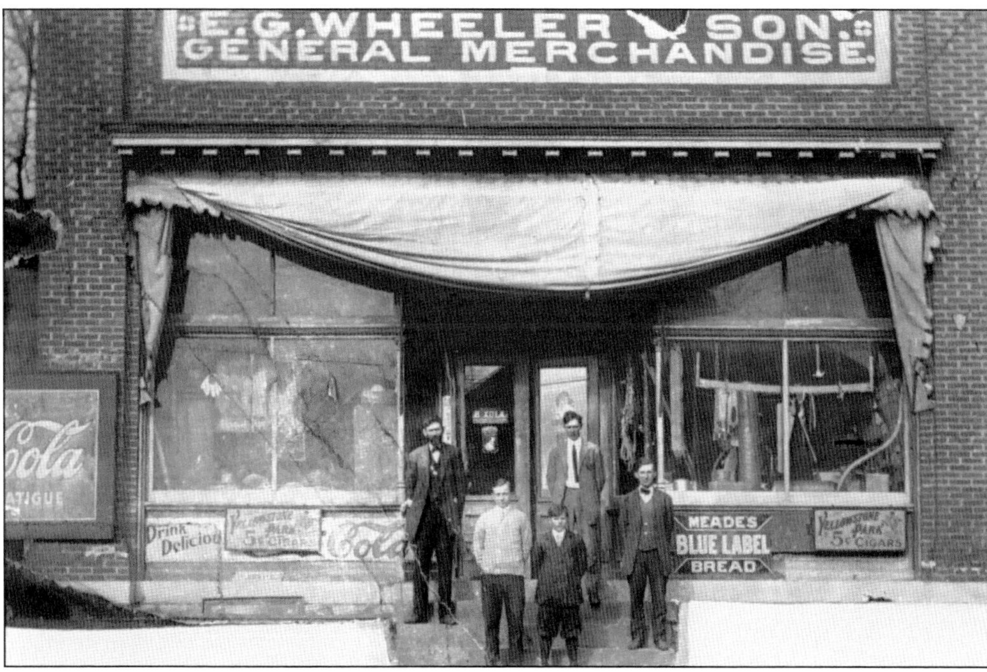

The E. G. Wheeler and Son General Merchandise store is shown here around 1910. Among those pictured are Edward Wheeler, proprietor; Pete Tawney; and Morris Stumpf. Gilbert Tillman appears in knickers, and Lester Wheeler is standing on the top step wearing a necktie. Mildred Wesley Loudon of the Loop House near Emory Grove donated the photograph to the Reisterstown Room. (Courtesy of the Reisterstown Room.)

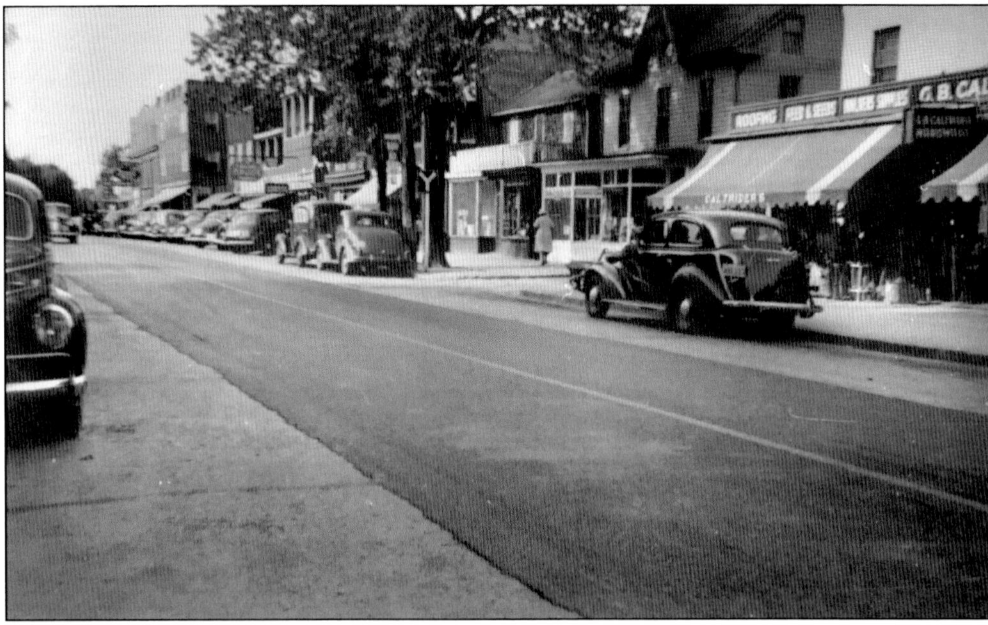

Looking north on Main Street, one is transported back in time to the year 1941. Caltrider's Hardware Store is most noticeable, with the awning and sign advertising roofing, feed and seeds, and building supplies. Louise Bland Goodwin photographed the busy street scene.

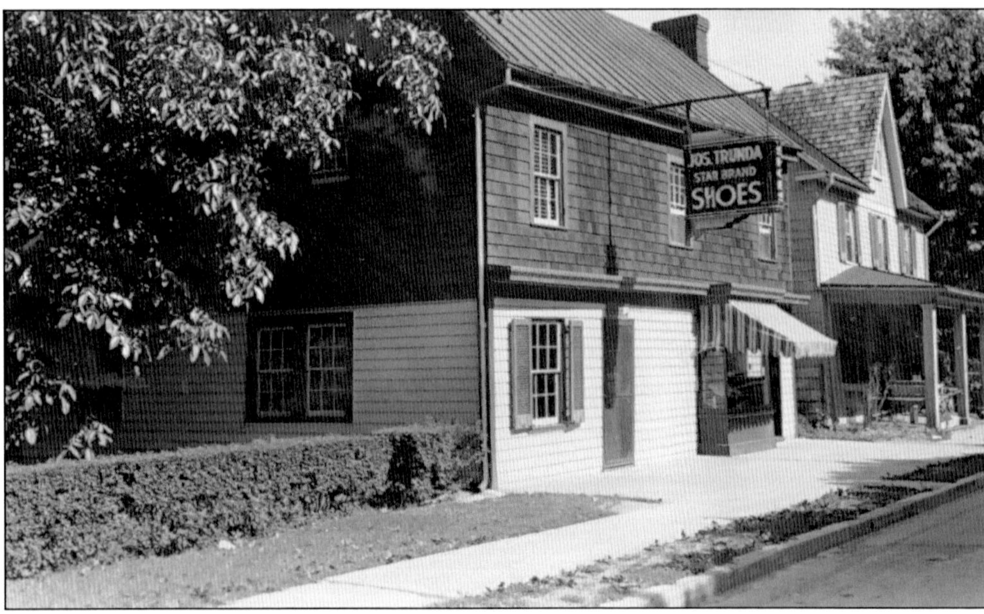

Featured is one of Reisterstown's oldest homes, located at 143 North Main Street, with log construction dating to the late 1700s. The building, enlarged at least three times, housed a residence and shoe shop for more than 100 years. In this image, the structure houses Trunda's Shoe Shop with an overhead sign that says, "Jos. Trunda Star Brand Shoes." Louise Bland Goodwin took the photograph in 1941.

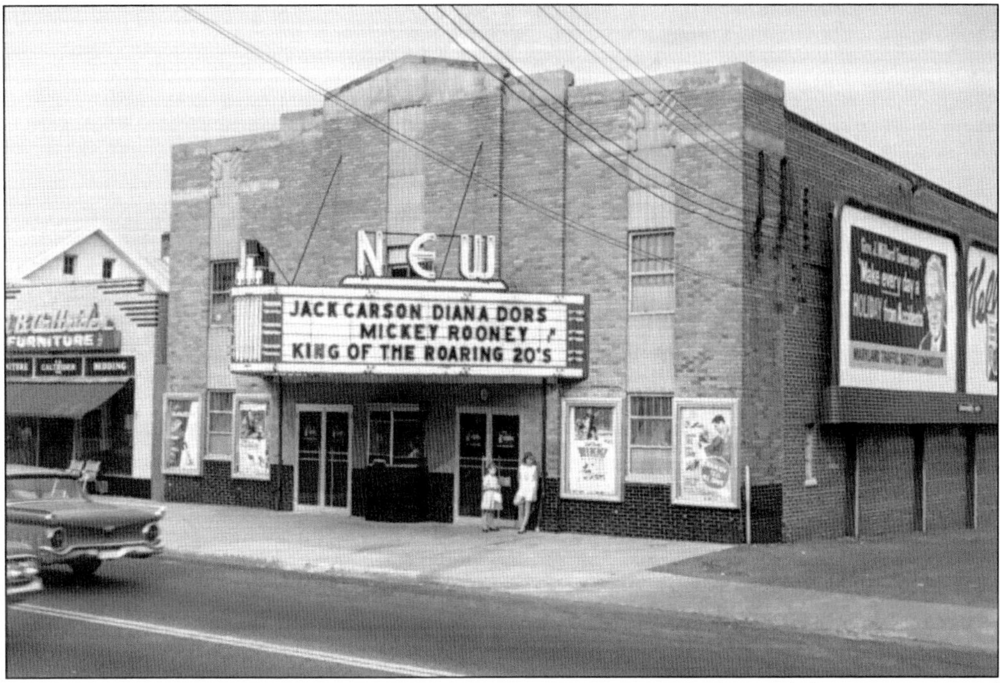

This 1950s image shows the New Theatre at 51 Main Street. It was the first real theater in town and was constructed in 1935. The theater reportedly had excellent movies. Prior to the New Theatre, residents were shown movies in Goodwin's Hall and later in a building on the Westminster Pike. (Courtesy of the Reisterstown Room.)

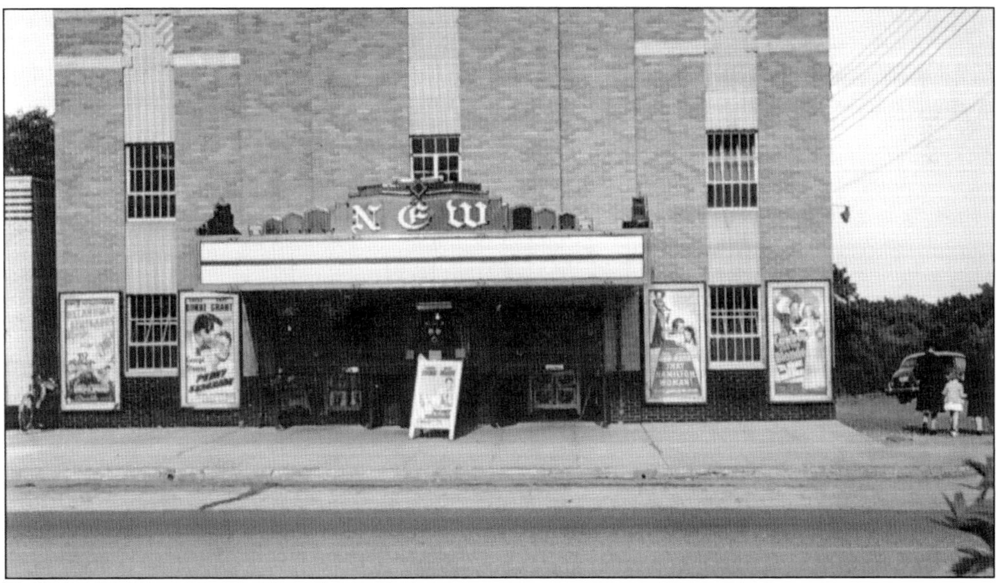

Louise Bland Goodwin took this photograph of the New Theatre in 1941. The New Theatre opened on October 19, 1934, showing *Hide Out*, featuring Robert Montgomery and Maureen O'Sullivan. In this 1941 photograph, the posters advertise *That Hamilton Woman!* The theater closed in the 1970s. (Courtesy of the Reisterstown Room.)

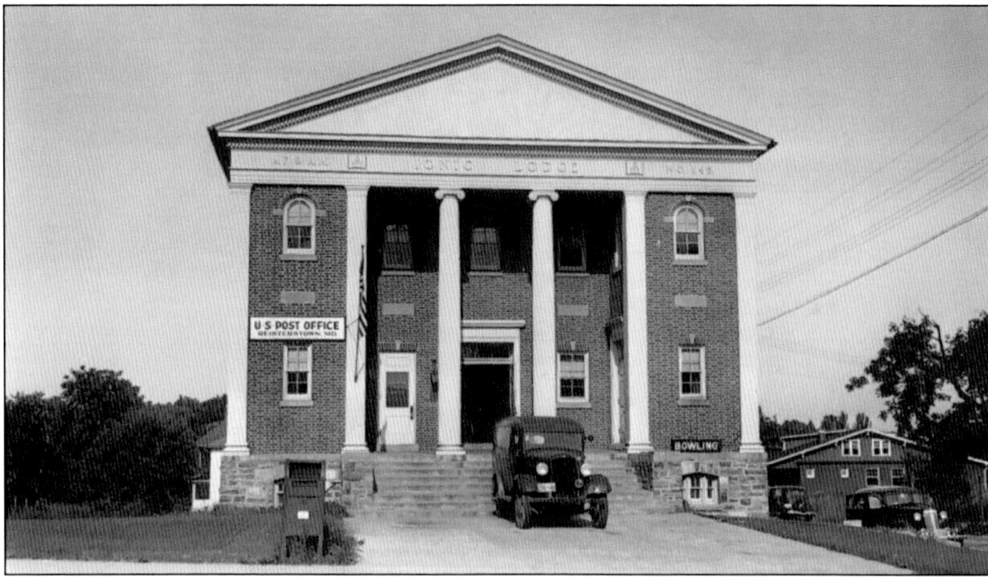

The Reisterstown Post Office can be seen on the left side of this image. It was housed in the Masonic Temple, located at 85 Main Street, where Main Street intersects Chatsworth Avenue. Since 1931, the post office had been located at the Masonic Temple, until it was moved in 1950 to a newly leased building on Chatsworth Avenue.

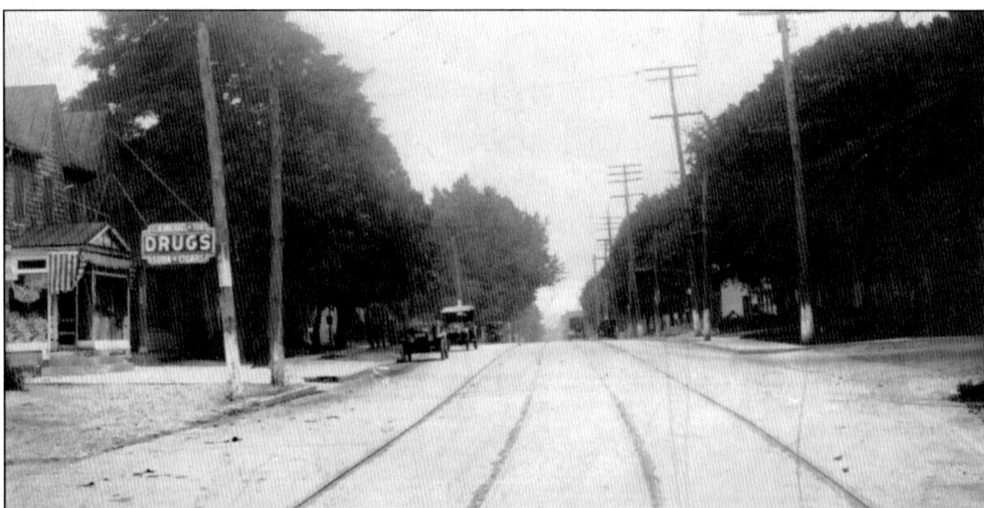

Dr. Michael's Drug Store on the east side of Main Street, opposite Westminster Road, burned to the ground in the fire of 1928. The story goes that Dr. Michael locked his store door and fled as the fire approached but later needed to borrow cigarettes since he forgot to take them with him when he left the store. Notice the streetcar lines in the road in this c. 1912 photograph. (Courtesy of the Reisterstown Room.)

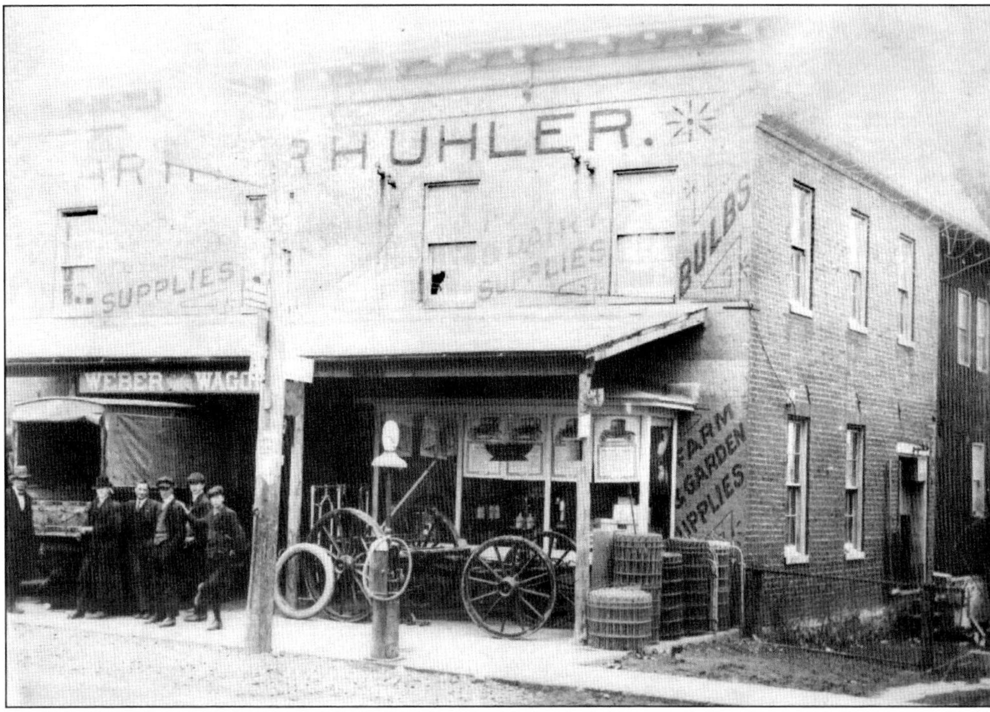

Arthur Uhler's Store is shown above around 1908. A few details can still be made out in the faded image. A group of well-dressed men and boys with caps are at left acknowledging the camera. The store advertises for sale farm and garden supplies, Weber wagons, and poultry and dairy supplies. Fencing for sale sits out front the brick store, along with a large wagon. (Courtesy of the Reisterstown Room.)

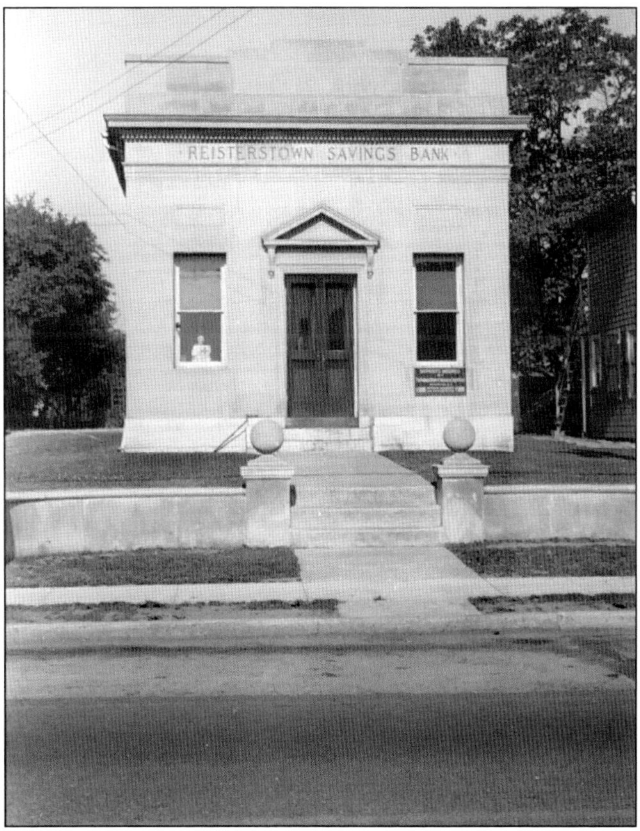

This photograph of 50 West Main Street was taken in 1941. It was the home of the Reisterstown Savings Bank at the time and was located north of the Will Stevenson home and the Odd Fellows Hall. The bank was demolished in the 1990s, paving the way for the Reisterstown Village Shopping Center and Food Lion grocery store.

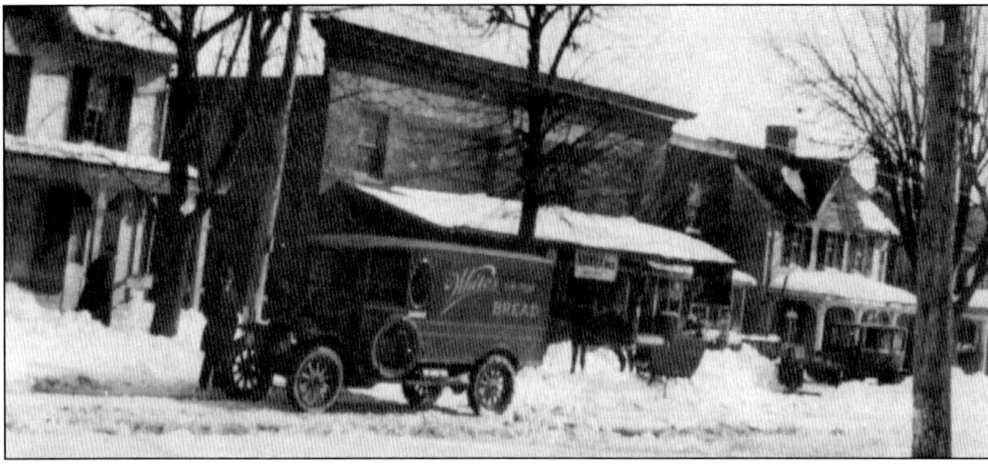

This c. 1922 image is from an unidentified publication. It shows Arthur Uhler's Feed Store at 43 Main Street. Stebbins Anderson Hardware later occupied the building until it closed around 1970. A White's Bread delivery truck is in the foreground in this snowy winter scene. The Akers' residence is shown at left. The Uhlers' residence is to the right of the store, and the Storms' residence is at the far right.

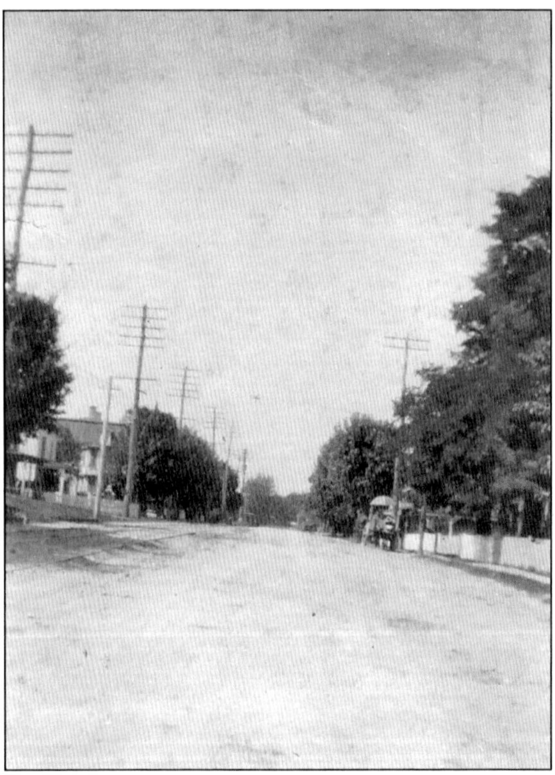

A. Zouck German took this photograph of Reisterstown Road in August 1908. Looking south, a horse and packed wagon is barely discernible on the right in the distance. A bit farther down the road and more toward the center stands a dark horse. Rail lines can be seen on the left side of the road. Streetcars came to Reisterstown in 1896, and electric streetlights came in 1902.

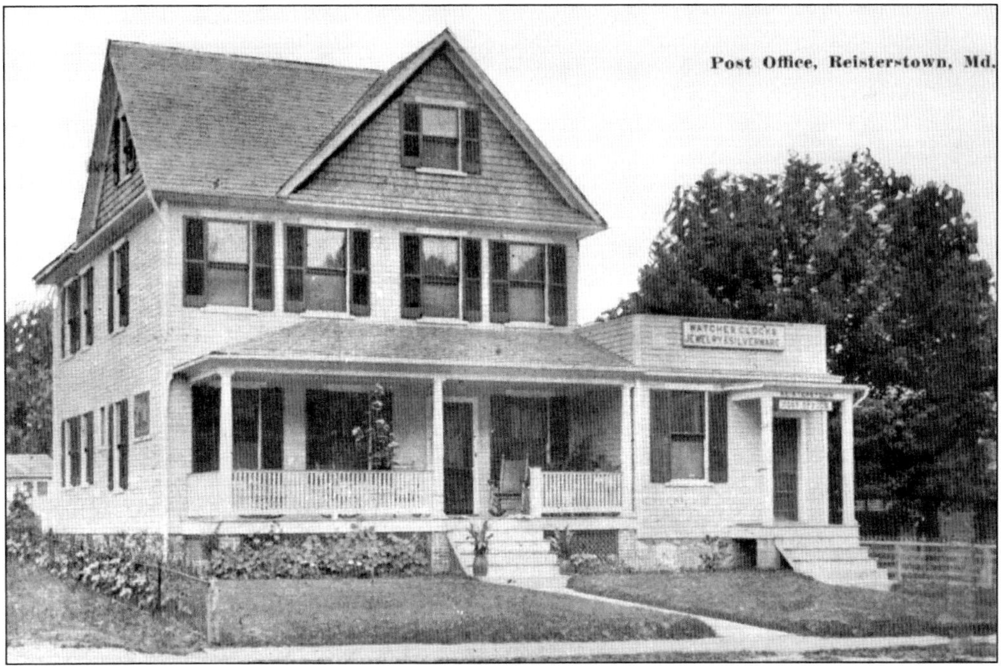

L. Kaufman and Sons of Baltimore published this postcard, stamped July 15, 1915. It shows an addition to the frame dwelling that houses the post office and a shop. The sign above the addition reads "Watches Clocks Jewelry Silverware." Above the addition's covered entrance another sign reads "Reisterstown Post Office." The rocking chairs on the porch give a hint to the pace at that time. (Courtesy of the Reisterstown Room.)

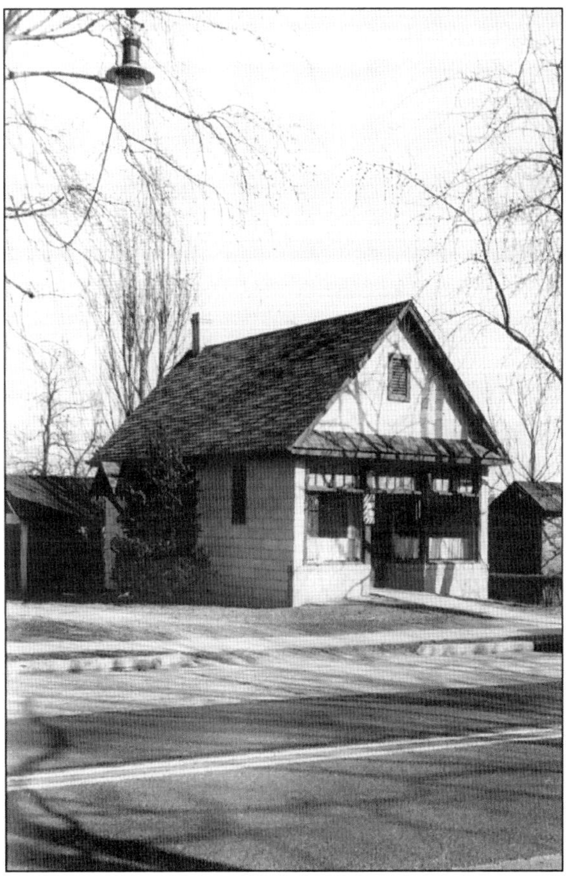

The undated photograph at right shows Mr. Tracey's Barber Shop, which operated between 1920 and 1930. "Shorty" Tracey lived in a house to the left. The building, located at 137 East Main Street, served as a place for Christian Scientists to hold church services and Sunday school from December 1942 until March 1947. The building later housed the Bound's Bakery. Today it is a tire and wheel business. (Courtesy of the Reisterstown Room.)

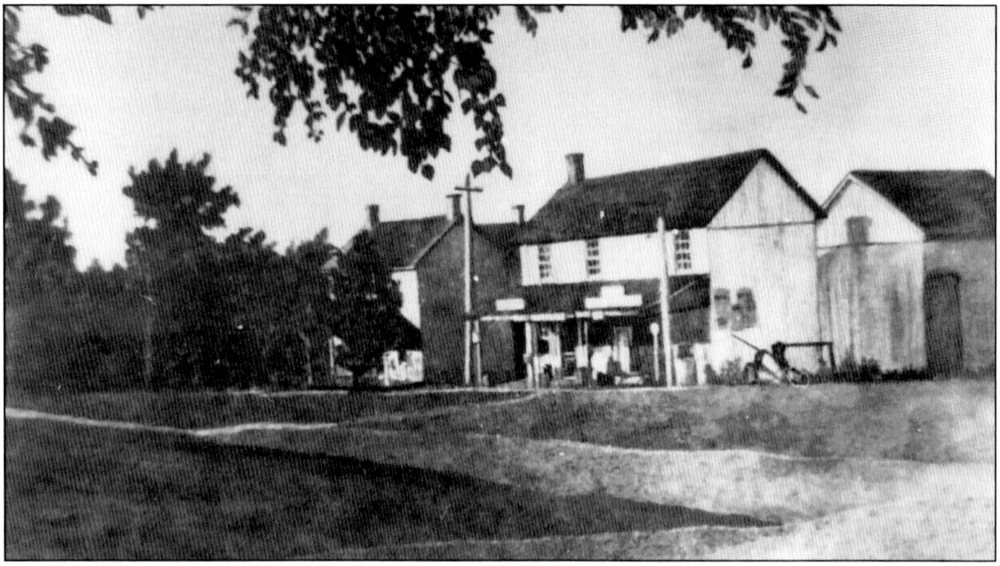

Shown is the original appearance of the Eckhardt Funeral Chapel on Reisterstown Road in what is now Owings Mills. At one time Robert Cross owned the 19th-century business. The structure shown is actually a log cabin since covered with siding that was built before the Civil War. An unknown photographer captured the image sometime in the early 20th century.

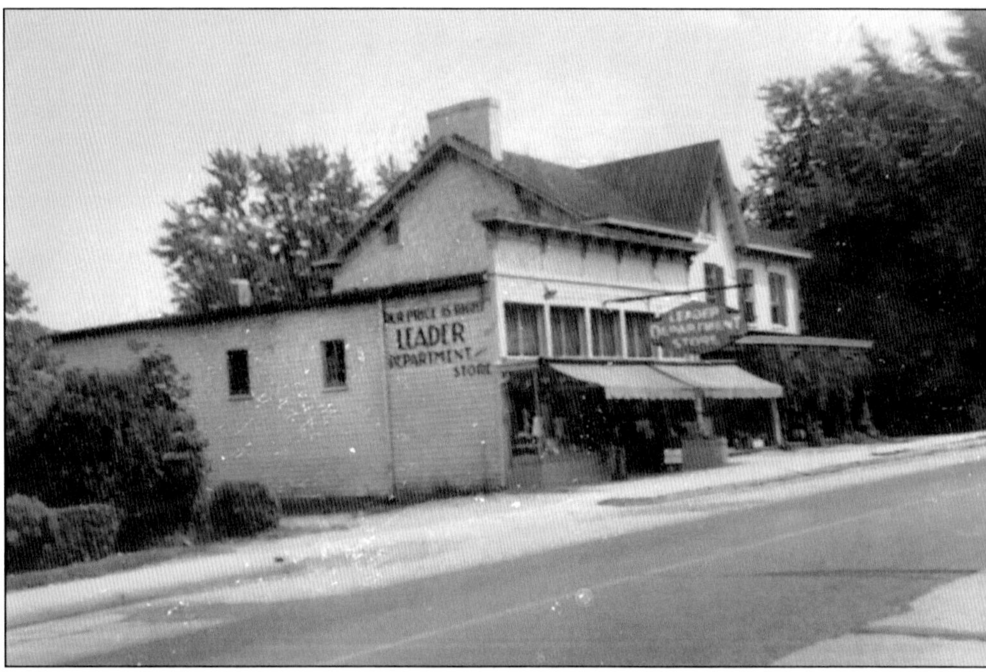

The Leader Department Store on Main Street was popular in the 1900s. On the side of the frame building, above the store's name, one could read the slogan, "Our Price is Right." The store formerly housed Currie's Store, another popular shopping stop. Today it is home to Tina's Antiques. Louise Bland Goodwin took this photograph in 1941.

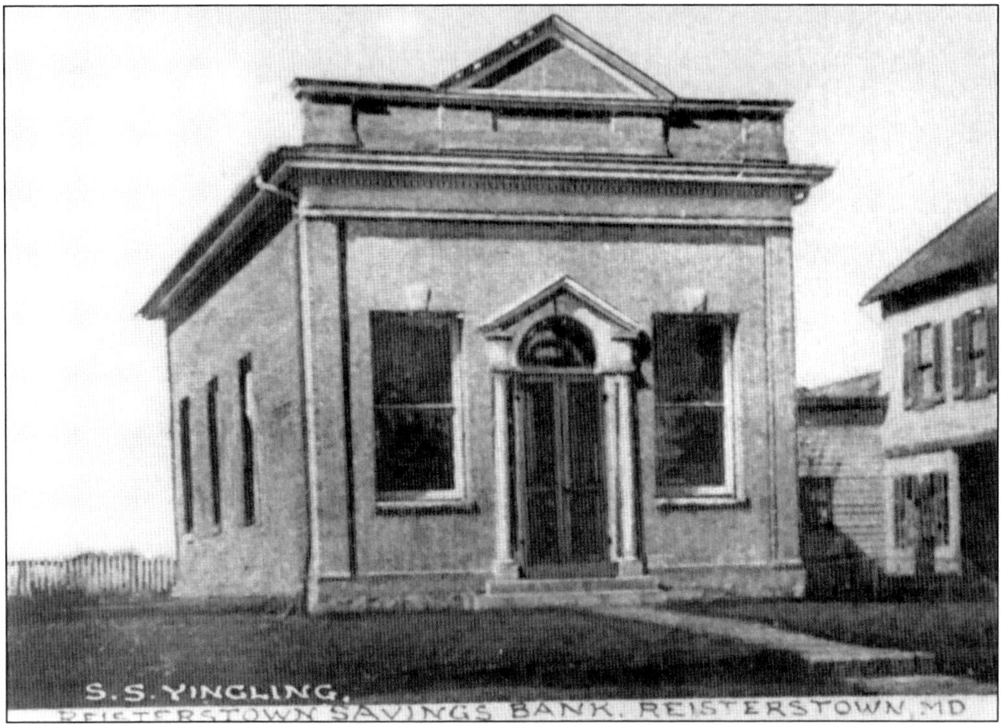

In 1907, an unknown photographer captured this image of the Reisterstown Savings Bank, which was located at 50 West Main Street. The bank began in 1901, with Frank H. Zouck serving as president for a time. Additions were made inside and out until the building was eventually demolished in the 1990s to make room for the Reisterstown Village Shopping Center.

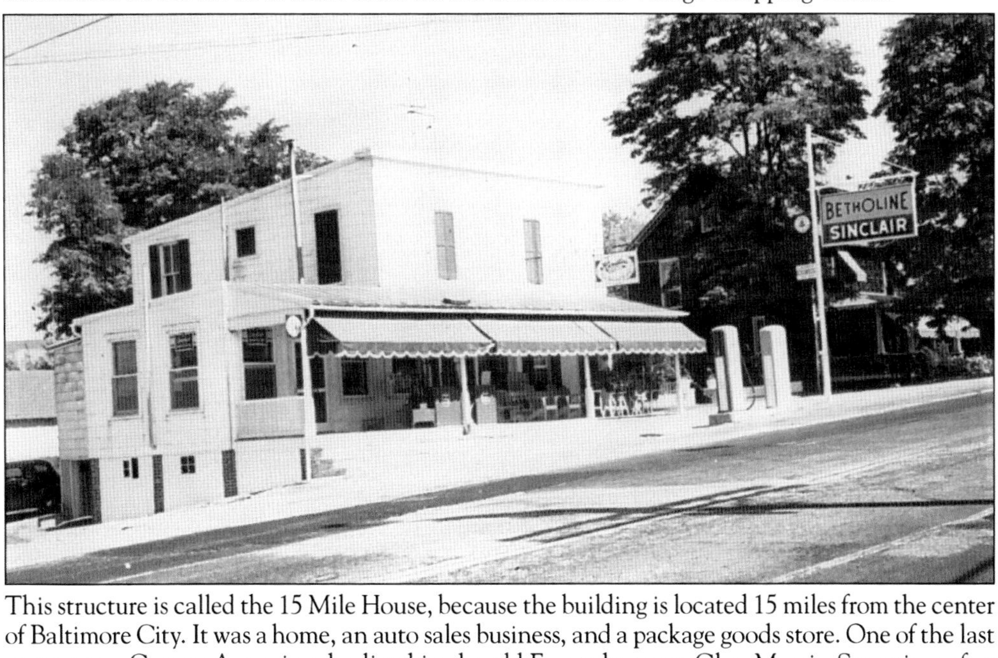

This structure is called the 15 Mile House, because the building is located 15 miles from the center of Baltimore City. It was a home, an auto sales business, and a package goods store. One of the last owners was George Antonis, who lived in the old Frantz home at Glen Morris. Sometime after Antonis's death, the property was sold to Fuddruckers. (Courtesy of the Reisterstown Room.)

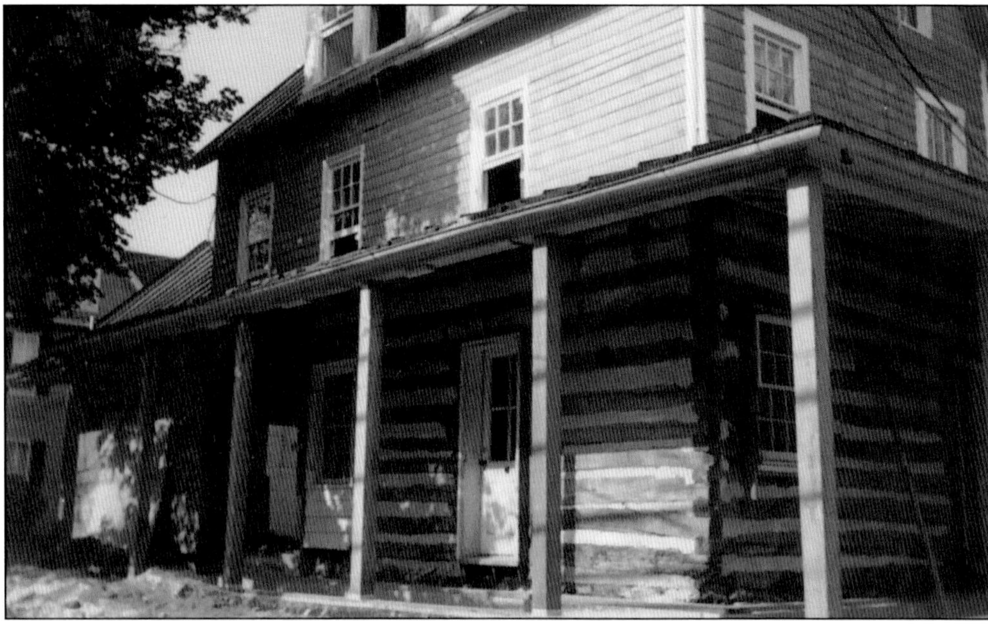

The chestnut and oak log cabin was built shortly after 1798 as a saddlery and harness shop. The core of the surviving structure remains at 340 West Main Street in Reisterstown. Samuel Harryman owned the land on which the house was built in 1814. In 1986, the house was remodeled and became the Harryman House Restaurant. It is one of the earliest homes constructed in Reisterstown that is still standing. (Courtesy of the Reisterstown Room.)

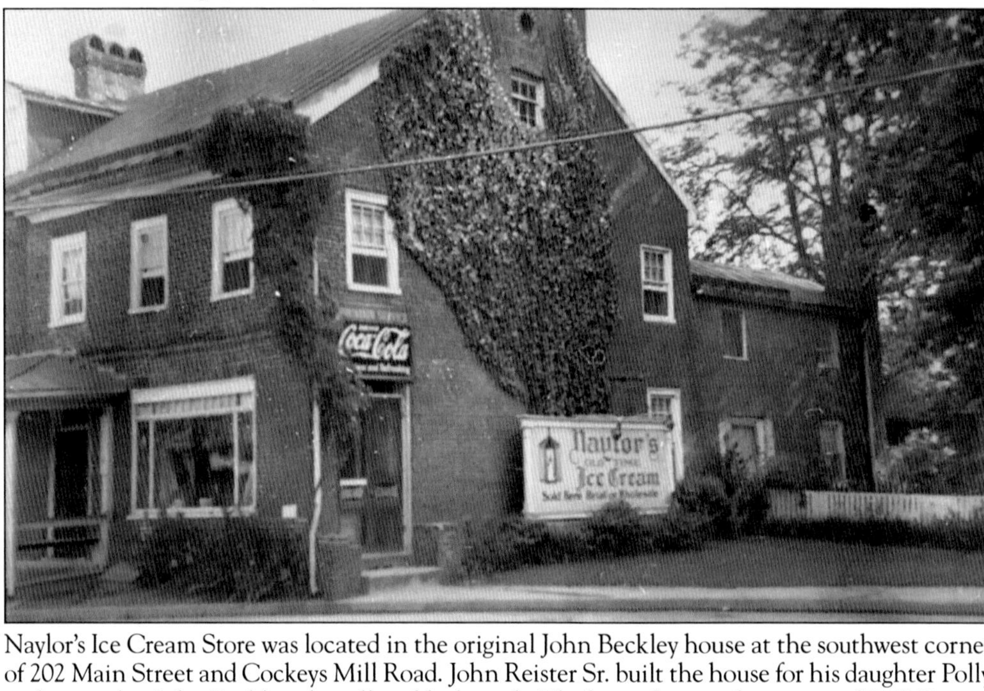

Naylor's Ice Cream Store was located in the original John Beckley house at the southwest corner of 202 Main Street and Cockeys Mill Road. John Reister Sr. built the house for his daughter Polly and son-in-law John Beckley, the village blacksmith. The house bears a date stone of 1779. Fannie Naylor acquired the building in 1909 and advertised an "ice cream parlor opposite the Central Hotel." Today it is a ski shop.

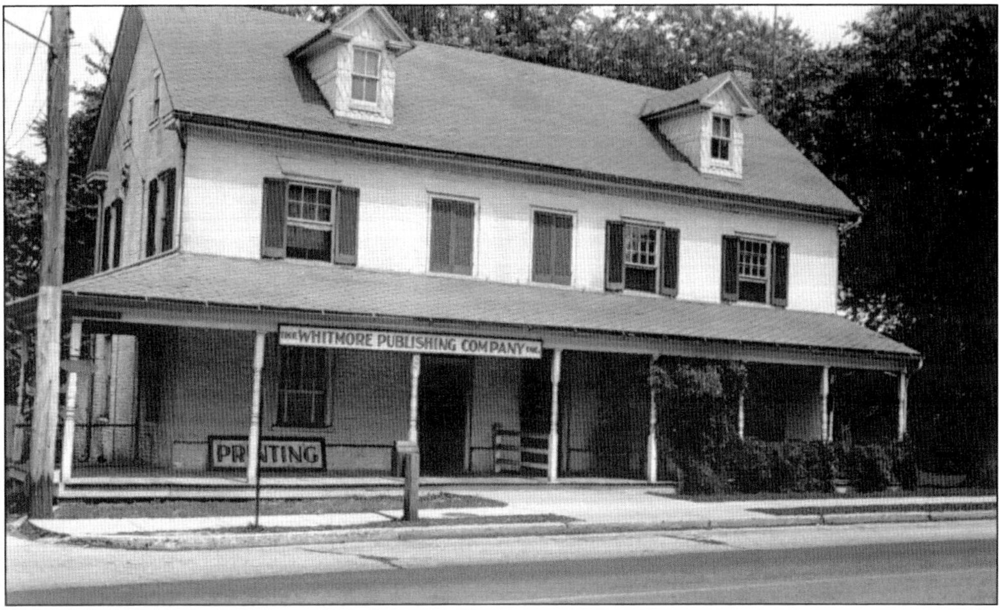

The Whitmore Publishing Company, Inc., publisher of the *Leader*, operated at 301–303 East Main Street at the time of this photograph. John Lanius and his wife, Catherine (the daughter of John Reister II), built the house between 1794 and 1798. The brick structure at the corner of Main and Bond Streets is now home to Constellation Books, an independent general bookstore. Louise Bland Goodwin photographed the historic structure in 1941.

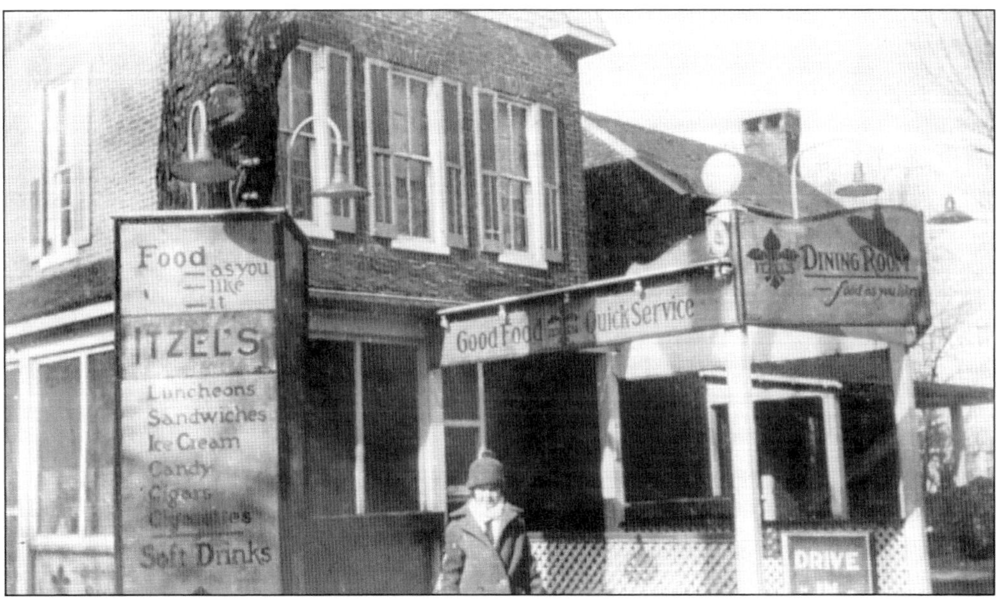

This 1929 photograph of Itzel's Dining Room on the west side of 324 Main Street shows an unidentified young girl standing out front. The business promised "food as you like it." The sign, complete with overhead lights, advertised luncheons, sandwiches, ice cream, candy, cigars, cigarettes, and soft drinks. Note the "Drive In" sign at the lower right of the picture. (Courtesy of the Reisterstown Room.)

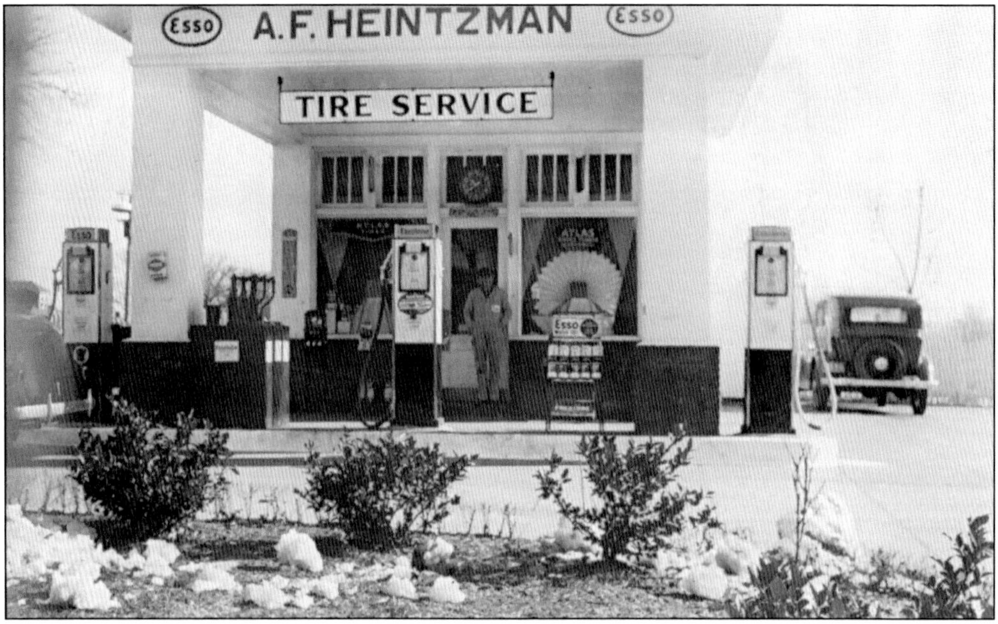

The 1941 Standard Filling Station stood at 101 Main Street on the southeast corner of Main Street and Chatsworth Avenue. The owner, A. F. Heintzman, had his name proudly advertised overhead. An unidentified man, possibly Heintzman, stands at the doorway of the station, which sold Atlas tires, batteries, and accessories. (Courtesy of the Reisterstown Room.)

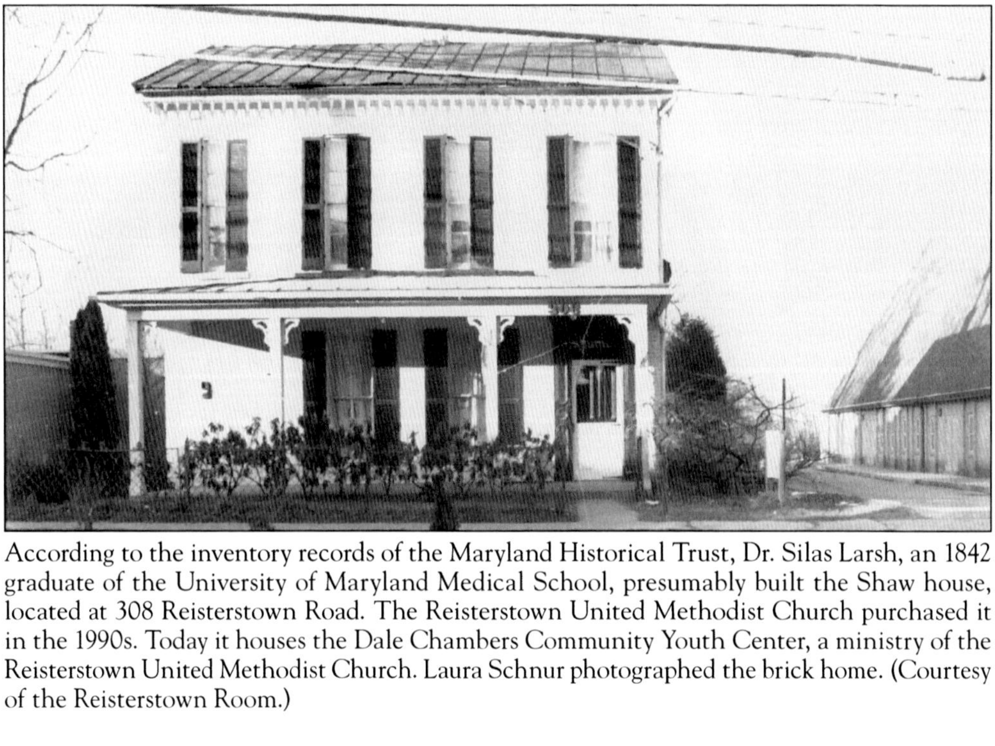
According to the inventory records of the Maryland Historical Trust, Dr. Silas Larsh, an 1842 graduate of the University of Maryland Medical School, presumably built the Shaw house, located at 308 Reisterstown Road. The Reisterstown United Methodist Church purchased it in the 1990s. Today it houses the Dale Chambers Community Youth Center, a ministry of the Reisterstown United Methodist Church. Laura Schnur photographed the brick home. (Courtesy of the Reisterstown Room.)

Three

The Great Fire

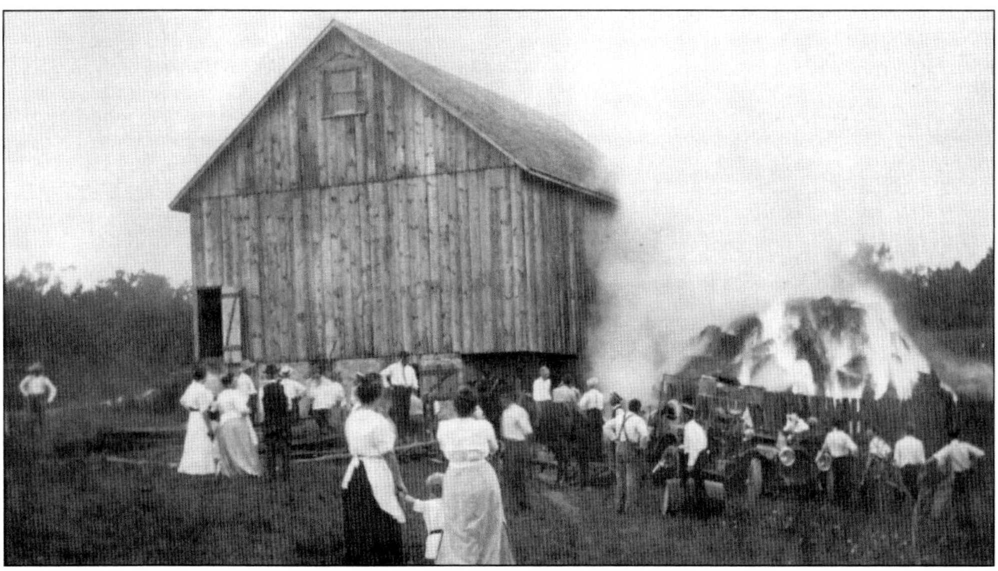

Reisterstown firemen came to the rescue of Delbert Green's barn, located in nearby Mechanicsville. The firefighters managed to drag the burning haystack a safe distance away, while onlookers watched with relief nearby. The fire took place in 1915, one of 28 fire calls that year; another being the train wreck and fire at nearby Fowblesburg. (Courtesy of the Reisterstown Volunteer Fire Company.)

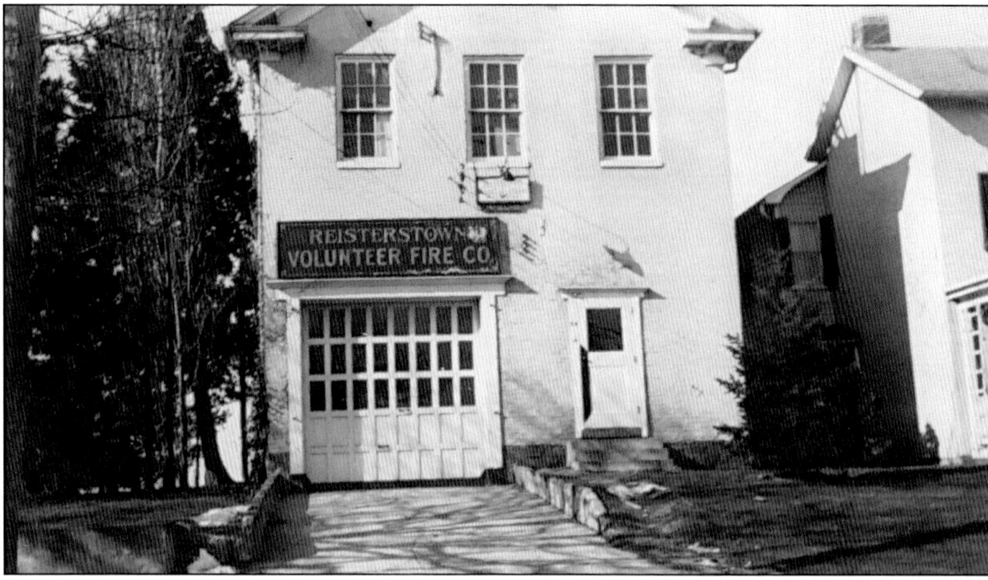

Reisterstown's first fire company called 56 West Main Street home. The equipment consisted of a hose, a hand pump, rubber buckets, and hand chemical tanks but no fire truck. Initial plans to purchase the vacant academy building were cancelled, primarily because it was too far from town. Instead the Odd Fellows Hall at 56 Main Street was purchased and became home for the fire company for the next 34 years. (Courtesy of the Reisterstown Room.)

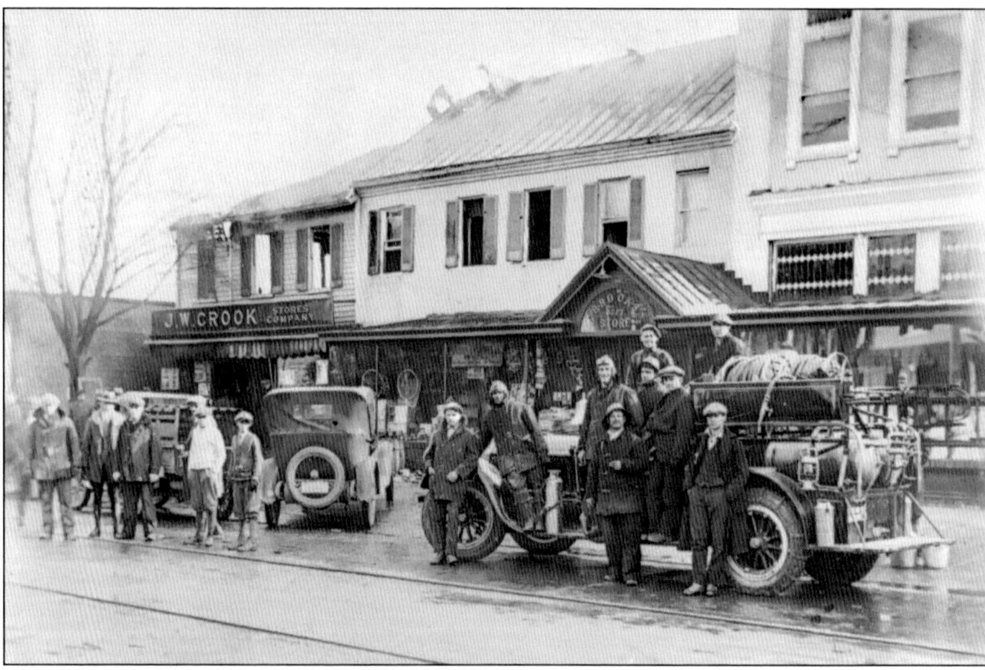

The J. W. Crook building marks the point where the fire was stopped. Eighteen fire companies responded in bitter cold to battle the inferno. The Glyndon Volunteer Fire Department truck with chains in the right foreground is surrounded by firefighters. Among those pictured are Sam Wesley, Eli Hewitt, Lloyd Clifton, Walter Snyder, Bill Linker, and Preston Bosley. Standing at the far left of the photograph are (from left to right) Edward Shaeffer, Edward Devese, and Edwin Eline.

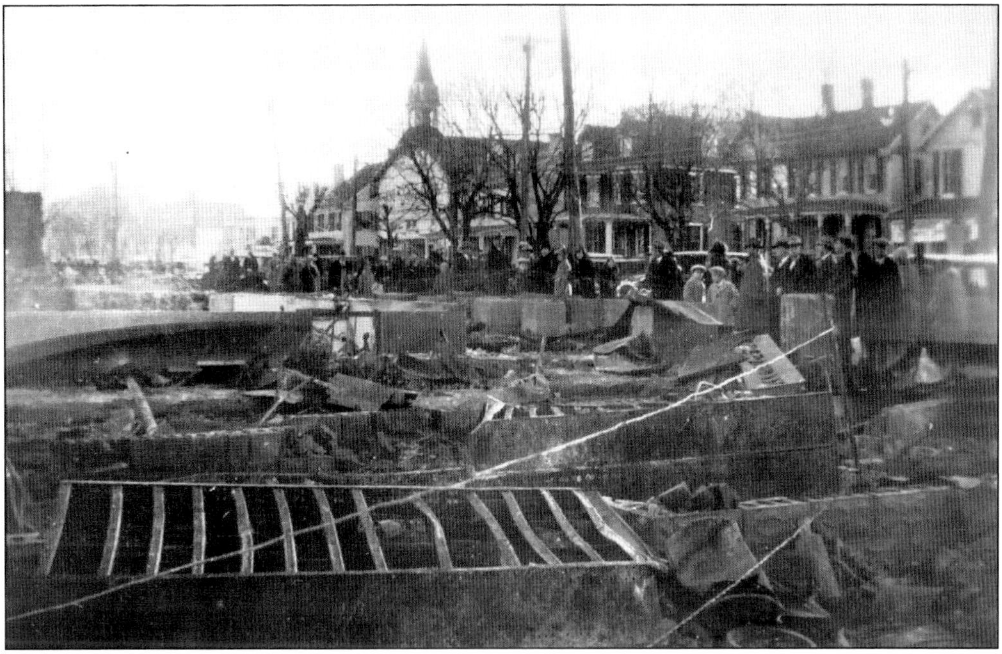

This view is looking west on Main Street from the vantage point of the smoldering ruins. The distinctive clock tower of Koenig's Garage, the former livery stable, can be seen in the center background. Crowds gather in the bitter cold, fixated by the enormity of the damages. The 1928 Great Fire was only one of 61 fires that the Reisterstown Volunteer Fire Company responded to that year.

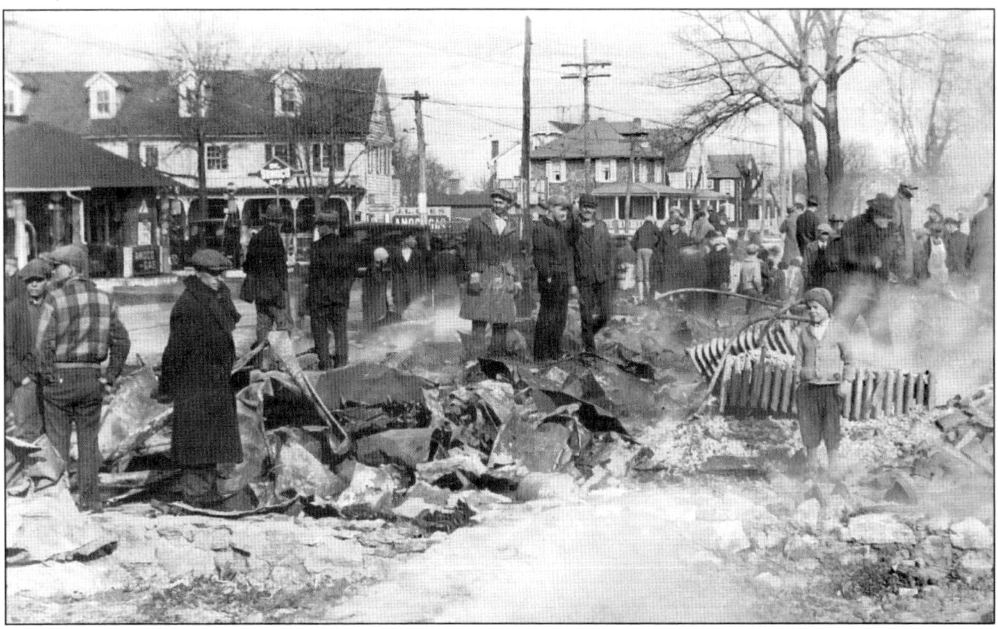

In a state of disarray, onlookers take in the smoking destruction of the Reisterstown fire of February 11, 1928. Looking north on Reisterstown Road, from where Lindy's Drug Store stood, one can see the large historic Hitshue Hotel at back left. In the center foreground, a young Dick Bond tilts his head in acknowledgment of the camera recording the historical moment.

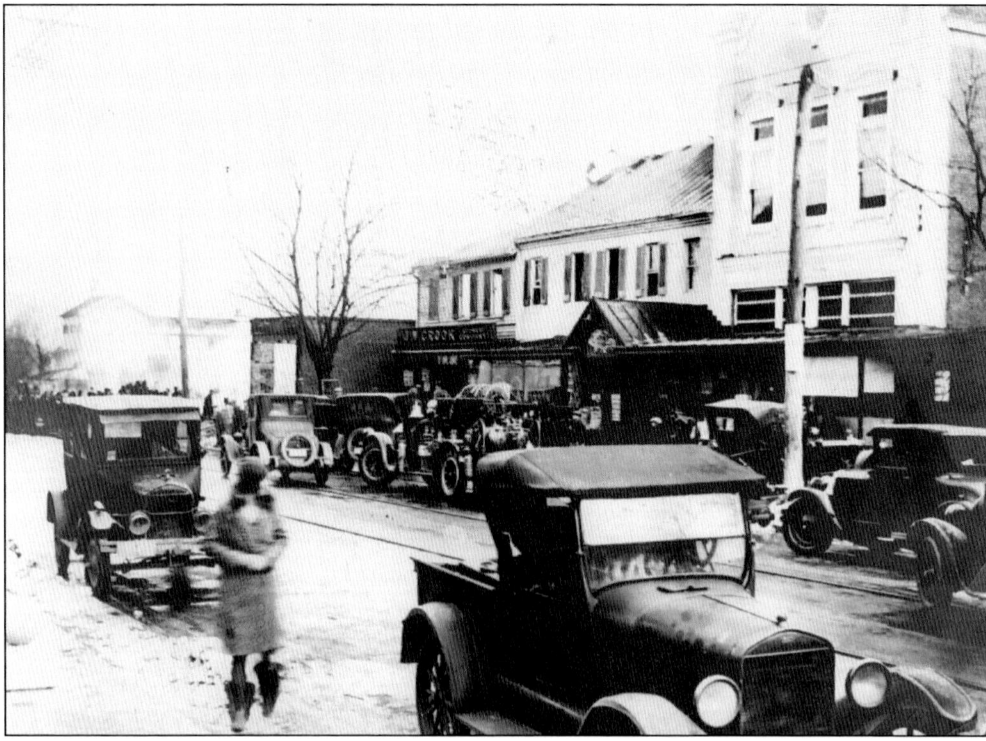

The Reisterstown Volunteer Fire Company, assisted by 17 other companies, valiantly fought the blaze that burned for 11 hours and threatened the entire business district. Having no convenient fire hydrants or pumpers, water was hand pumped from Johnson's Ice Pond, located approximately 2 miles west of town. A majority of the business district was destroyed, but fortunately no lives were lost. In the distant background, the fire damage on East Main Street can be seen.

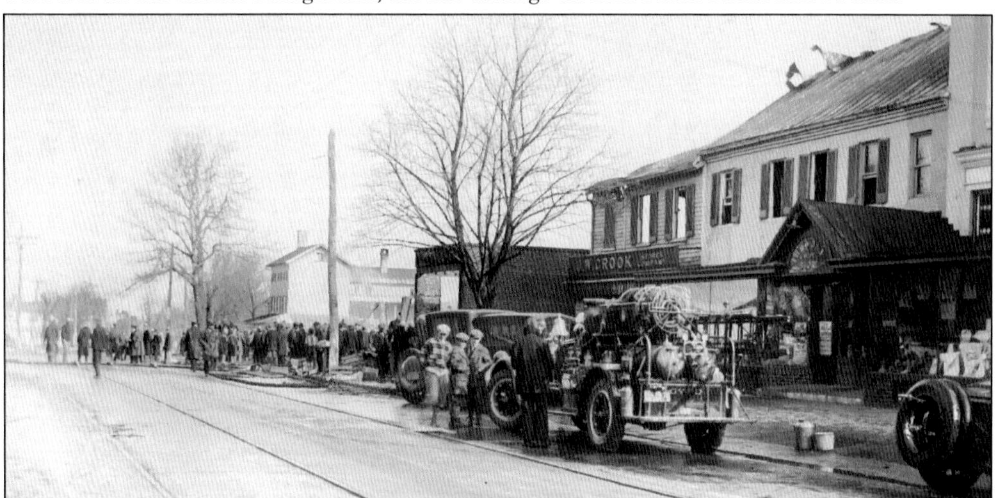

Crowds and equipment are shown in the aftermath of the fire that destroyed eight stores on Main Street. Marion H. Michael discovered the fire at 3:45 a.m. in Sander's Meat Market. Seventeen-year-old Evelyn Cook, on duty at the telephone exchange, called neighboring communities for help. Residents pushed for dynamite to be used to stop the spread of the fire, but it was finally stopped at the brick walls of Brook's Hardware Store.

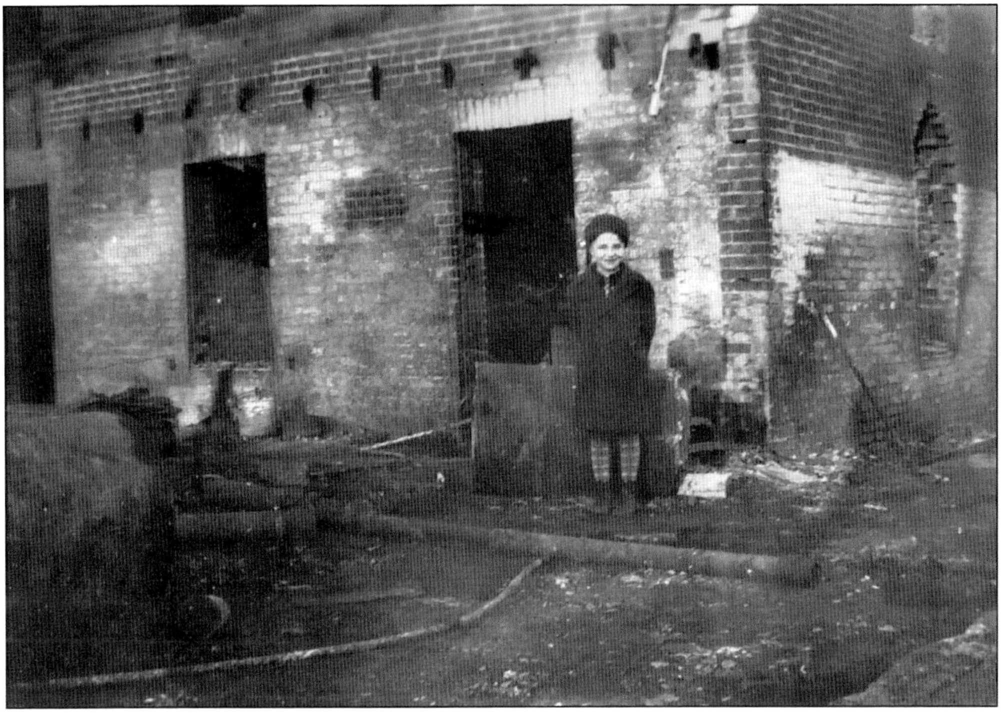

A young, smiling Reisterstown resident poses for the camera against the backdrop of the ruins of the Great Fire. The disaster marked an important event, which would never be forgotten but was recorded forever in the annals of history. The unidentified child was likely one of many who recorded the event for posterity. (Courtesy of the Reisterstown Room.)

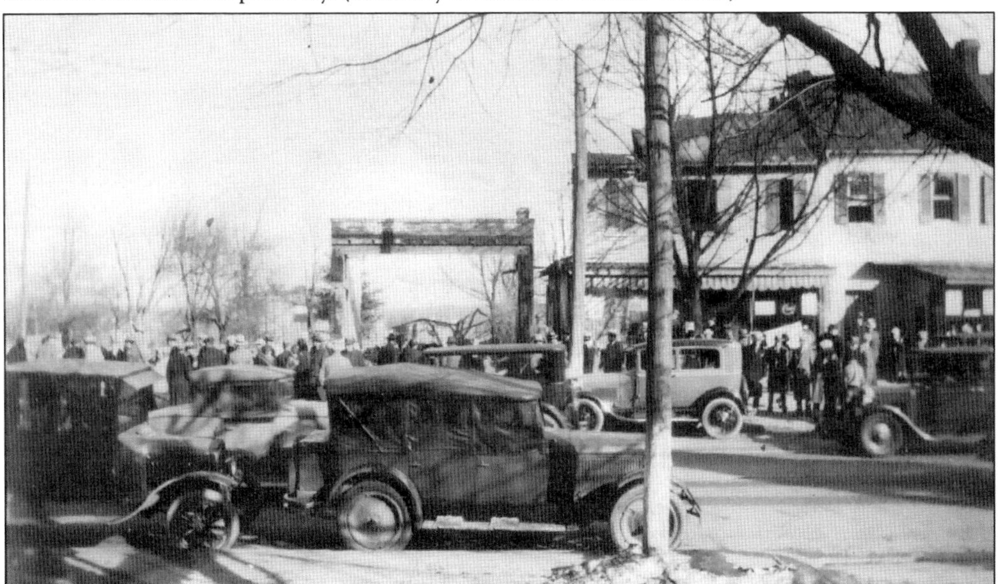

Looking east across Main Street, one can see where the fire stopped. J. W. Crook's store, with its striped awning, is still standing. Immediately to the right of the store is Brook's Hardware Store, and directly in the center of the picture are the remains of Hill's store. Crowds gather in disbelief, taking in the historic spectacle. (Courtesy of the Reisterstown Room.)

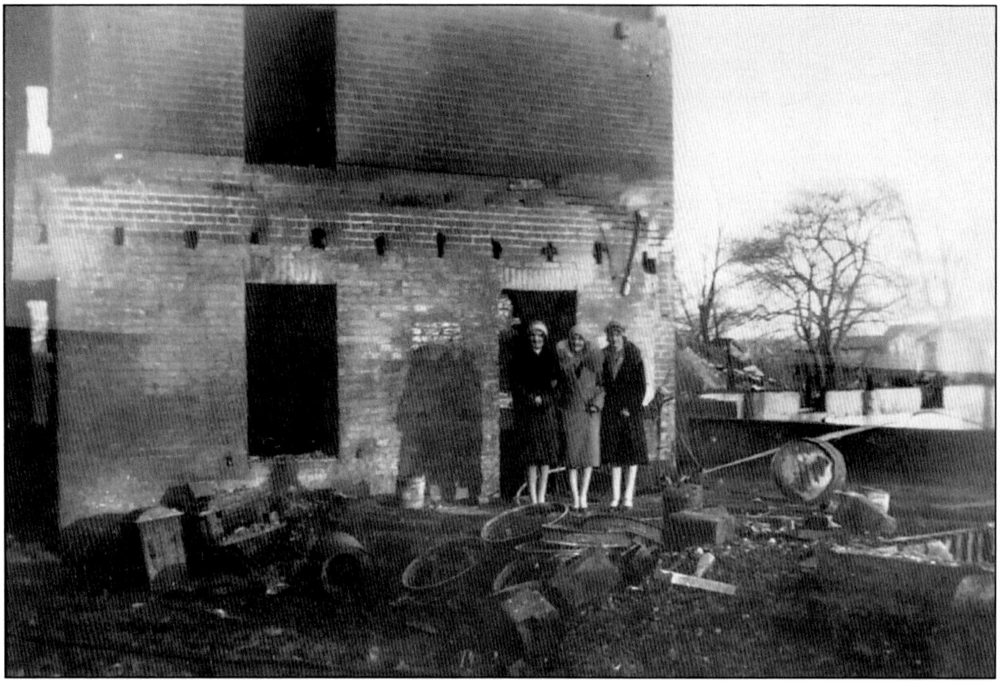

On the back of the photograph above are written the words, "Me, Rosie, and Zorah," and on the back of the photograph below is the name "Gingrich." Both photographs show people posing against the backdrop of the devastation from the Great Fire of 1928 that almost wiped out the business district. It destroyed the Tourist's Lunchroom, a vacant dwelling at the rear of the Christholf Apartments, John Sander's Meat Market and dwelling, Rimby Brothers Bowling Alley, the A&P store, John Yingling's Confectionery Store, Dr. C. H. Michael's Drug Store and dwelling, T. K. Hill's Store and dwelling, and the Smith Chevrolet Agency. J. W. Cook's Store and Harry Brook's home were partially destroyed. (Courtesy of the Reisterstown Room.)

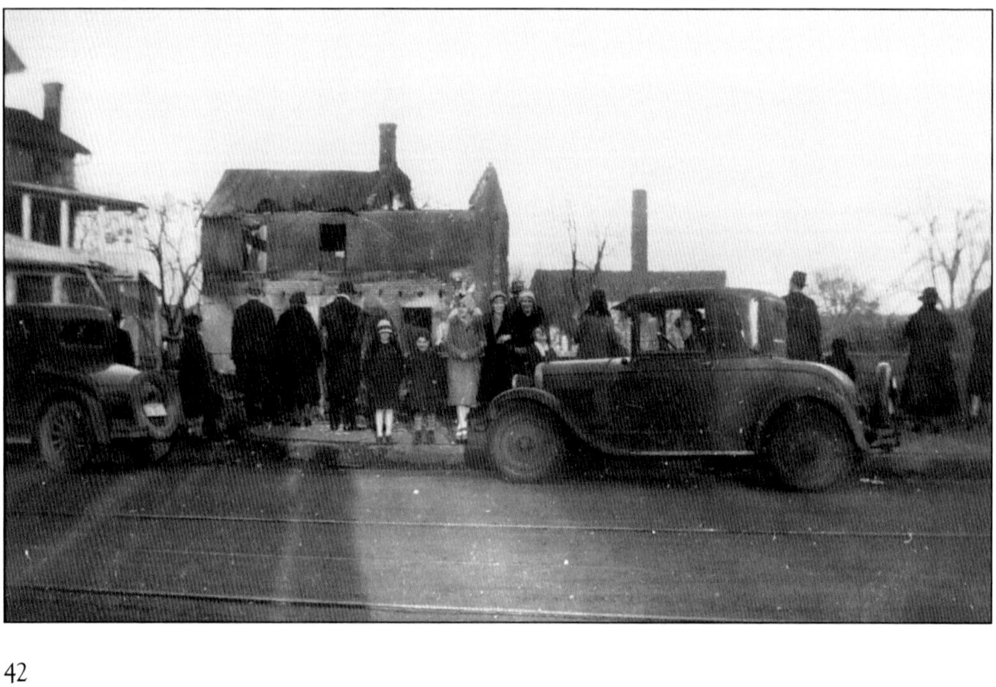

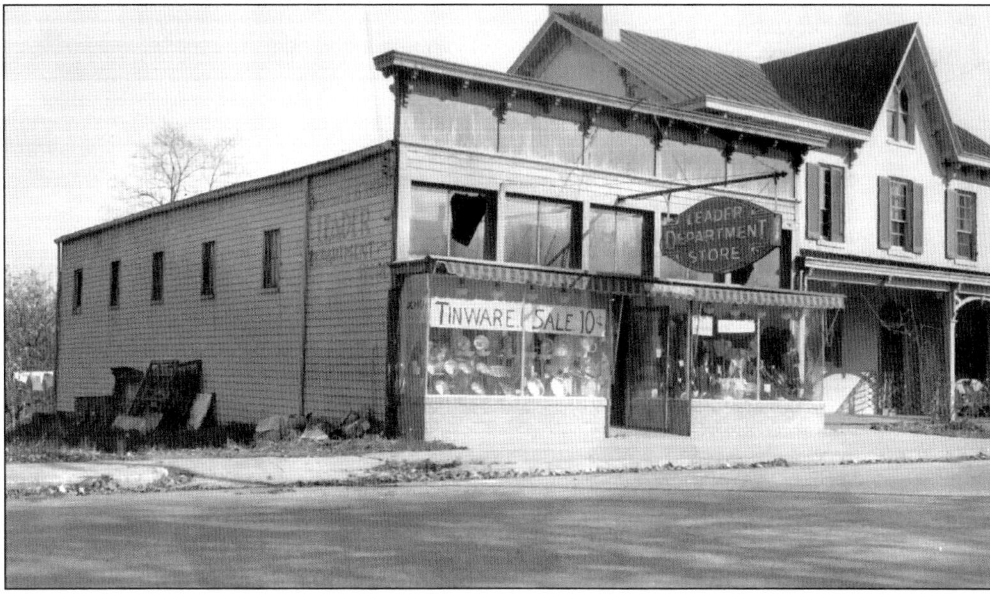

The Leader Department Store is shown almost six years after the Great Fire of 1928. The front door stands ajar, welcoming customers, and the sign in the store window offers tinware for only 10¢, not a bad price even for decorative and utilitarian tin pieces of what is oft-called "poor man's silver." The photograph is dated November 2, 1934. (Courtesy of the Reisterstown Room.)

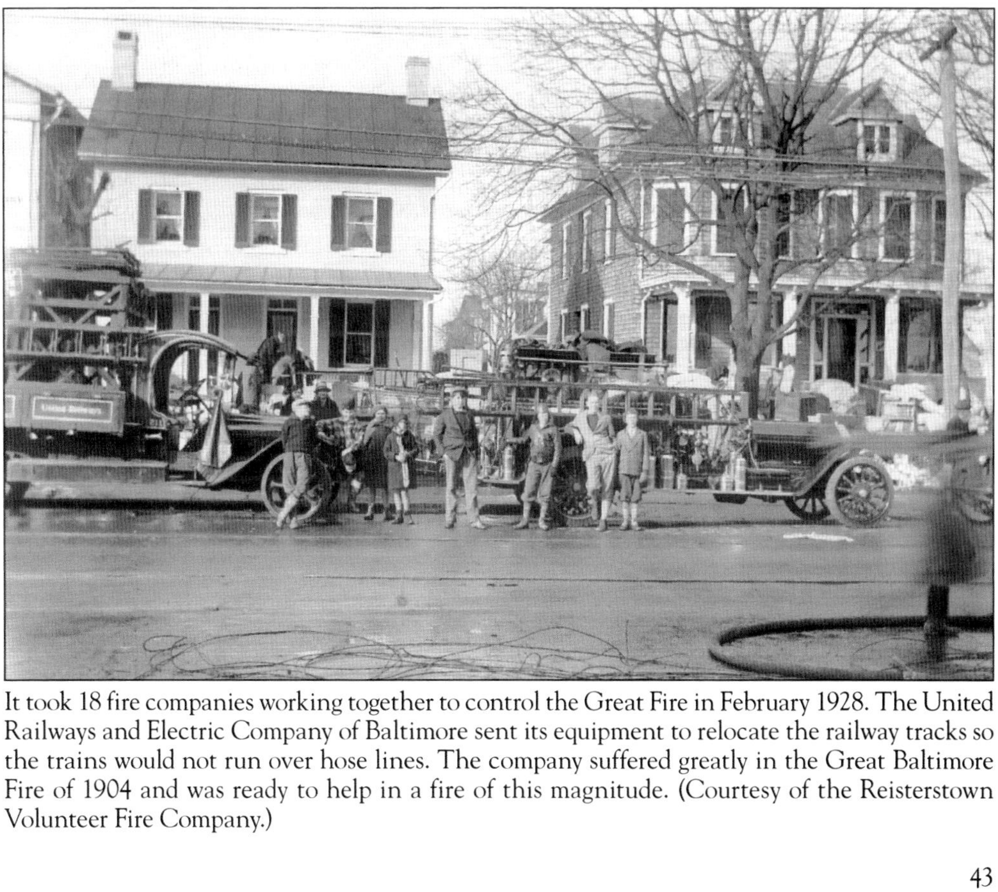

It took 18 fire companies working together to control the Great Fire in February 1928. The United Railways and Electric Company of Baltimore sent its equipment to relocate the railway tracks so the trains would not run over hose lines. The company suffered greatly in the Great Baltimore Fire of 1904 and was ready to help in a fire of this magnitude. (Courtesy of the Reisterstown Volunteer Fire Company.)

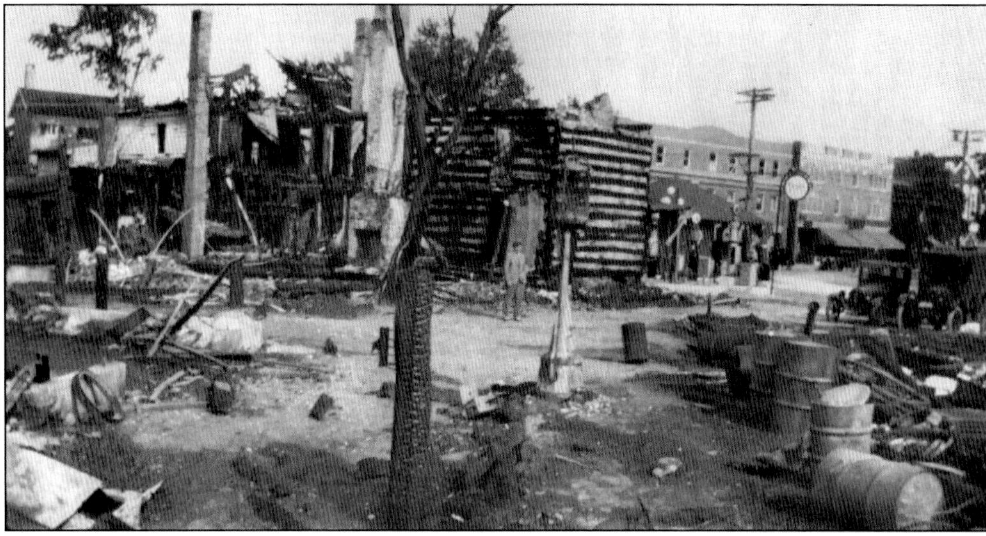

On May 29, 1930, another fire roared through Reisterstown, destroying the Neil Buick garage where it originated, the J. L. Gies store, and a meat house. Hitshue's Hotel, shown in the background, a landmark originally built by Capt. Jeremiah Ducker in 1818, with additions by John Hitshue, was damaged severely. The ruins of Gies Store and the Neil Buick Garage are shown in the foreground. (Courtesy of the Reisterstown Volunteer Fire Company.)

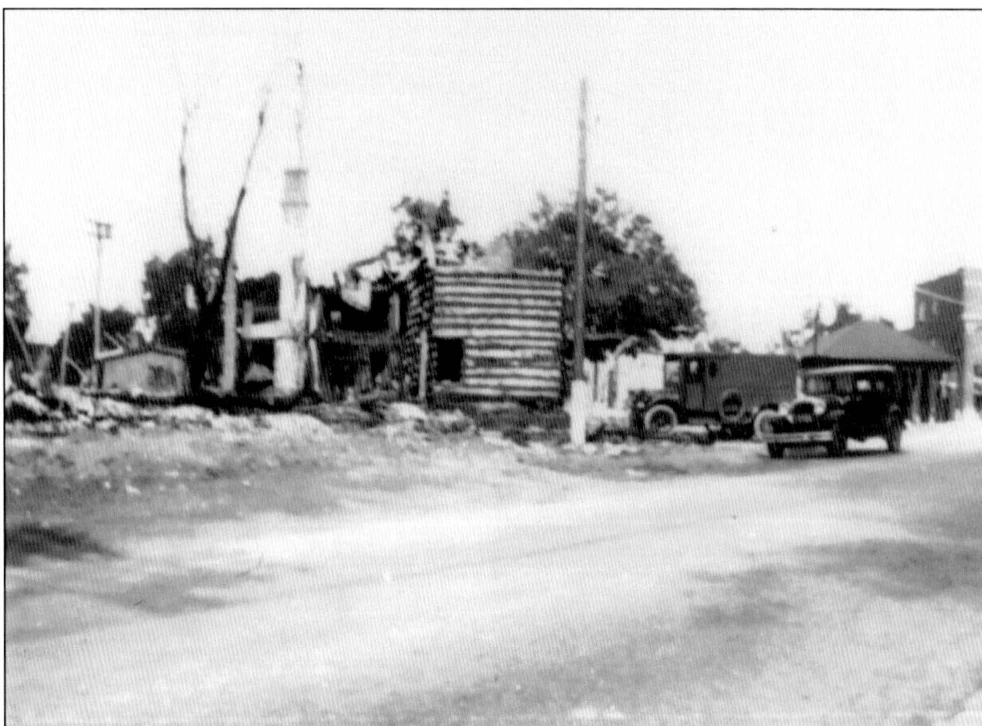

The fire of 1930 was severe, although it was only one of 69 fires that the Reisterstown Volunteer Fire Company battled that year. The old flint mill at Glen Morris and Samuel Yeatts's ice storage house in nearby Glyndon also went up in flames. The scene shows the devastation of the Hitshue Hotel and surrounding buildings from the vantage point of Westminster Pike.

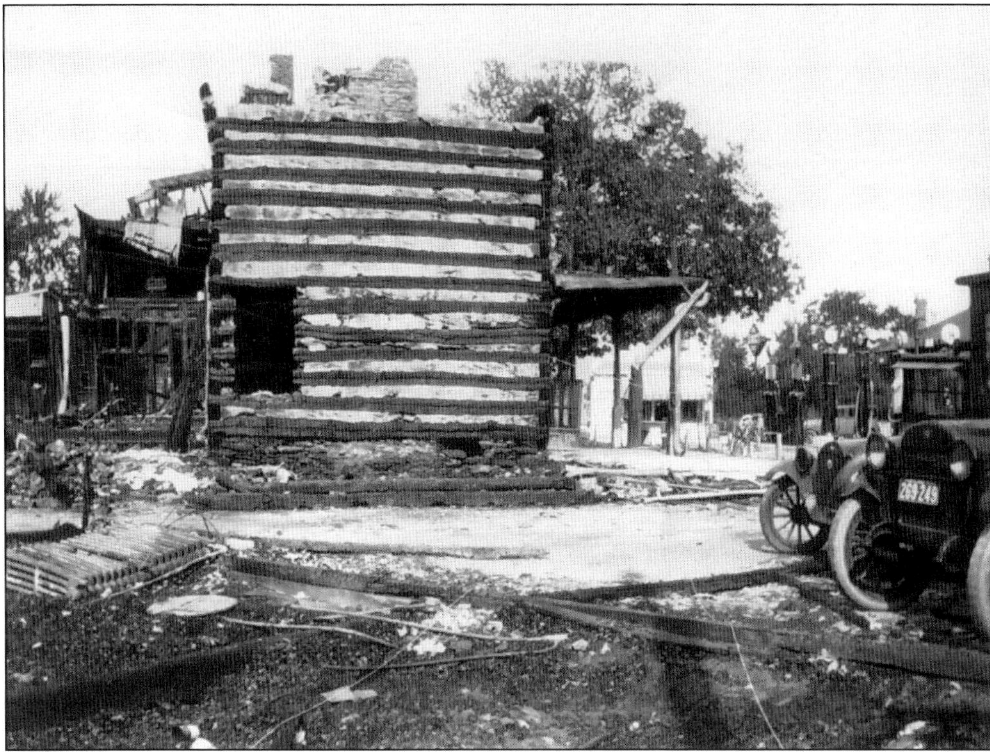

This burned-out shell was all that remained of the historic Hitshue Hotel. The log cabin stands in ghostly tribute to Capt. Jeremiah Ducker, who built the hotel in 1818. Although the 1930 fire was not as large or destructive as the Great Fire of 1928, it took its toll on the cherished history of Reister's Town.

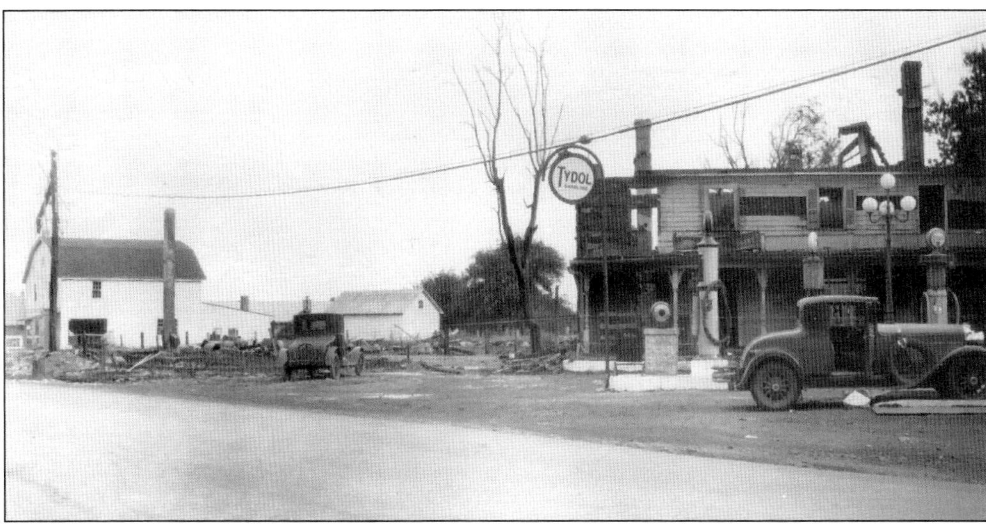

This May 29, 1930, photograph looks northwest from the corner of Westminster Pike at Main Street near the location of the Hitshue Hotel fire. On the left were the J. L. Gies Store and the Neal Buick Garage (formerly the hotel stable), both completely destroyed. The Hitshue Hotel was a town gathering place, as well as a polling place during elections. (Courtesy of the Reisterstown Volunteer Fire Company.)

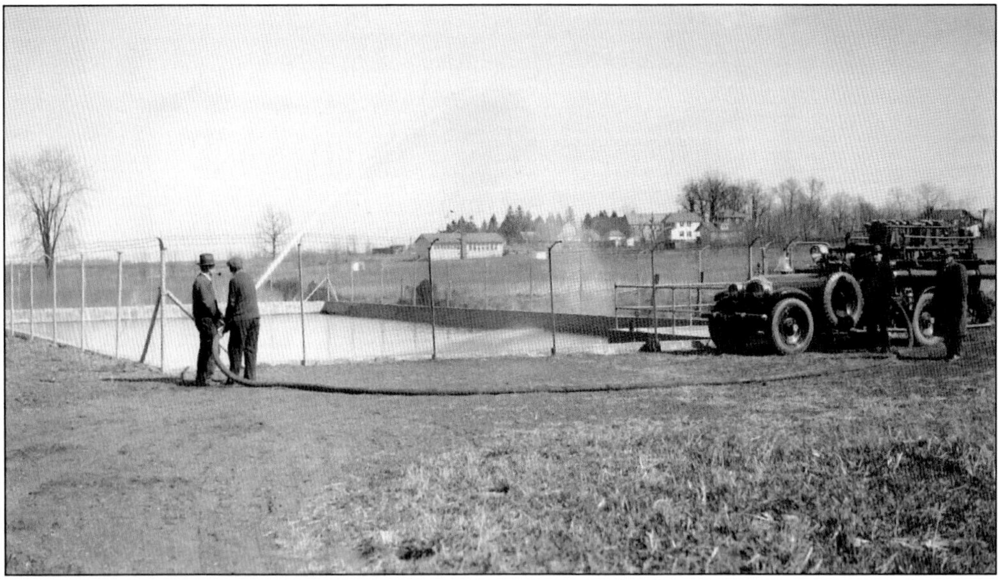

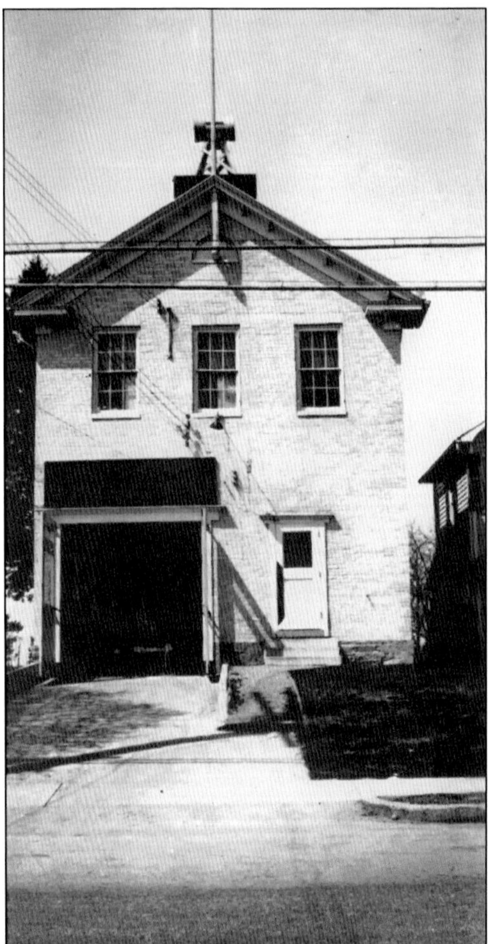

In 1931, the fire company constructed a desperately needed 300,000-gallon reservoir on land located behind Hobbs Hotel. The land was rented from Lee J. Hobbs for the sum of 1¢ per year. At right is a 1922 Packard pumper truck. The firemen pictured from left to right are Edward Schaeffer, John Eline, Edward Eline, and Clyde Palmer. (Courtesy of Reisterstown Volunteer Fire Company.)

At a special meeting in Uhler's store on May 25, 1914, it was voted to buy the Odd Fellows Hall at 56 Main Street for the sum of $1,500 to house the Reisterstown engine. The location served as a firehouse for the next 34 years. The building, erected in 1852, required significant remodeling to fit the company's needs. The members did much of the work. (Courtesy of the Reisterstown Volunteer Fire Company.)

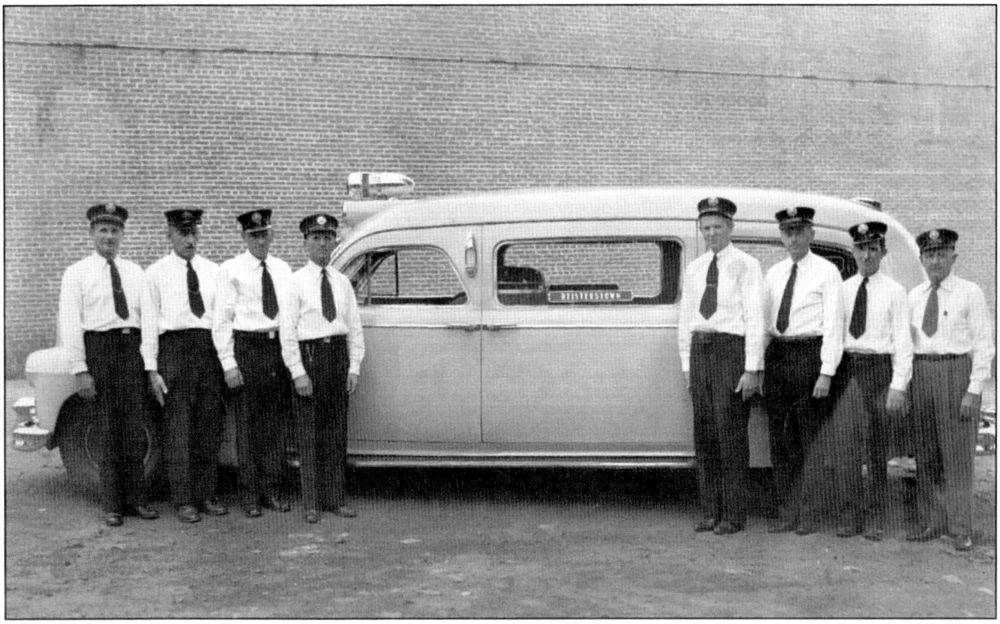

On display is the first ambulance donated by the Reisterstown Kiwanis Club in 1948. There were 189 ambulance calls that year. The crew is shown with the ambulance. From left to right are (standing) Richard Isennock, Walter Merkle, William Peeling, Calvin O. McElhattan Sr., William Leppo, Robert Stansfield, William Hickman, and William Linker Sr. (Courtesy of the Reisterstown Volunteer Fire Company.)

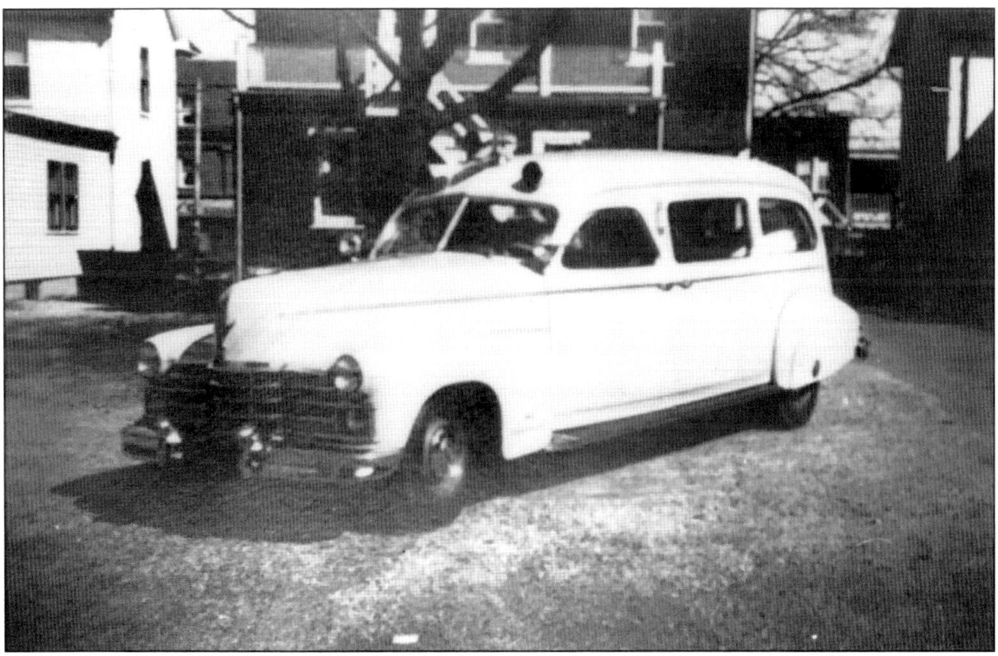

The ambulance was received on January 21 and was put into service on January 22, 1948. The Cadillac ambulance cost $6,155. It was housed in the garage of the Eline Funeral Home until a new station house was built. Plans for a new station began after World War II ended in 1945. The new building was dedicated on January 30, 1949.

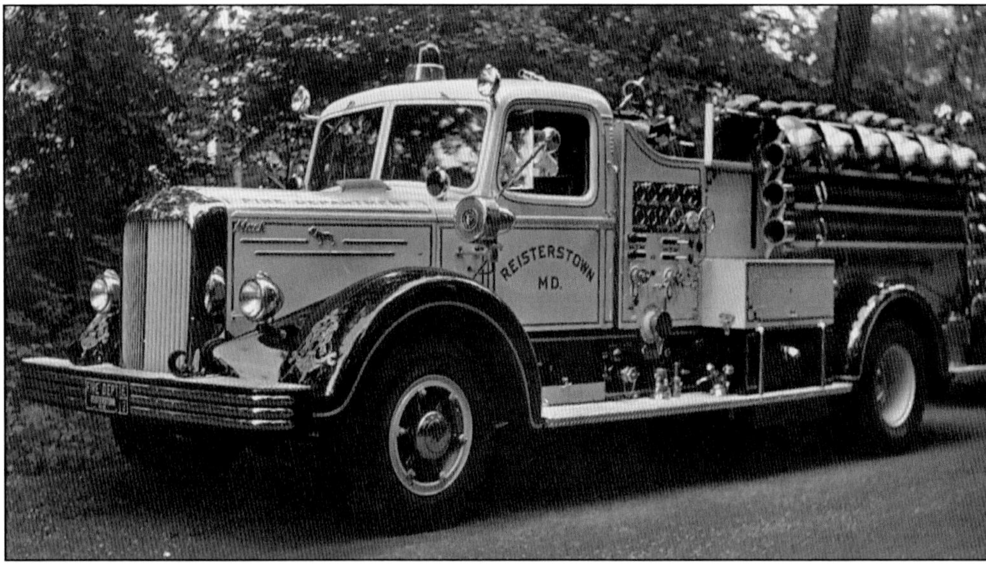

In July 1953, the Reisterstown Volunteer Fire Company started a replacement program for all of its firefighting equipment. The first step was the purchase of a 1953 Mack 1,000 GPM (gallons per minute) pumper with a 400-gallon water tank (shown above). The price of the unit at the time was $29,800. (Courtesy of the Reisterstown Volunteer Fire Company.)

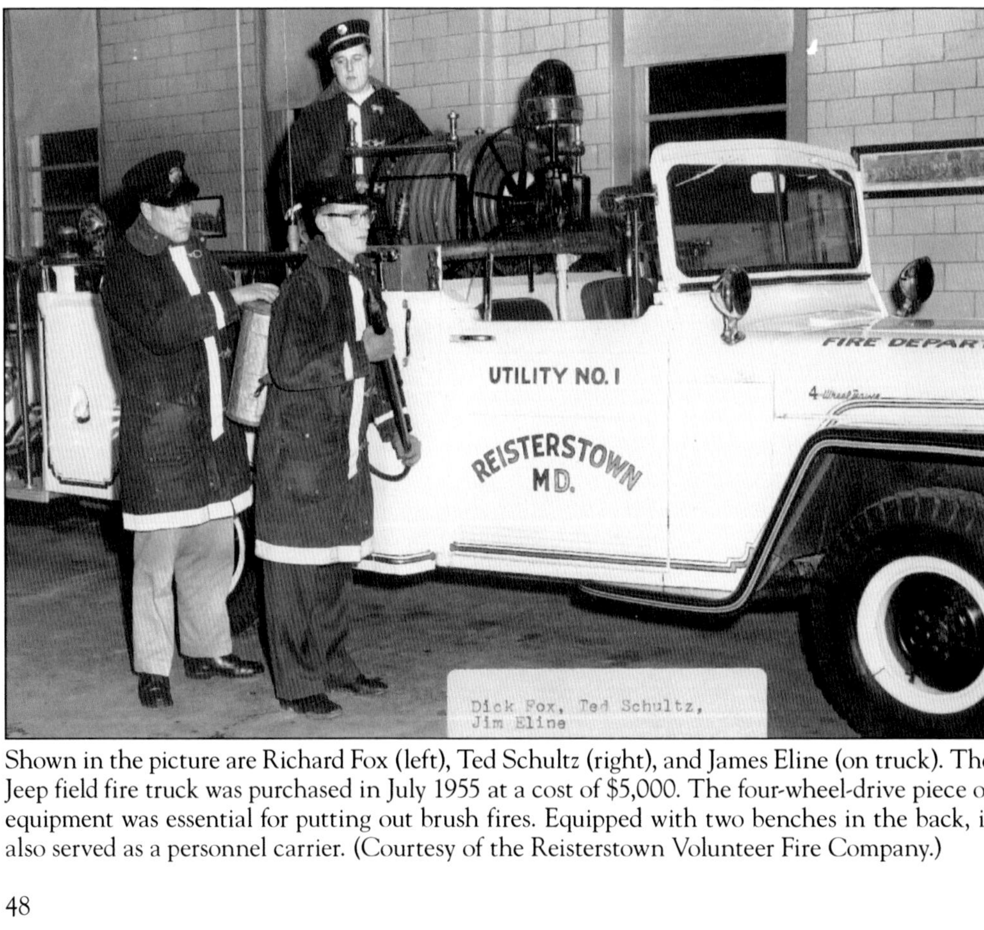

Shown in the picture are Richard Fox (left), Ted Schultz (right), and James Eline (on truck). The Jeep field fire truck was purchased in July 1955 at a cost of $5,000. The four-wheel-drive piece of equipment was essential for putting out brush fires. Equipped with two benches in the back, it also served as a personnel carrier. (Courtesy of the Reisterstown Volunteer Fire Company.)

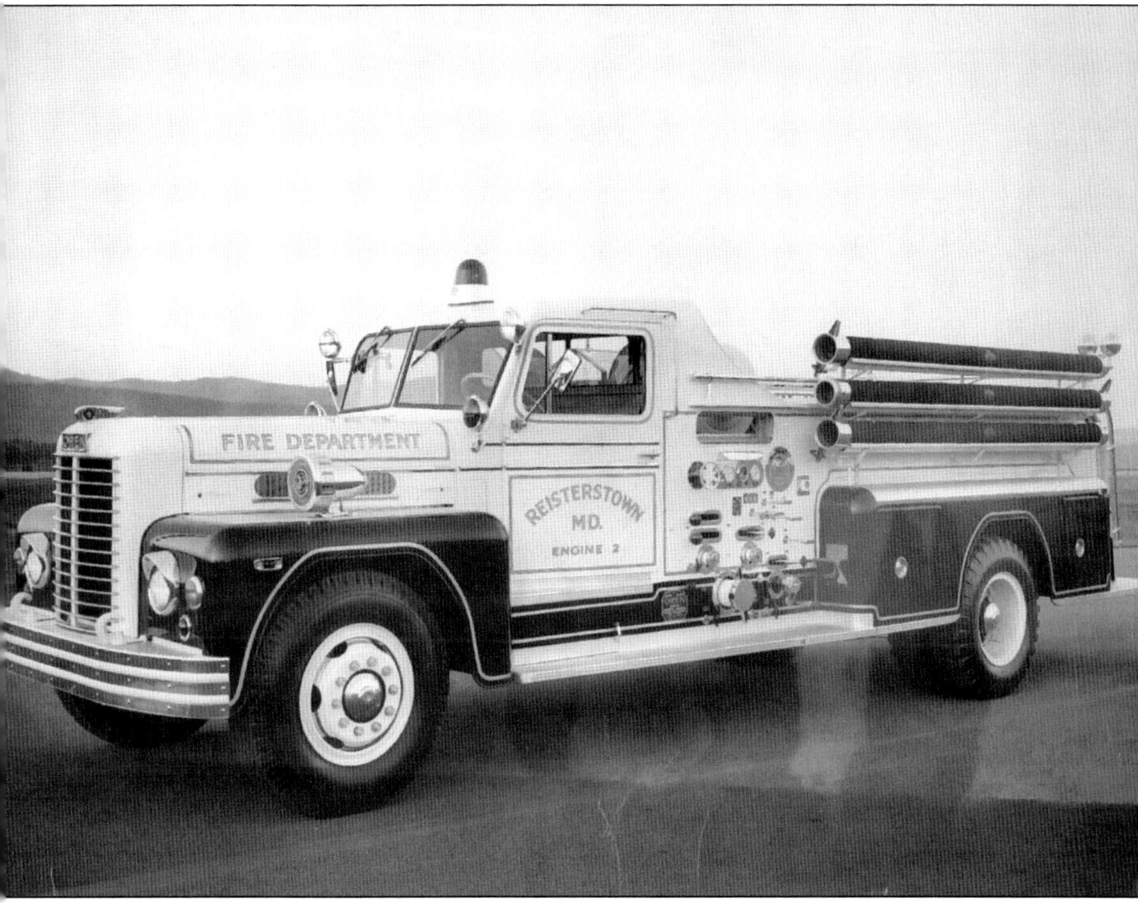

In July 1953, the Reisterstown Volunteer Fire Company started a replacement program of all of its firefighting equipment. After purchasing the Jeep field fire truck, the fire department purchased an Oren 750 GPM pumper with an 800-gallon water tank at a cost of $20,000. The pumper truck, shown here, sports "Engine 2" on its door. (Courtesy of the Reisterstown Volunteer Fire Company.)

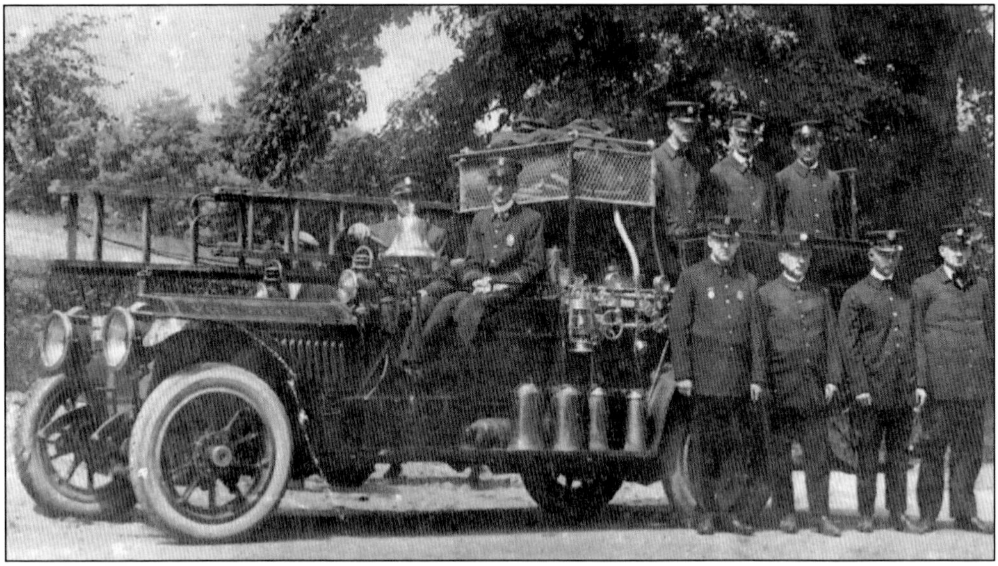

The first truck, a converted 1912 Packard chemical truck costing $3,400, was right-hand drive with carbide headlamps that had to be hand lit for night driving. Seated in 1919 are Thomas Poe (left) and William Stevenson. Standing in front of the truck are, from left to right, George Gillman, unidentified, Edward Schaeffer, and Wade Walters. Standing on the truck are, from left to right, Thomas Rawlings, Orrick Naylor, and Emory Peregoy. (Courtesy of the Reisterstown Volunteer Fire Company.)

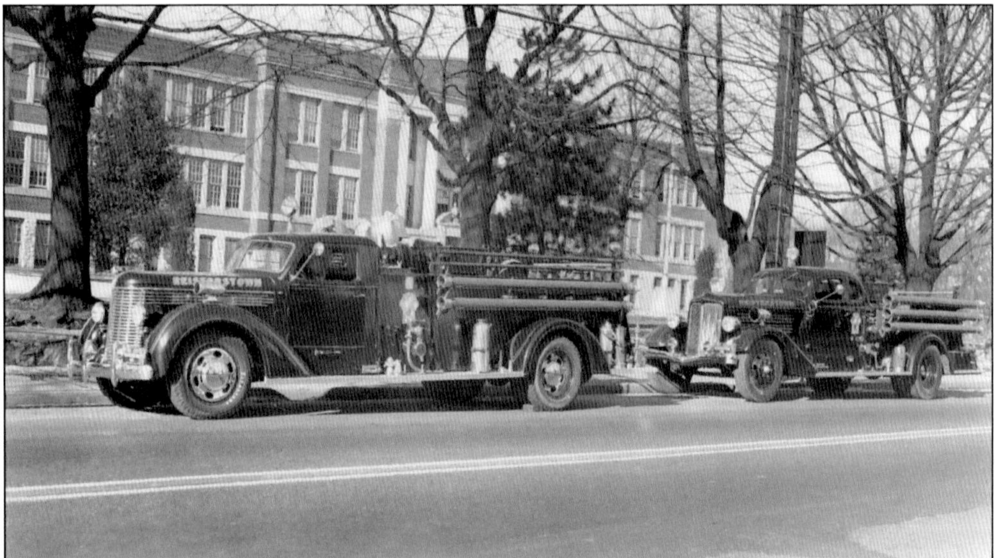

Firefighting equipment is shown parked in front of Franklin High School (now Franklin Middle School) on Reisterstown Road at Cockeys Mill Road. At left is a 1939 Diamond T truck next to a 1937 Packard. The 1939 Diamond T was manufactured at the Diamond T Motor Car Company of Chicago, responsible for more than 50,000 heavy-duty military vehicles used in World War II. (Courtesy of the Reisterstown Volunteer Fire Company.)

Four

POMP AND CIRCUMSTANCE

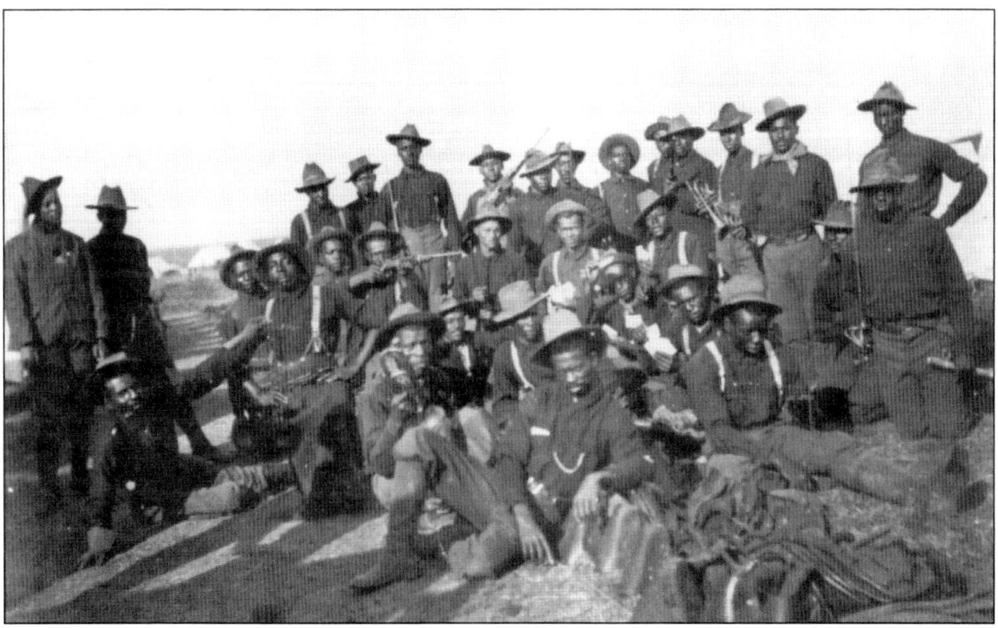

This postcard image shows Buffalo Soldiers of the 9th Cavalry at Camp Wikoff in Long Island in September 1898. The regiment's motto was "We Can, We Will." Shown second from right in the third row wearing a bandana is 1st Sgt. Augustus Walley, a 19th-century Congressional Medal of Honor recipient for bravery. Walley (1856–1938) is interred in the cemetery behind St. Luke's United Methodist Church in Reisterstown. (Courtesy of the Reisterstown Room.)

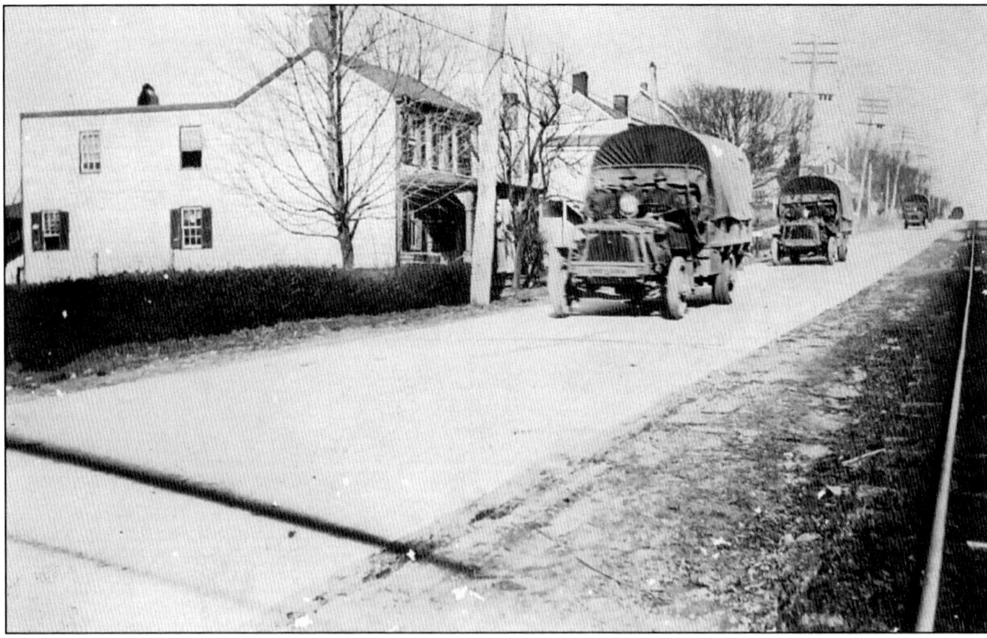

A convoy of World War I army trucks is pictured traveling south along Reisterstown Road. The memorable event was photographed in 1918 as the convoy passed by the houses on the east side of the 400 block of Main Street in the area known as "Smoketown." Mary Syous donated the photograph. (Courtesy of the Reisterstown Room.)

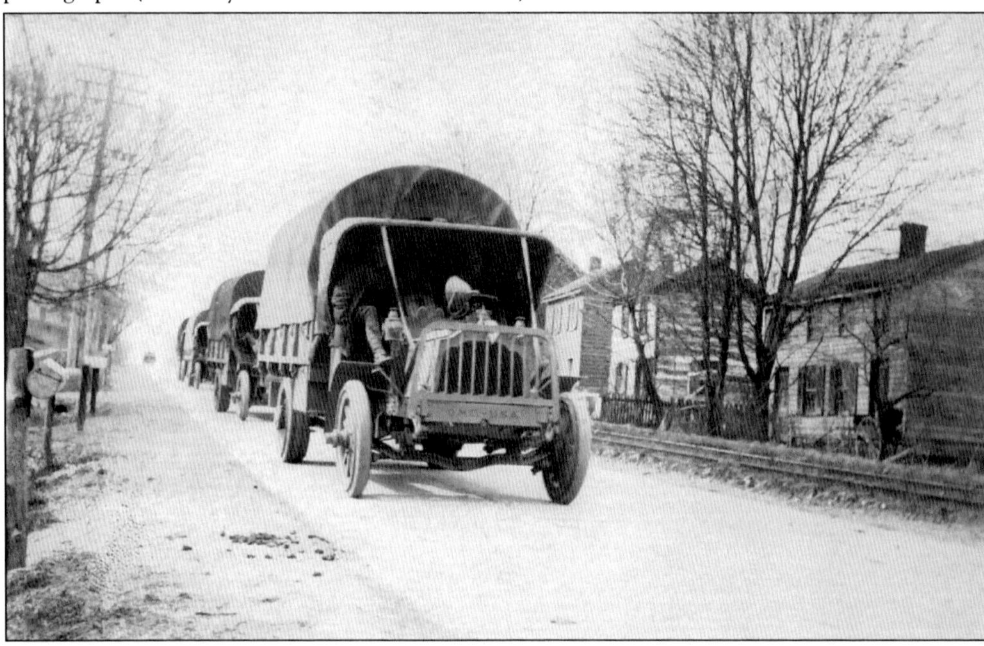

This convoy of covered army trucks from World War I proceeded south past houses on the east side of the 700 block of Reisterstown Road. In 1917, many of the country's men and boys were drafted or signed up to fight. Women were busy knitting sweaters, gloves, and stockings to send to the men at camp. At home, war supporters held war bond rallies, planted war gardens, canned foods, and endured a sugar shortage.

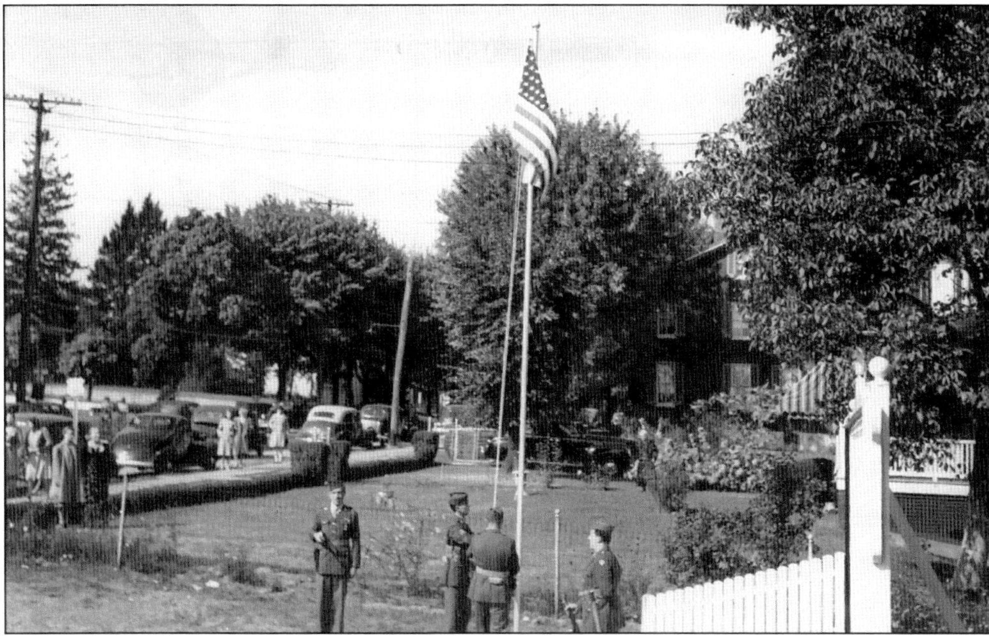

The ceremony marks an unidentified event at the Masonic Temple on Main Street. The brick Dickson home at 67–69 Main Street can be seen through the trees at the far right. The striped awning at the Arnold Ducker house can be seen at the center far right. Lawrence Reter donated this photograph to the Reisterstown Room. (Courtesy of the Reisterstown Room.)

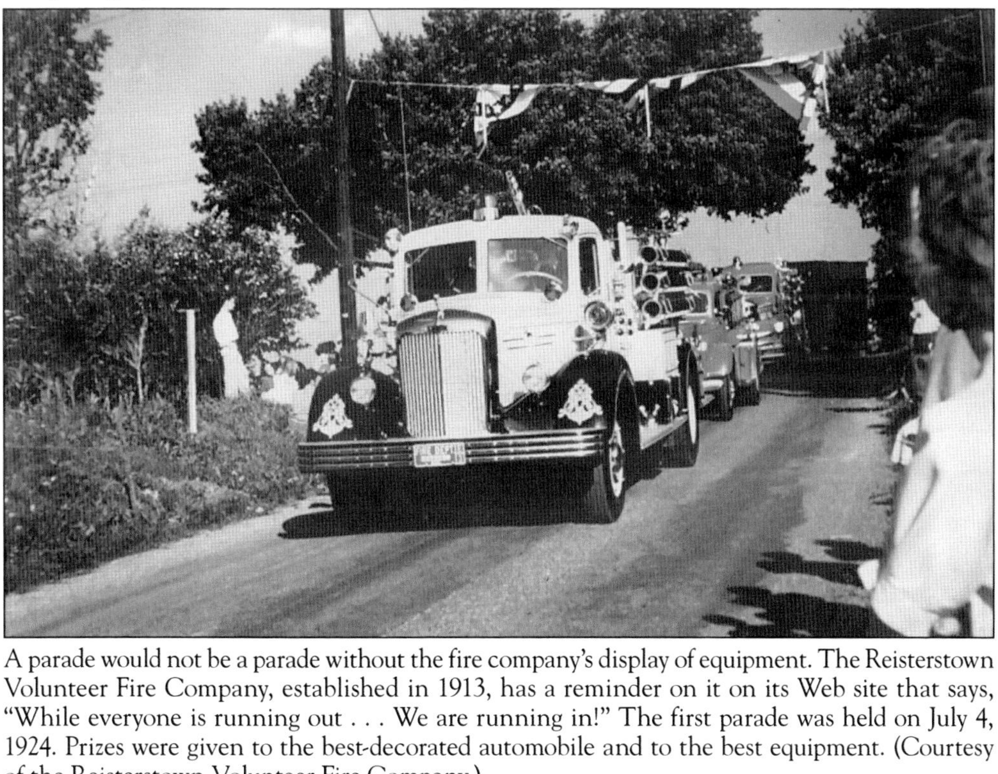

A parade would not be a parade without the fire company's display of equipment. The Reisterstown Volunteer Fire Company, established in 1913, has a reminder on it on its Web site that says, "While everyone is running out . . . We are running in!" The first parade was held on July 4, 1924. Prizes were given to the best-decorated automobile and to the best equipment. (Courtesy of the Reisterstown Volunteer Fire Company.)

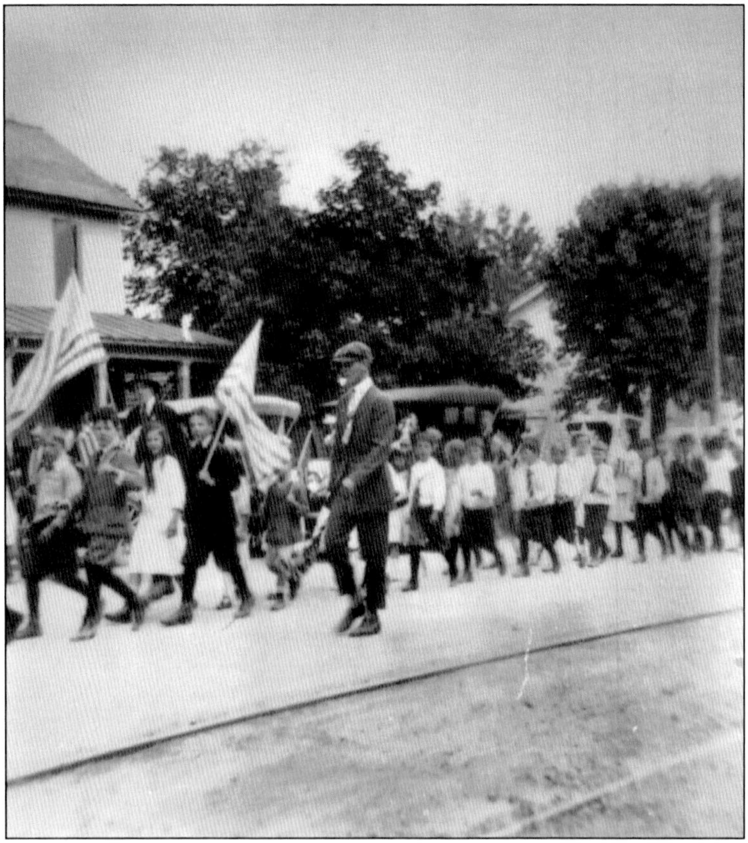

Young boys and girls march by carrying flags, followed by a group of young boys in white shirts and ties passing by what is possibly Hobbs Hotel or Naylor's Ice Cream Parlor. Streetcar tracks can be seen in the bottom right corner. The c. 1917 or 1918 photograph was taken by an unidentified photographer to commemorate a Fourth of July parade during the World War I period.

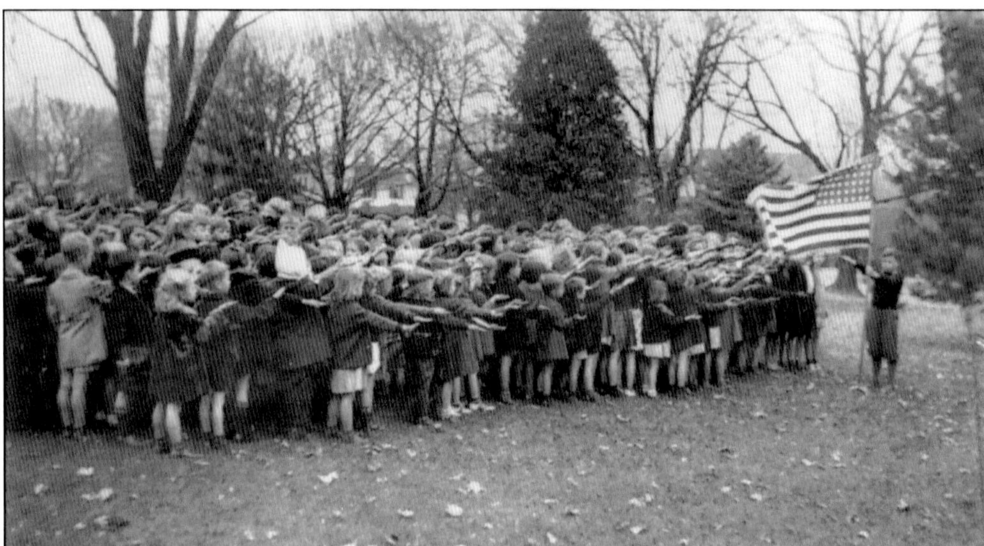

Students from Franklin Elementary are seen here celebrating Armistice Day. Louise Bland Goodwin photographed the event on November 11, 1940. Armistice Day or Remembrance Day was proclaimed a national holiday by Pres. Woodrow Wilson to recognize the armistice signed between the Allies of World War I and Germany near Compiegne, France.

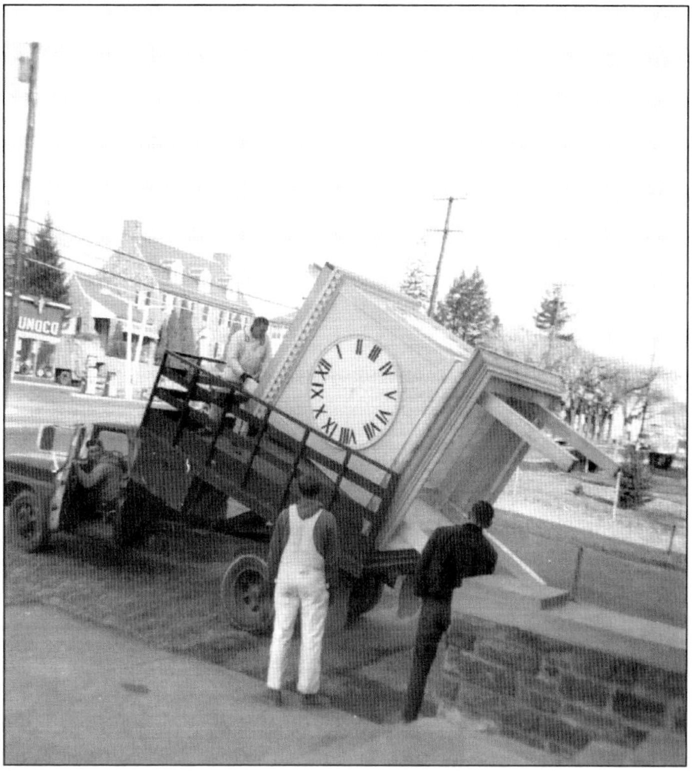

The town clock and bell were bought in 1887 with money raised from door-to-door subscriptions and an oyster supper, the first event held in Goodwin Hall. The great clock was nicknamed "Big Ed" by Col. Edwin D. Selby, James Eline's great-grandfather. Selby was a carpenter, cabinetmaker, and undertaker whose business was located two doors away. He maintained and wound the clock weekly, a family tradition that continues to this day. (Courtesy of the Reisterstown Room.)

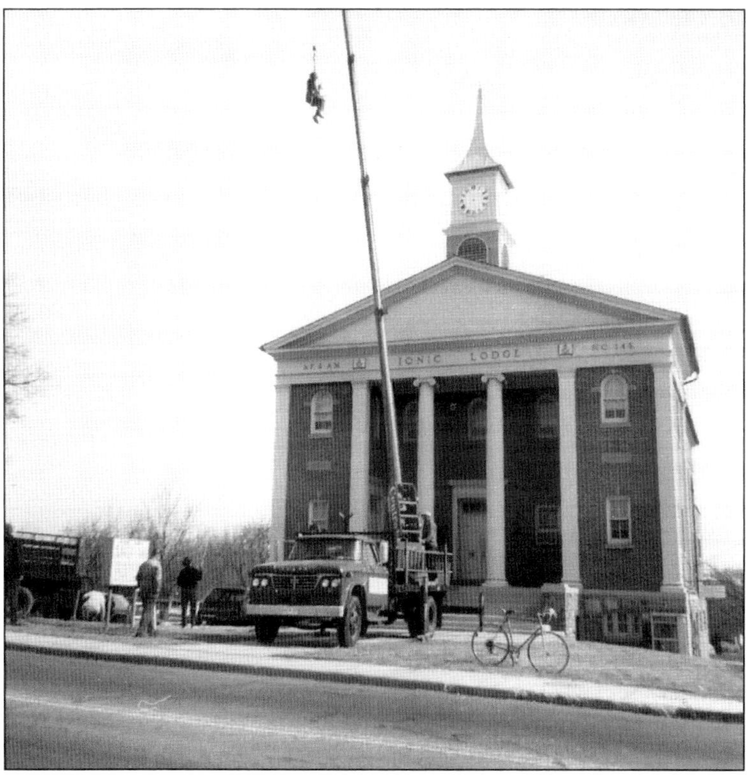

On February 27, 1968, the bell, clock, and weather vane were relocated to the top of the Masonic Temple through public donations and proceeds from the Tic Tock Ball. The Selby-Eline family wound the clock, and Harry Russell and others rang the bell to sound an alarm of fire. Before traffic, both the bell and the clock could be heard from one end of town to the other. (Courtesy of the Reisterstown Room.)

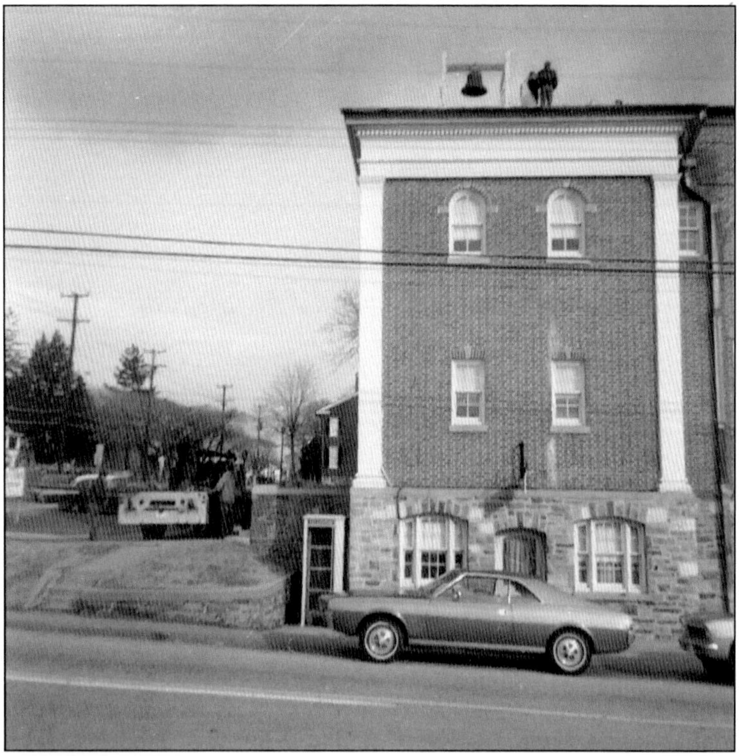

After grappling the clockworks into the attic and hoisting the clock into place with a crane, the beloved clock from the Howard Clock Company of Boston sits atop its new home at the Masonic Temple, located at 85 Main Street. "Big Ed" is equipped with 1,500 pounds of counterweights; a 7-foot, 150-pound pendulum; a 500-pound bell; and a legacy of 123 years of service. (Courtesy of the Reisterstown Room.)

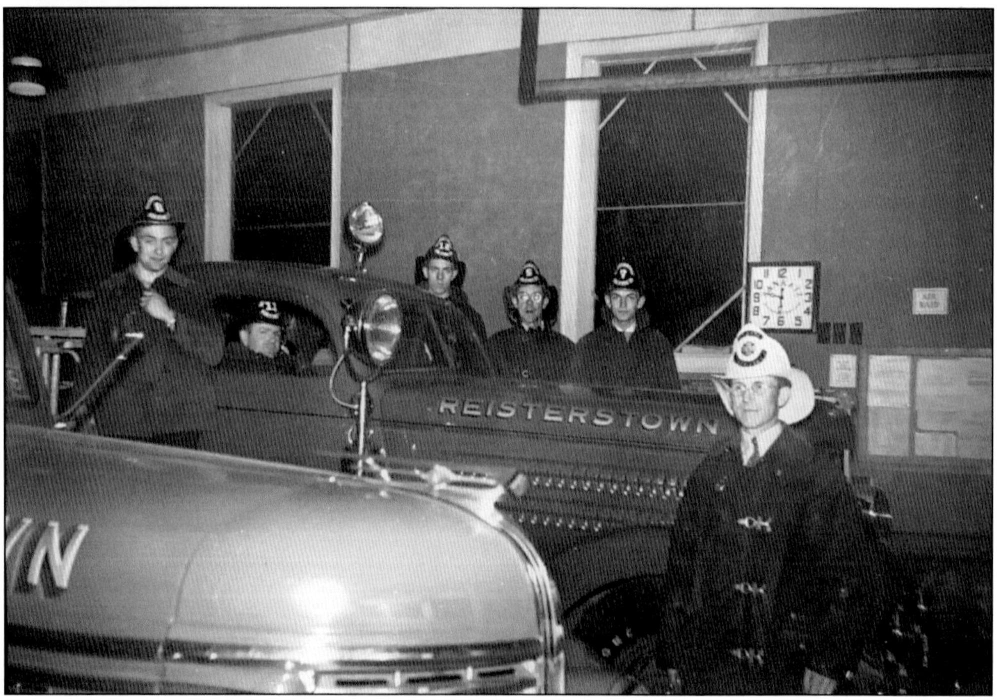

Posing from left to right are William Linker Jr., William Linker Sr., Wilbur Williams, unidentified, Roland Stansfield, and Calvin O. McElhattan Sr. The photograph was taken in the 1940s. (Courtesy of the Reisterstown Volunteer Fire Company.)

Children carrying U.S. flags in a *c.* 1917 Fourth of July parade march past what appears to be the side of a large wooden structure resembling the Hitshue Hotel. Spectators look on as the parade passes. The streetscape includes the interesting mix of horse and buggy and a Ford Model T car, typical of that period.

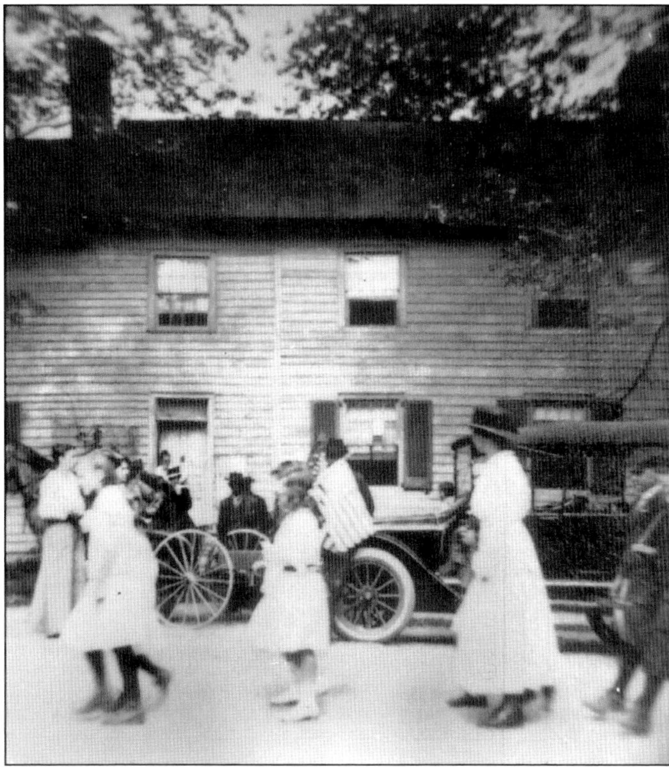

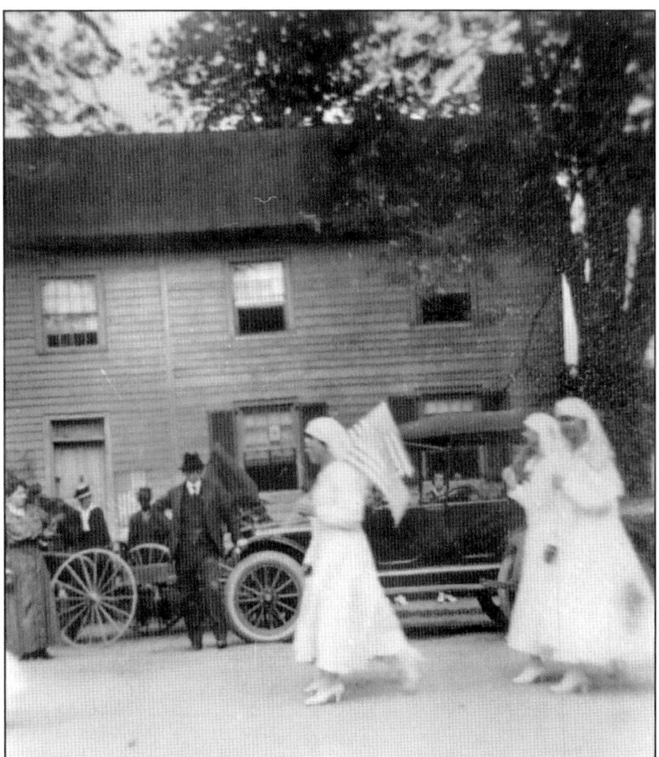

Women wearing Red Cross uniforms make a striking appearance in this Fourth of July parade during the World War I period. Showing pride and patriotism, they march past what appears to be the Hitshue Hotel at Main and Westminster Streets.

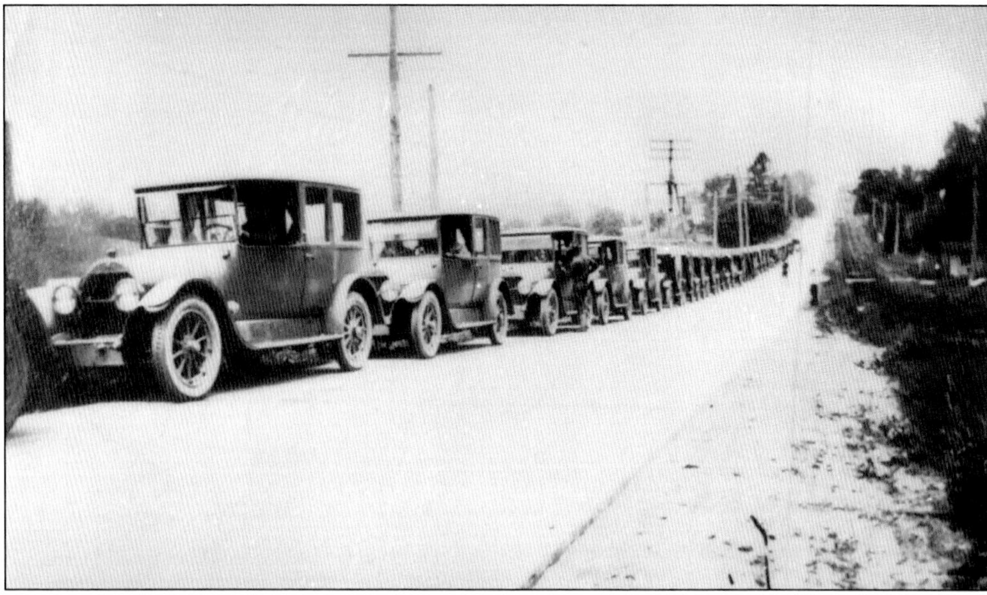

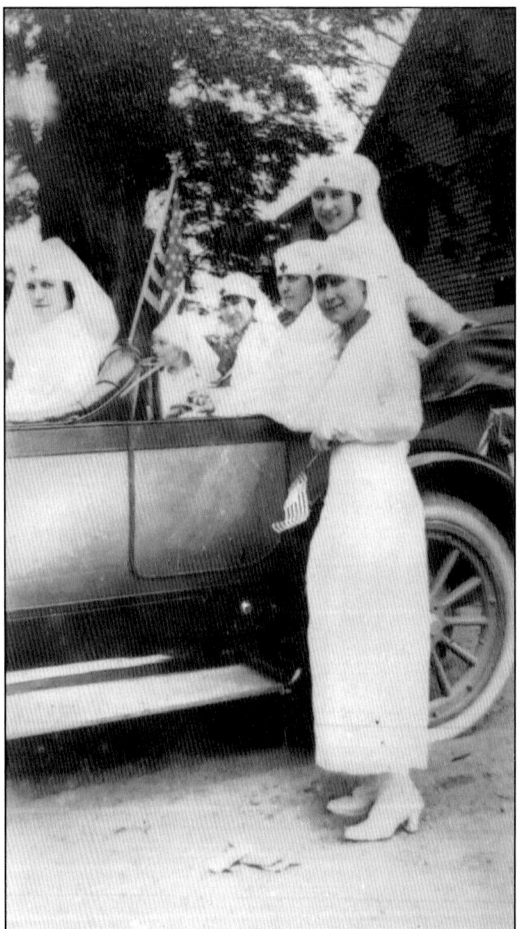

A long line of parked period cars with drivers at the ready appears to be waiting to enter the parade. The cars appear to be Ford Model Ts, which were produced between 1908 and 1927. The *c.* 1917 image by an unidentified photographer is testimony to Henry Ford's vision to build an affordable car for the great multitude.

Six unidentified women wearing the Red Cross uniform are shown participating in a Fourth of July parade in Reisterstown. The women in this *c.* 1917 image are standing beside a touring car during the World War I period. The Red Cross recruited more than 29,000 nurses to serve during World War I.

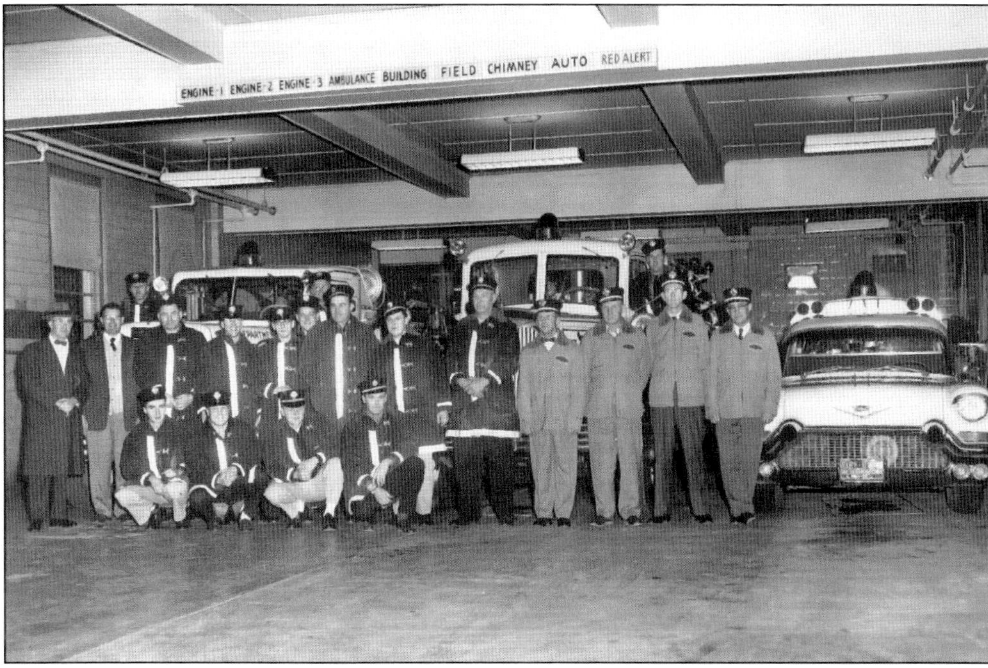

Firefighters pose for this photograph. From left to right are (kneeling) Robert Holtz, Fred Linker, Bud Houck, and S. Y. Hammond; (standing) Carroll Saumenig, Yates Wilson, Jack Shultz, John Folkert, Dudley Cook, Ted Schultz, Preston Patterson, Roland Hipple, Earl Tawney, James Eline, August Heise, Calvin O. McElhattan Sr., Ben Cook, Richard Fox, William Lentzner, and Spurgeon Wolf.

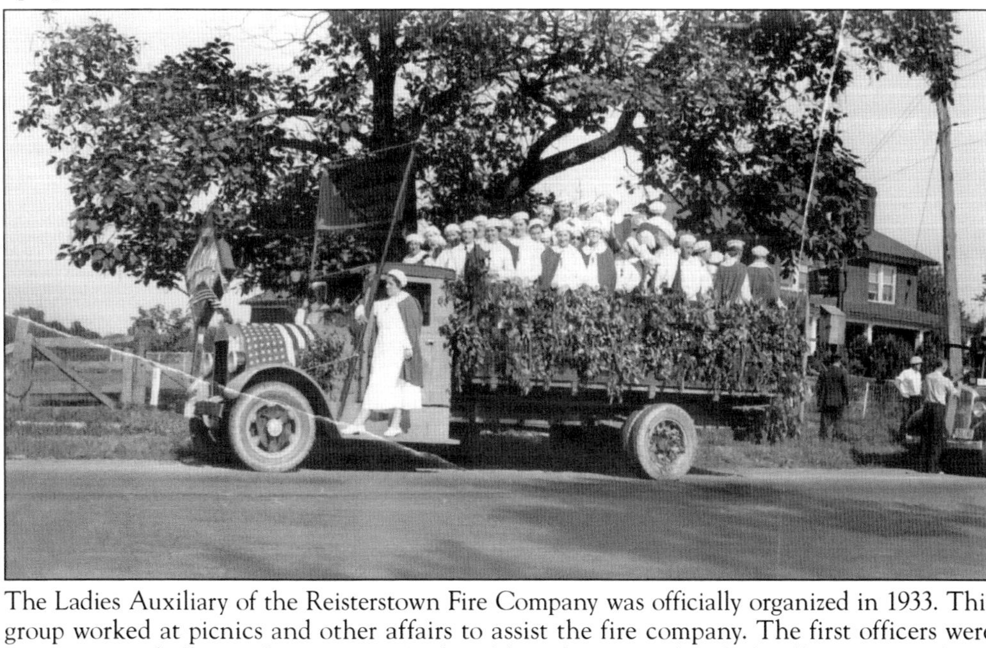

The Ladies Auxiliary of the Reisterstown Fire Company was officially organized in 1933. This group worked at picnics and other affairs to assist the fire company. The first officers were Bessie S. Marshall, president; Mrs. A. Earl Welsh and Mrs. J. Edward Shaeffer, vice presidents; Helen A. Ruley (now Mrs. Carroll E. Saumenig), secretary; and Mrs. Elmer H. Peregoy, treasurer. (Courtesy of the Reisterstown Room.)

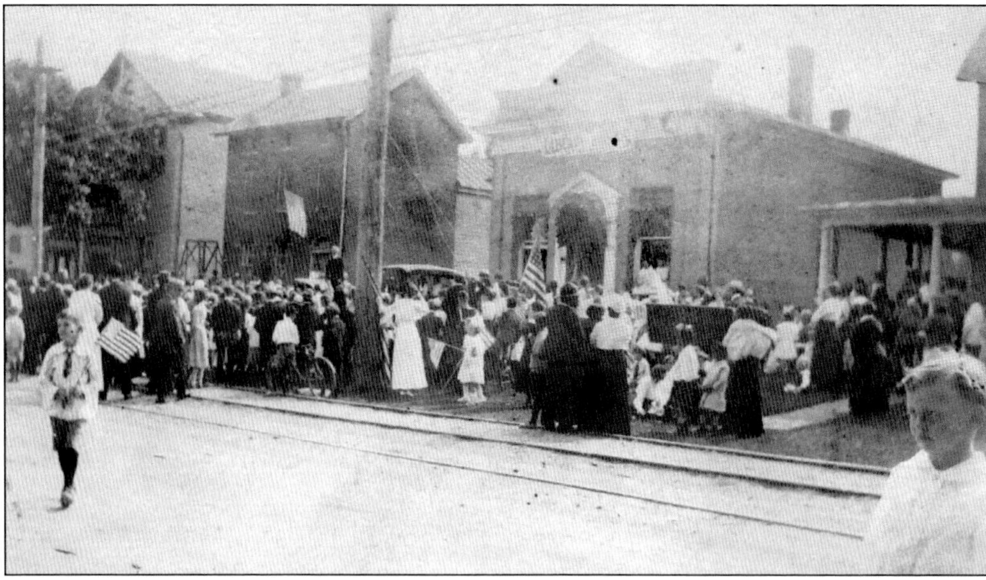

Patriotic citizens supported the Liberty Bond Rally at 50 Main Street around 1917. The crowd surrounds a speaker in front of the Reisterstown Savings Bank. Situated from left to right are the Odd Fellows Hall, the Larsh house (later residence of Mr. and Mrs. Will Stevenson), the Reisterstown Savings Bank, and the Ruley home. The bank and Ruley home were demolished in the 1990s to make room for the Reisterstown Village Shopping Center. (Courtesy of the Reisterstown Room.)

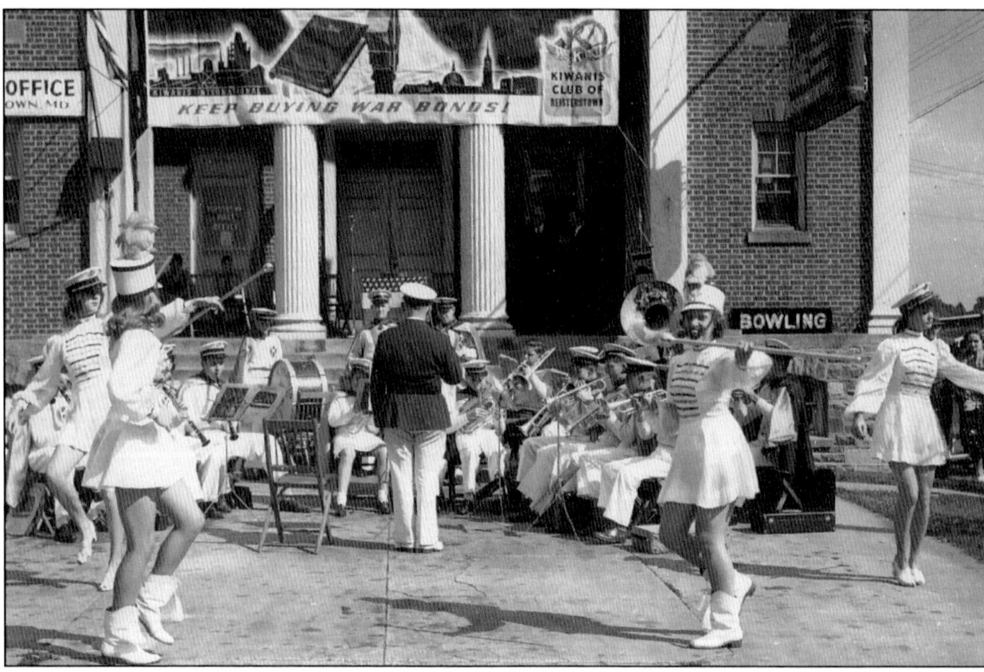

Majorettes in uniform twirl their batons in front of the Masonic Temple and post office in 1945. Majorette Elaine Frederick is in the front right smiling at the camera. The band plays on, encouraging people to perform their patriotic duty and "keep buying war bonds!" Lawrence Reter donated the photograph to the Reisterstown Room. (Courtesy of the Reisterstown Room.)

Five

For One's Edification

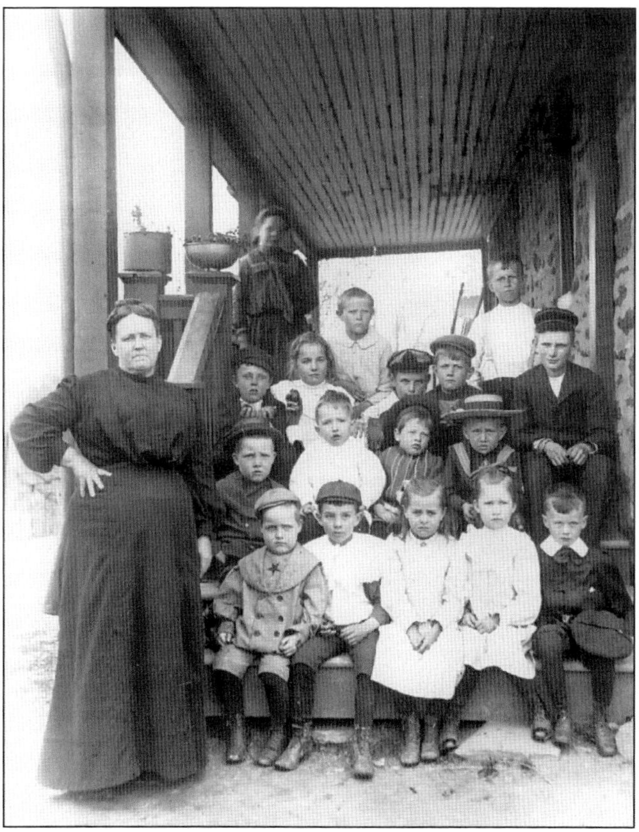

The members of the West Point church group were connected to the Grace Methodist Church South, located at 321 Main Street in Reisterstown. Some members at West Point in the 1880s planned to build a church called Church of the Holy Communion, but it did not pan out. The photograph of Laura Schwartz (standing, far left) and her Sunday school class was taken at the Brentwood farmhouse in April 1906.

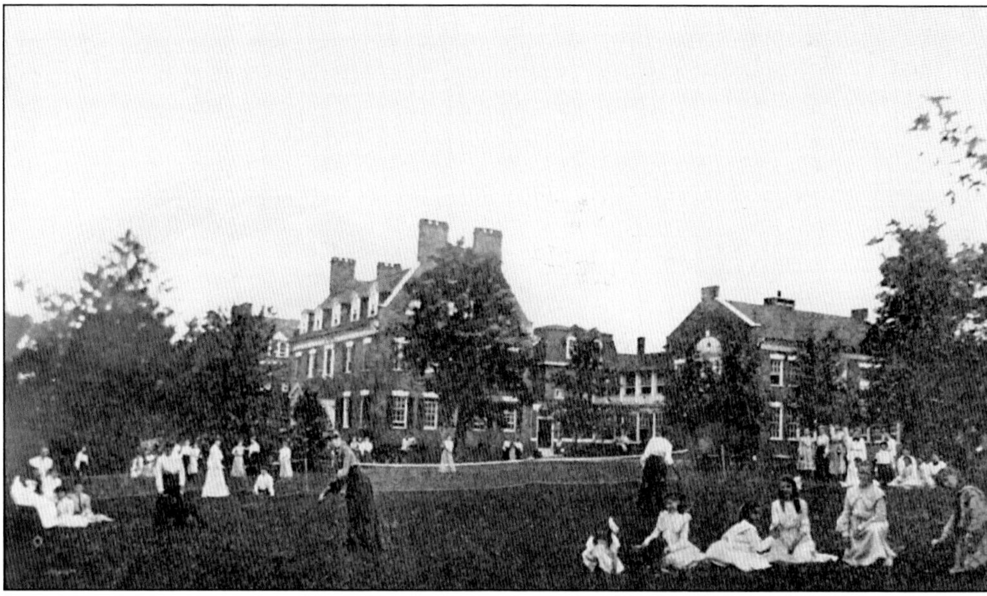

Students and staff enjoy croquet and badminton on the grounds of Hannah More Academy in this undated photograph. The school closed in July 1974 after its merger with St. Timothy's School. The county purchased the site a few years later, and it is now known as Hannah More Academy Park. Hannah More School leases 21 acres of the grounds. A county health center and skate park is also located there. (Courtesy of the Reisterstown Room.)

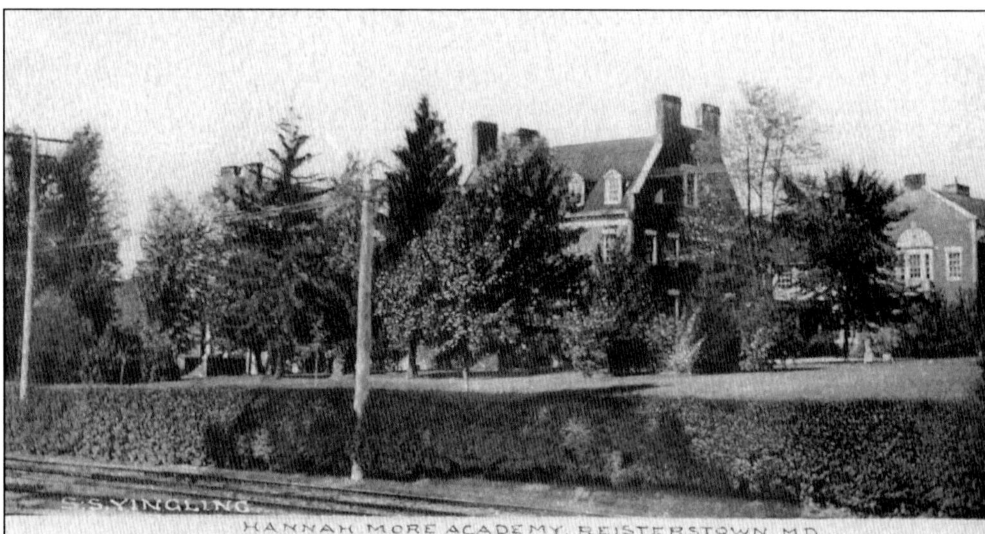

This postcard, published by S. S. Yingling, is dated May 28, 1907. It gives tribute to the oldest Episcopal boarding school for girls in the United States, founded in 1832. Anne van Bibber Neilson gave the school $10,000 and 3 acres for the building of the school to be modeled after the educational philosophy of Hannah More, an English author and educator of poor women. (Courtesy of the Reisterstown Room.)

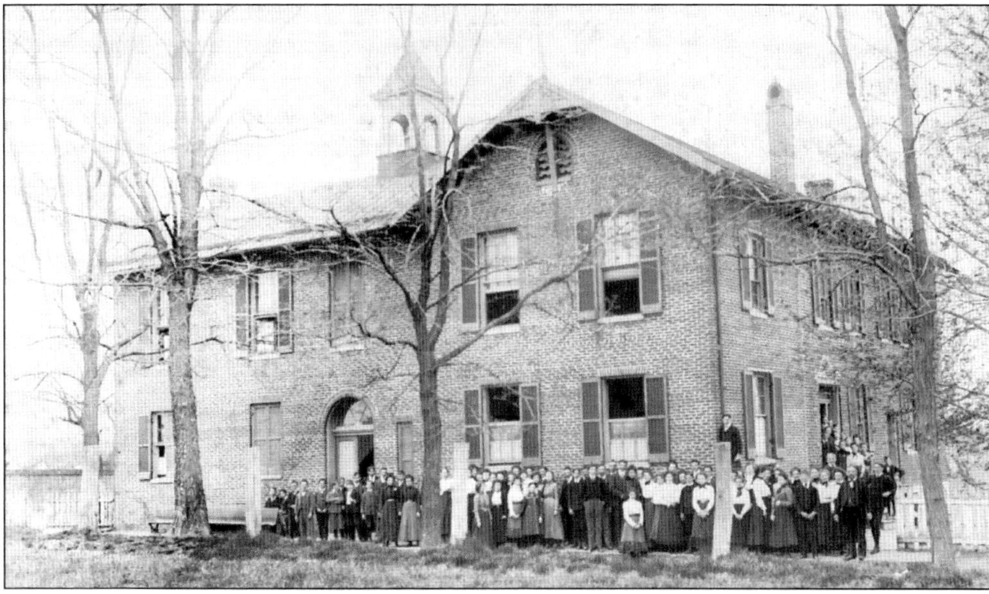

In 1901, the students and staff of the Old Franklin Academy posed for the history books. The building housed the first public high school in Baltimore County from 1874 until the early 1900s. Additions were constructed to accommodate the growing number of students. Today the structure serves as the Reisterstown branch of the Baltimore County Public Library. (Courtesy of the Reisterstown Room.)

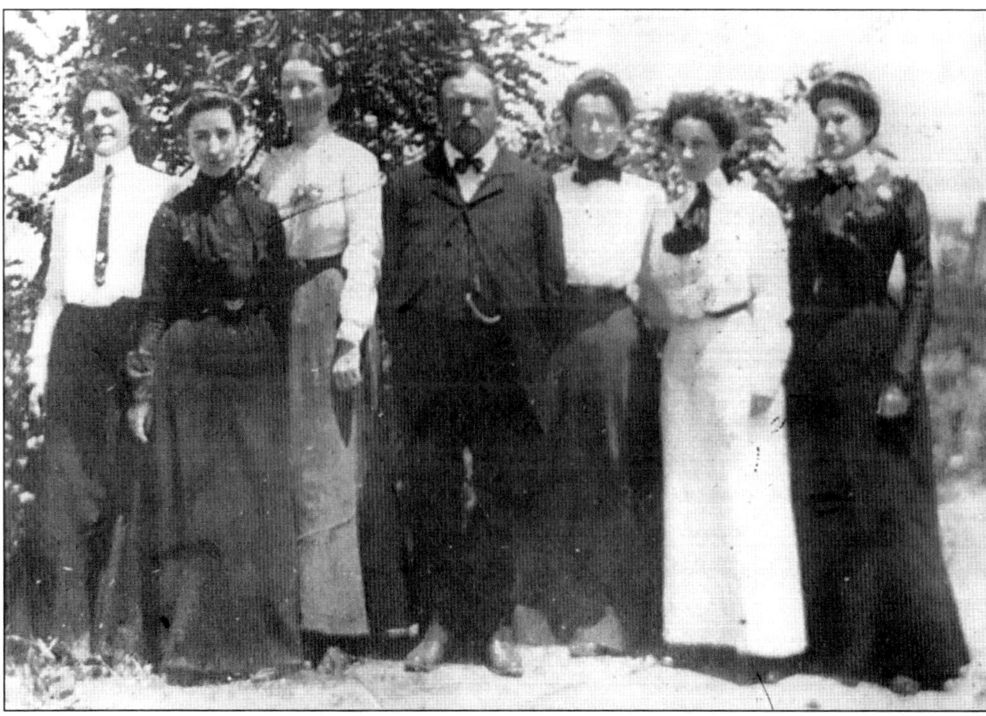

The Franklin High School faculty poses outdoors in this photograph, taken in 1902. They are, from left to right, ? Murray, E. Georgian Ewing, Lena Stansfield, Zachariah C. Ebaugh (principal), ? Miller, Ella Kane, and Gertrude M. Michael. (Courtesy of the Reisterstown Room.)

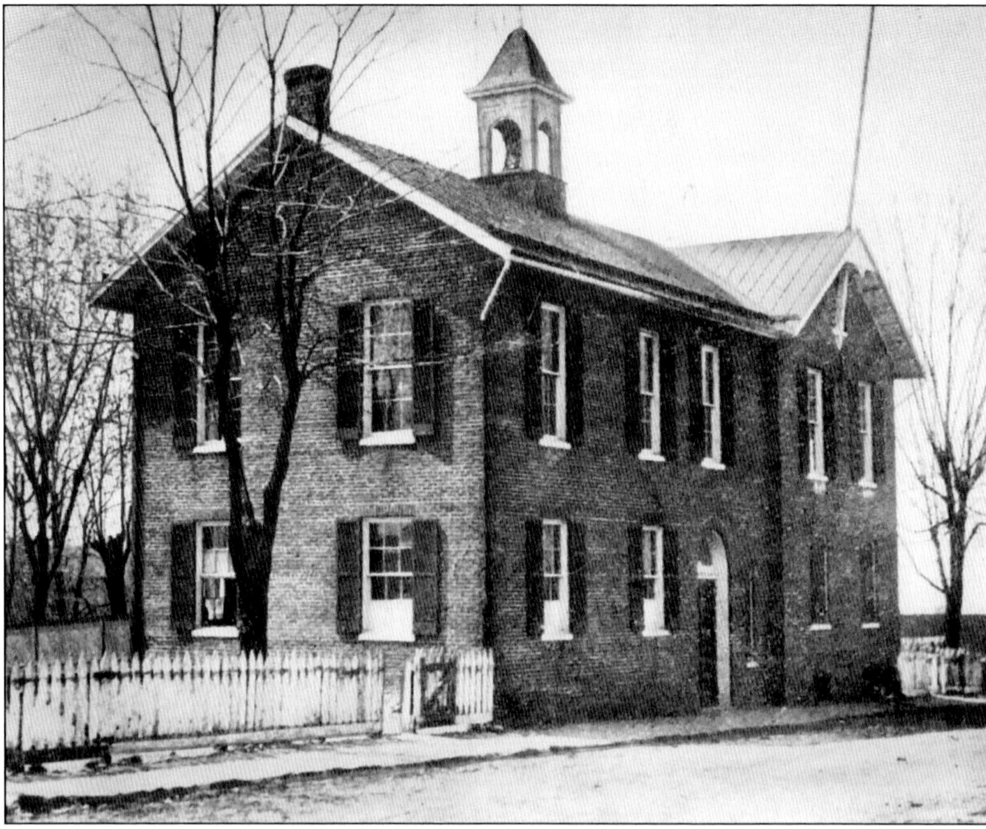

The Franklin Academy on Cockeys Mill Road, formerly known as Academy Lane, is shown here as it looked sometime before 1900. The school was built in 1824 with money raised by public subscription, and it became a public school in 1874. It holds the honor of being the oldest school in Baltimore County. In the 1870s, it became part of the Baltimore County school system. Rettberg Brothers Photographers, located at the time at 5802 York Road, took the photograph.

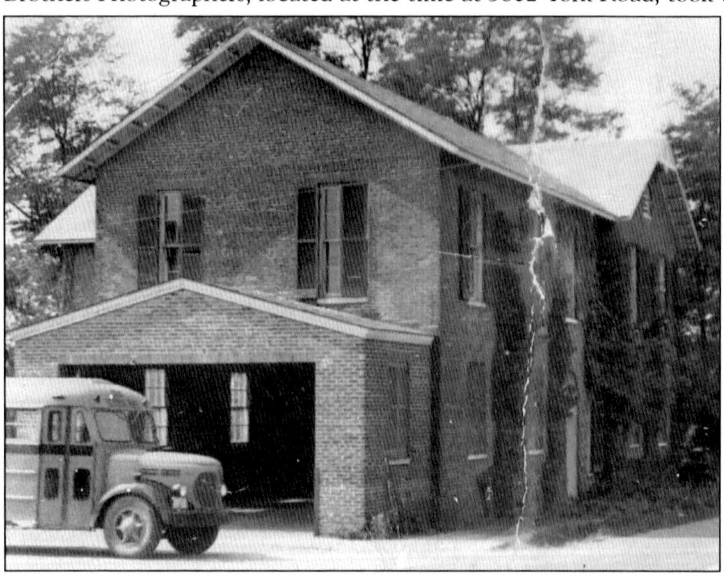

The image shows a *Federation News* photograph of the Old Franklin Academy, taken in 1901. In 1826, the town folk installed a cupola and school bell that now stands at the entrance of the Franklin High School. Adjacent to the Old Franklin Academy is the Old Lutheran Cemetery, holding the unmarked plot of the Reister family. (Courtesy of the Reisterstown Room.)

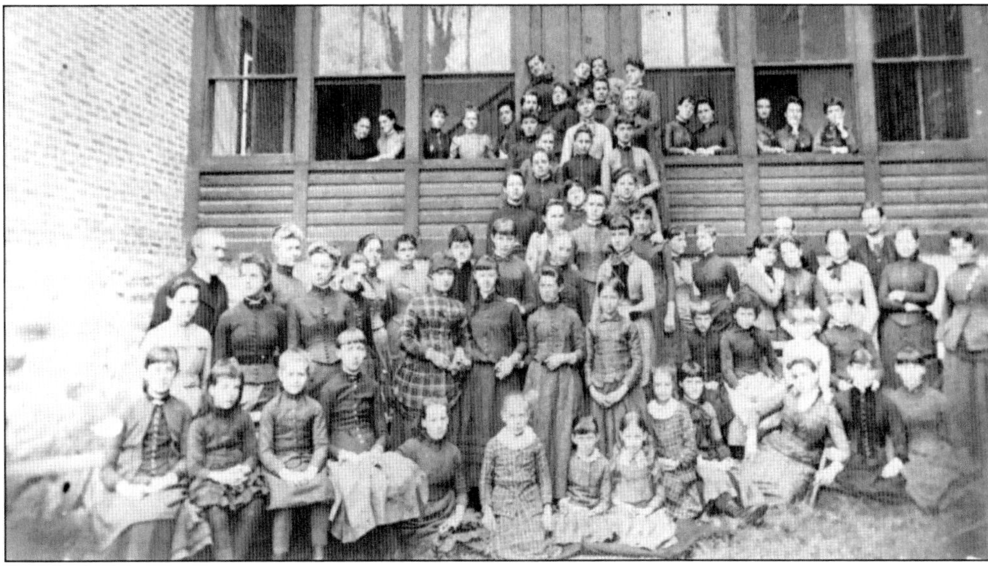

This *c*. 1890 photograph shows a large group of girls from the Hannah More Academy. Some of the girls are holding croquet mallets, while others have tennis rackets. They are posed standing inside and outside a frame structure adjacent to a brick building on the school's campus. Two male teachers are seen to the right just in front of the building.

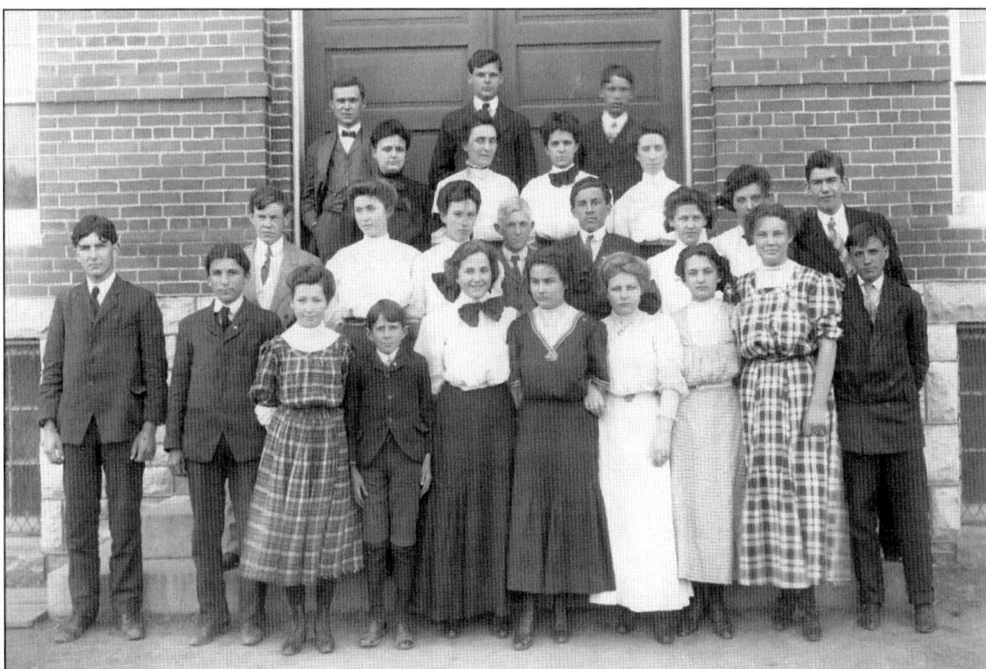

Franklin High School students are photographed in 1908. From left to right are (first row) Oscar Gorsuch, Charles Ebaugh, Mattie Hipsley, Arthur Brooks, Edith Tracey, Naomi Chen, Ellice Kinsey, Alice Wheeler, Margaretta Pearce, and Donald Munroe; (second row) James Currie, Mary Uhler, Nellie Burke, Alivett Chaney, John Reese, Beryl Owens, Laura Keyes, and Cameron Hoffman; (third row) J. Ebaugh, Jane Alford, Nell Zouck, and G. Ewing; (fourth row) Clyde Baker, William Kemp, and Howard Bollinger. (Courtesy of the Reisterstown Room.)

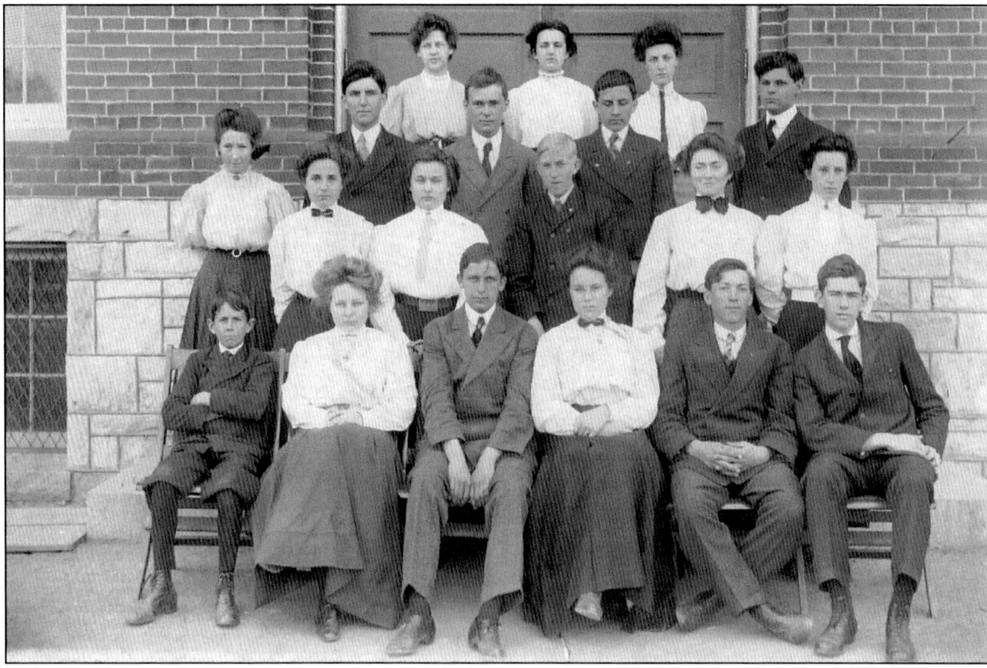

Among those shown in this 1908 photograph of Franklin High School students are Isabel Disney, Alice Wheeler, Laura Keyes, Oscar Gorsuch, Clyde Baker, John Reese, William Kemp, Mattie Hipsley, Edith Tracey, Naomi Chen, Alivett Chaney, Mary Upperco, Nellie Burke, Arthur Brooks, Ellice Kinsey, Howard Bollinger, Margaretta Pearce, Leslie Oursler, and Cameron Hoffman. (Courtesy of the Reisterstown Room.)

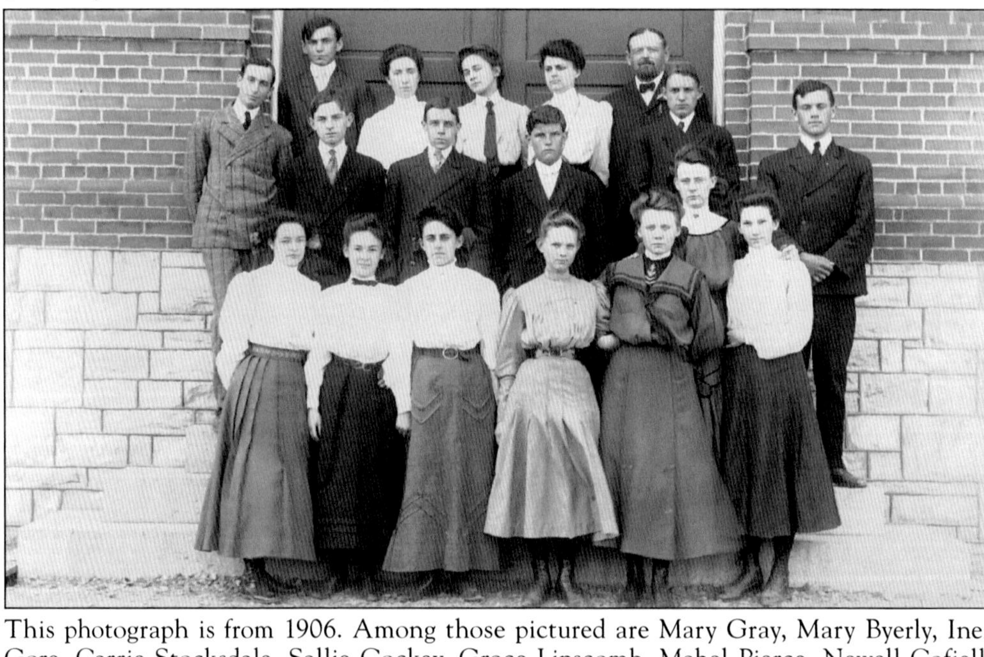

This photograph is from 1906. Among those pictured are Mary Gray, Mary Byerly, Inez Gore, Carrie Stocksdale, Sallie Cockey, Grace Lipscomb, Mabel Pierce, Newell Cofiell, Lawrence ?, Clinton Goodson, James ?, Walter ?, Kenneth Munroe, and Lewis Reese. (Courtesy of the Reisterstown Room.)

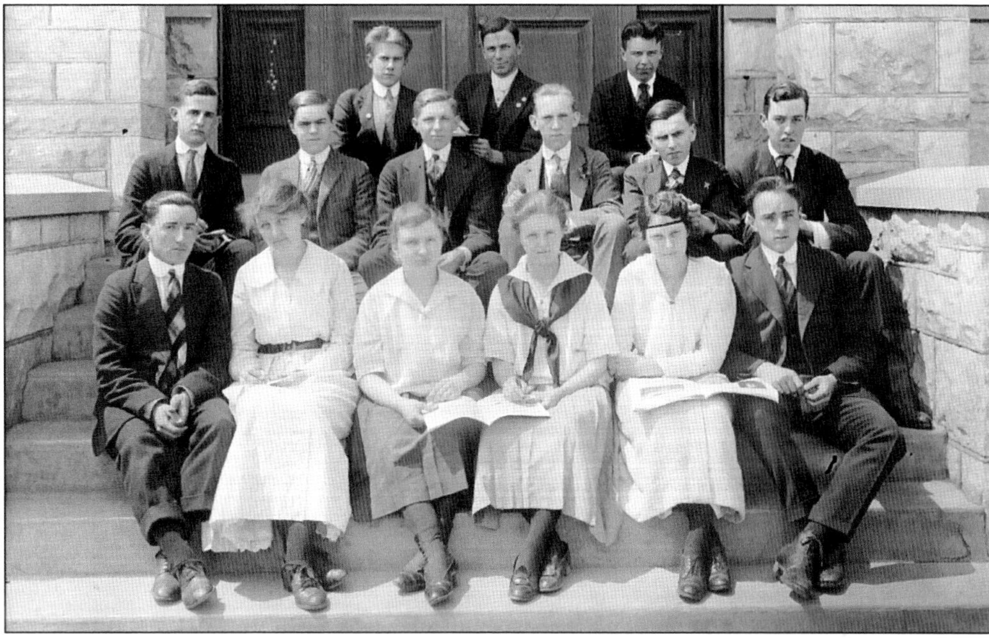

The members of the class of 1919 of Franklin High School are, from left to right, (first row) Ed Fromm, Edna Kelly, Eva Schultz, Ruth Fenby, Fannie McCubbin, and John Smith; (second row) Baker Clarke, John Yingling, George Lippy, Carl Eppers, Raymond Hyson, and Clarence Fischer; (third row) Ernst Roschen, Maurice Boring, and William Hammond. (Courtesy of the Reisterstown Room.)

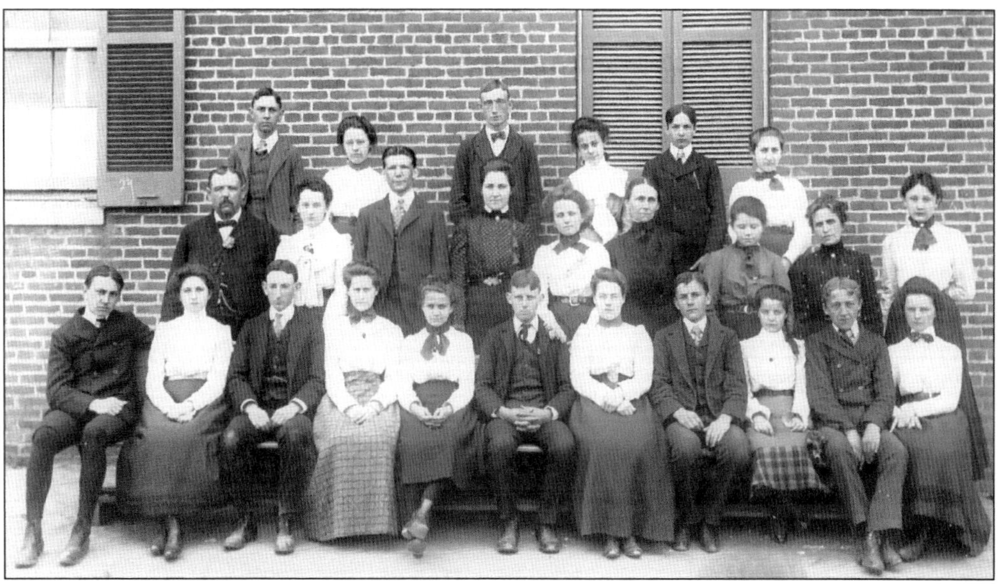

The class of 1902 is seen here having its picture taken in 1901. From left to right are (first row) Albert Sisk, Anna Brown, George Gist, Jessie Raine, Ina Marriott, Gist Cockey, Verna Scott, Grover Danner, Ellen Gray, Judson Wilson, and Lois Benson; (second row) Zachariah C. Ebaugh, Edna Tracey, Elmer Bennett, Olive Cole, Alta Swamm, Bessie Davis, Eleanor Wright, Ida May Riley, and Helen McCloskey; (third row) Arthur Harris, Nannie Benson, Harry Eckhardt, Minna Hentz, Benjamin Benson, and Grace McCoy. (Courtesy of the Reisterstown Room.)

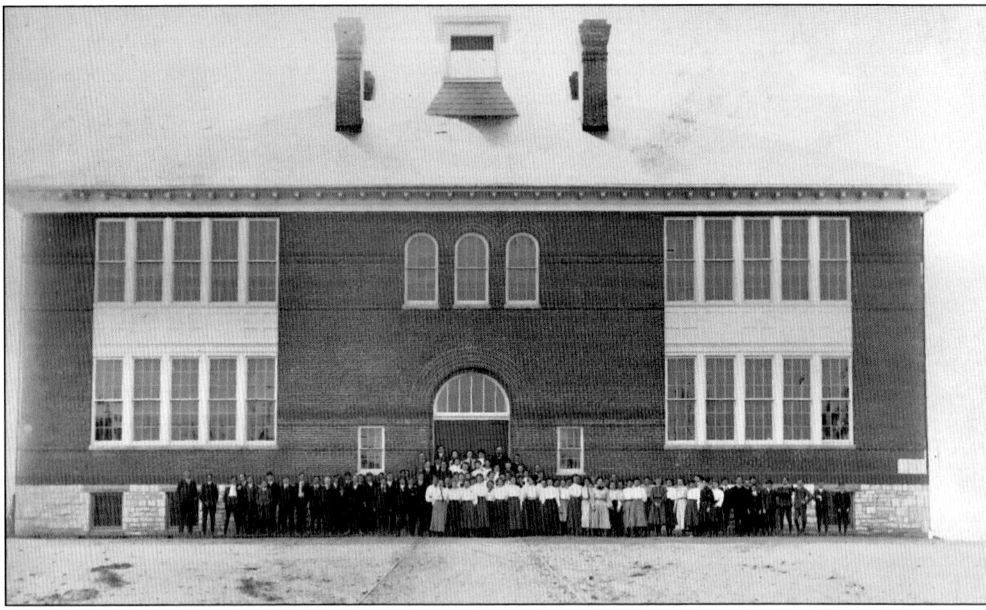

The new Franklin High School, erected in 1906, is shown in this photograph, donated by Louise Bland Goodwin. The building sits at the corner of Main Street and Cockeys Mill Road, formerly known as Academy Lane. According to lore, the school was named after Benjamin Franklin, who was the patron saint of high schools. It was the only high school in Baltimore County for many years. (Courtesy of the Reisterstown Room.)

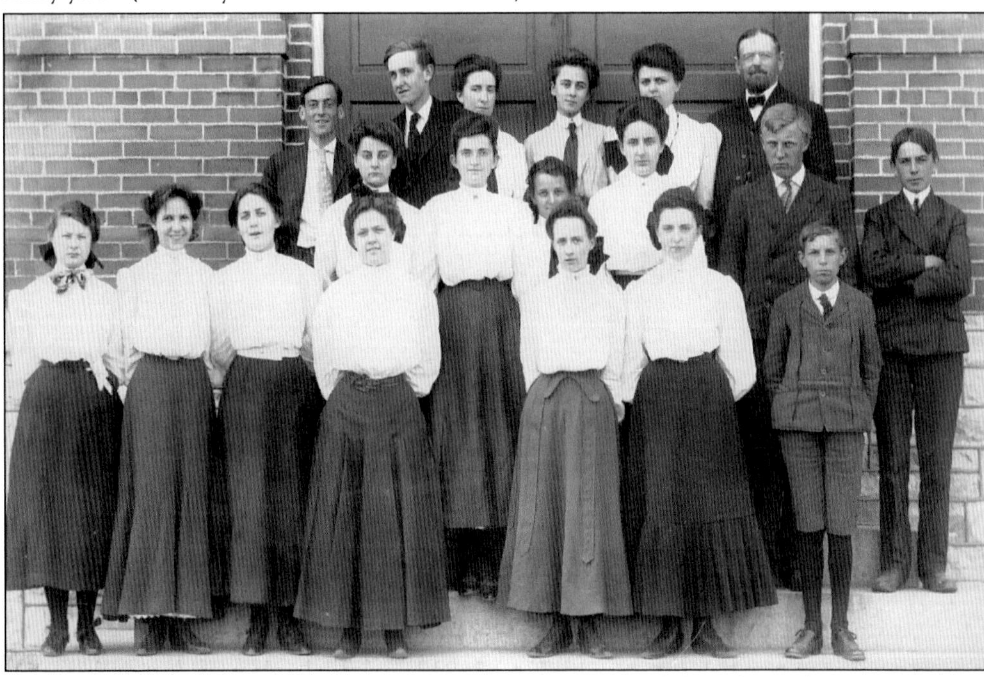

Among those shown in this 1907 photograph are Bessie Rohrbaugh, Pauline Derr, Aileen McKenney, Naomi Lowry, Pauline Sisk, Lucy Clark, ? Pfeffer, Rebecca Cockey, Mabel Slacksdale, May Armacost, Margaretta Pearce, Edin Graefe, Claude Leight, Donald Reitz, Charles Waters, and Peter Zouck. (Courtesy of the Reisterstown Room.)

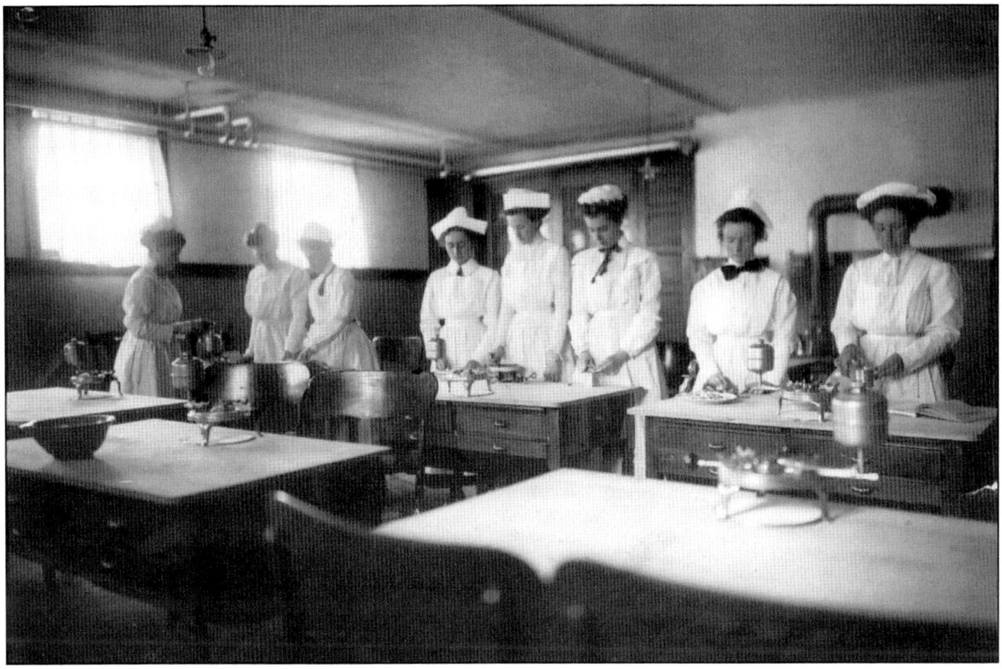

Girls of the class of 1910 are participating in a domestic science class at Franklin High School. Between 1907 and 1914, manual training, domestic science, and the commercial department were added to the curriculum. Among those pictured are Dora Elizabeth Schwamb, Mary Isabel Disney, Clara Gertrude Marshall, Mildred S. Warfield, Alice Marguerite Zouck, and Della Myrel Houck. (Courtesy of the Reisterstown Room.)

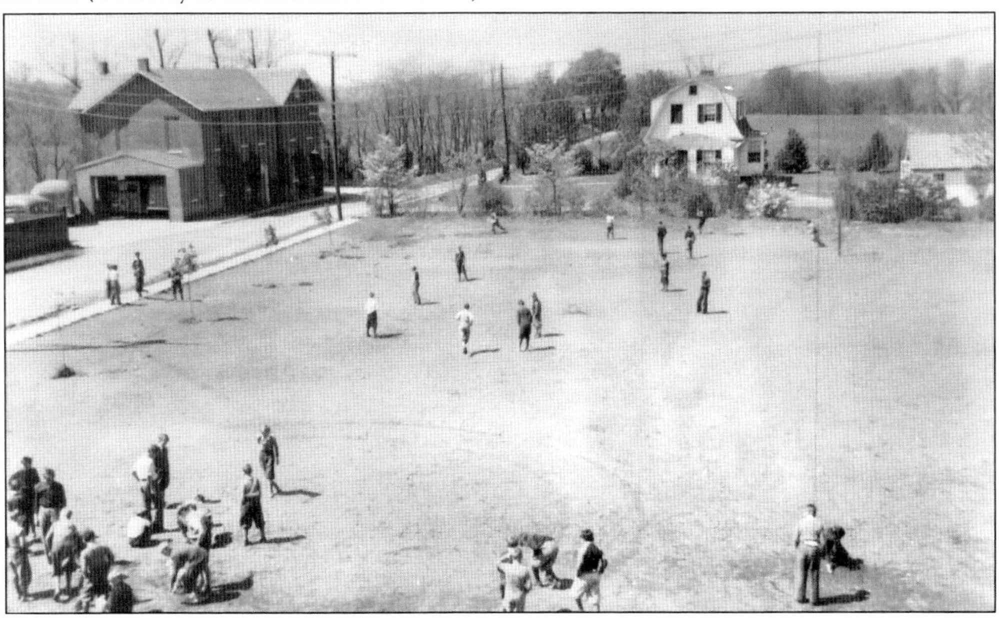

The fields across from the Franklin Academy were used as athletic fields for the students in this early-1900s photograph. All of the students are boys, and many appear to be wearing knickers. At the far left center of the picture one can see the wall surrounding the Old Lutheran Cemetery, where the early town folks and the Reister family were buried. (Courtesy of the Reisterstown Room.)

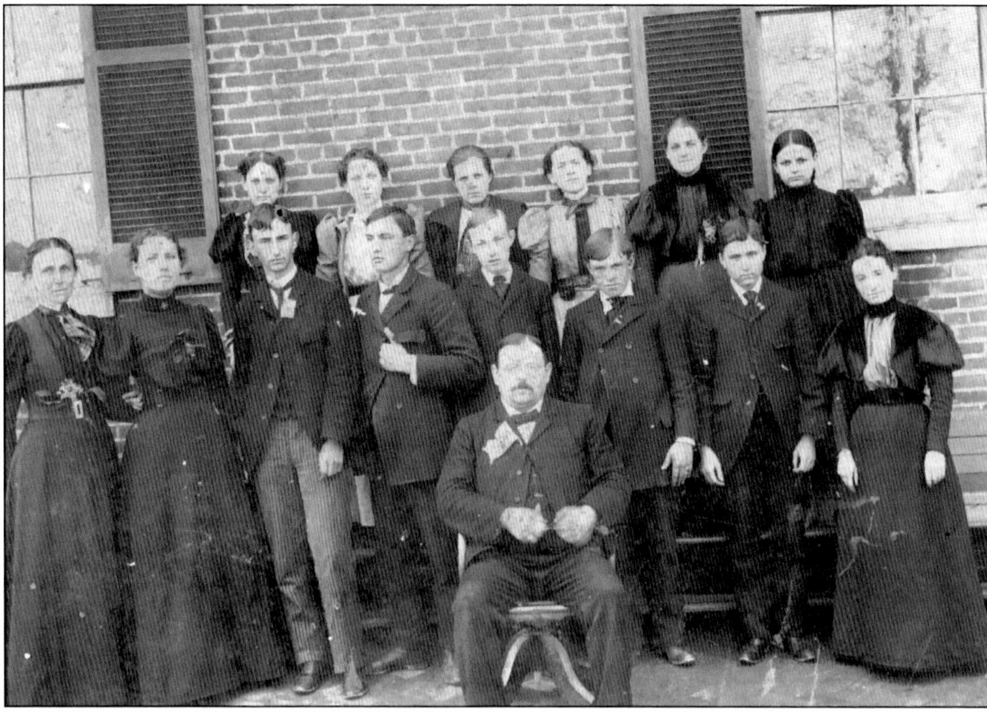

Zachariah C. Ebaugh sits on a stool in front of students and teachers of Franklin High School. They are, from left to right, (first row) Bessie Davis, Mary Scarborough, ? Beam, Robert Davis, George Muares, Raymond Russell, Simpson Ebaugh, and Jessie Wenner; (second row) Lutie Berryman, Emma Little, Edith Zouck, Lunsfield or Dunsfield, Bonnie Chick, and Jessie Ebaugh. (Courtesy of the Reisterstown Room.)

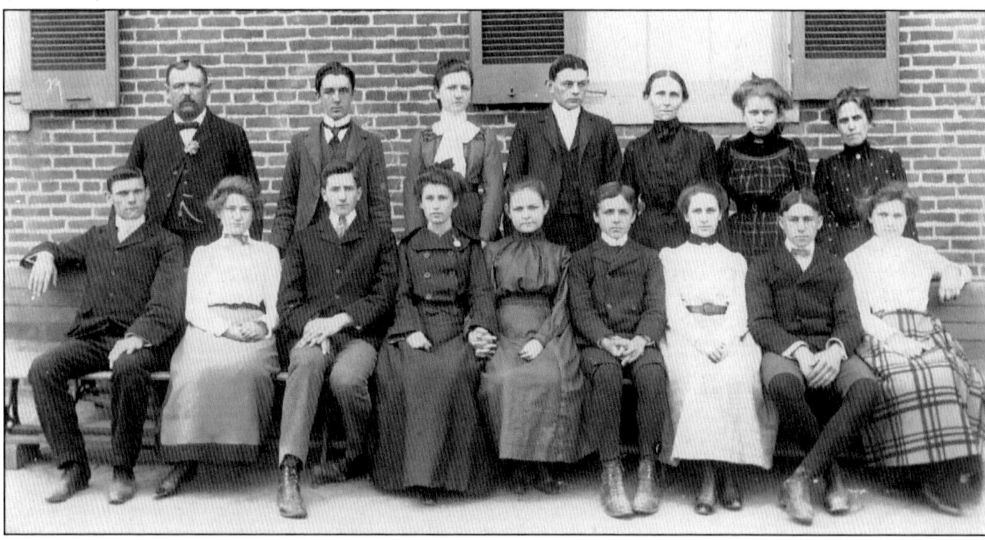

Zachariah C. Ebaugh poses with what appears to be his staff. Sitting from left to right are (first row) John McEwen, Rosa Gill, Irving Tracey, Bessie Waggoner, Mary Ebaugh, Ernest Wooden, Etha Frantz, Charles Wooden, and Ethel Hall; (second row) Zachariah C. Ebaugh, Thomas Campbell, Nellie Bly Gore, Marion Wilson, Bessie Davis, Edith Haughey, and ? Riley. The photograph was taken in 1901. (Courtesy of the Reisterstown Room.)

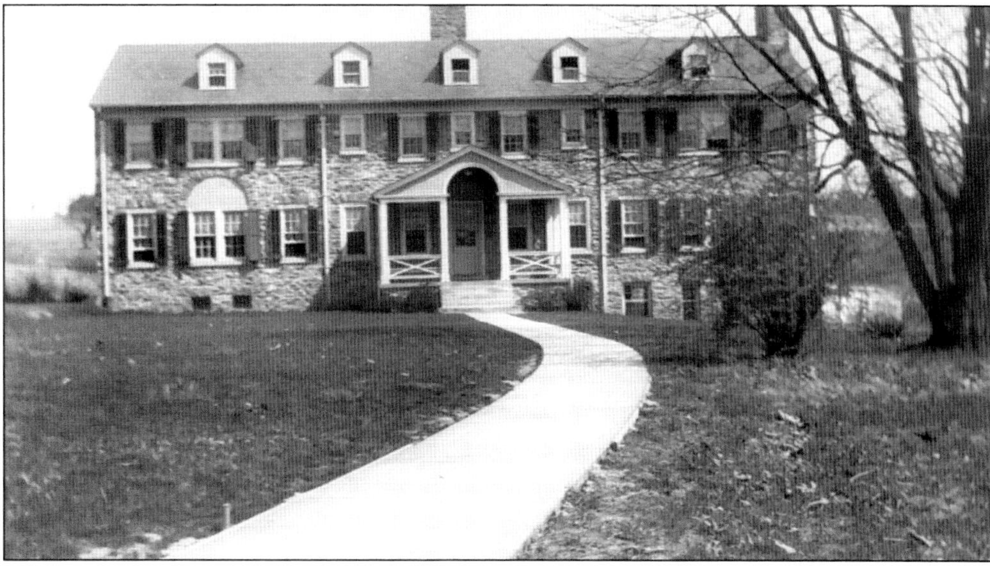

The Montrose Mansion is located at 13700 Hanover Road in Reisterstown. The granite, 24-room mansion played host to lavish balls and parties in its heyday. It was renowned for its landscaped gardens of boxwoods and roses. In 1920, it was purchased by the state for a delinquent girl's school. Today it houses Camp Fretterd, a National Guard facility. The photograph was taken around 1928. (Courtesy of the Reisterstown Room.)

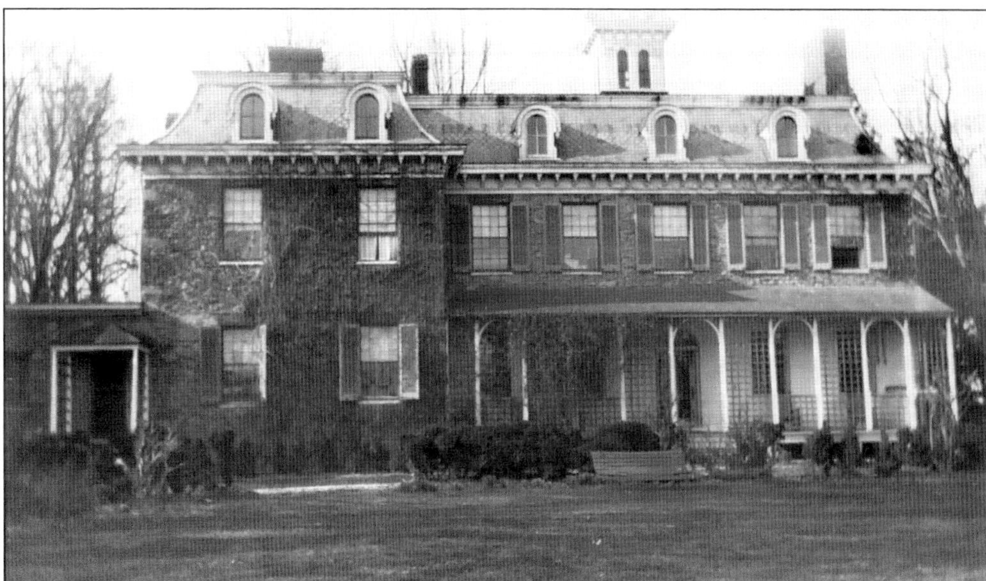

Montrose Mansion, as seen in this c. 1928 image, was built in the 1820s for Napoleon's exiled brother, Jerome Bonaparte, and his wife, Elizabeth, by his father-in-law, William Patterson. Jerome complied with his brother Napoleon's demands that he leave his wife and return home to become the first king of Westphalia. Elizabeth, learning that Jerome had married Princess Catherine of Wertemburg, was forced to divorce him. (Courtesy of the Reisterstown Room.)

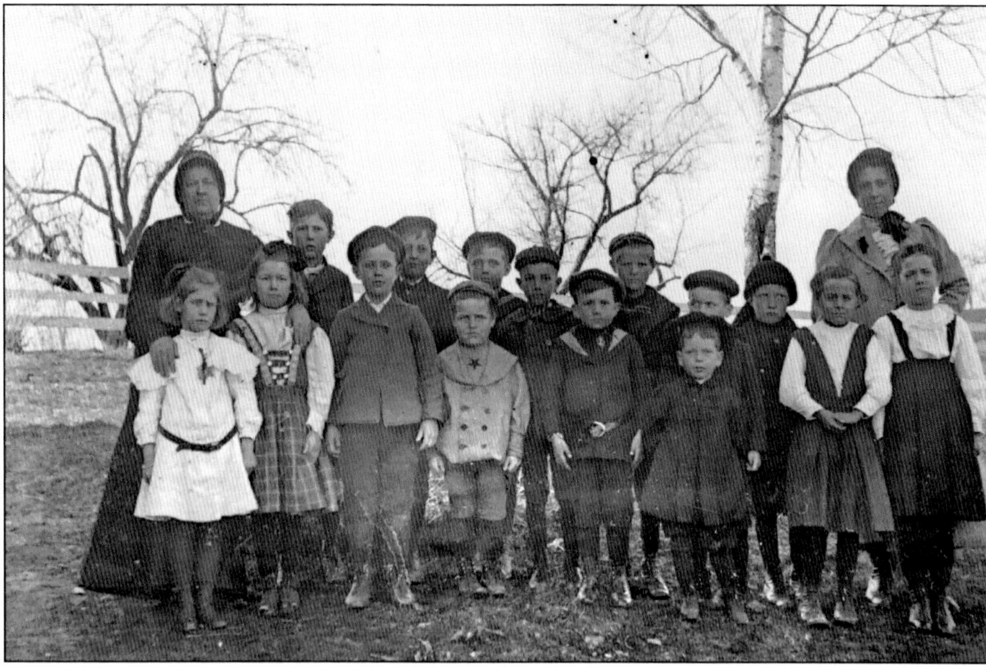

Laura Schwartz's Sunday school class is seen in an outdoor pose at West Point. The children all appear to be on their best behavior while wearing their Sunday best. The setting has been identified as the Brentwood farm on Cockeys Mill Road. Joshua Fitze took the photograph on April 16, 1906. (Courtesy of the Reisterstown Room.)

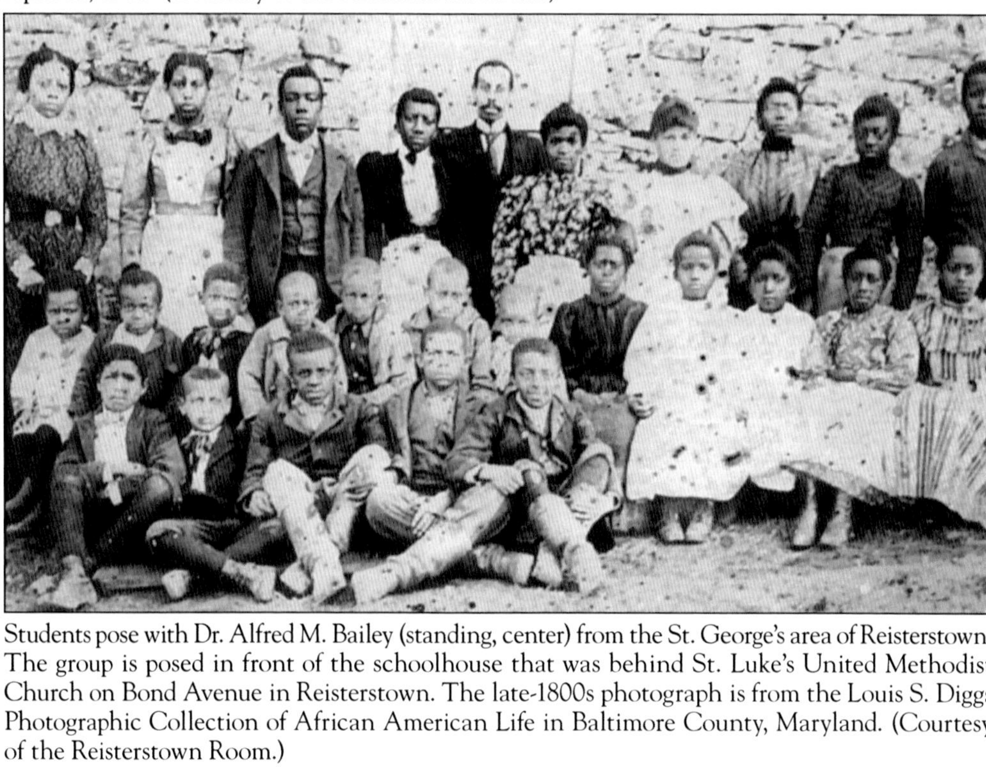

Students pose with Dr. Alfred M. Bailey (standing, center) from the St. George's area of Reisterstown. The group is posed in front of the schoolhouse that was behind St. Luke's United Methodist Church on Bond Avenue in Reisterstown. The late-1800s photograph is from the Louis S. Diggs Photographic Collection of African American Life in Baltimore County, Maryland. (Courtesy of the Reisterstown Room.)

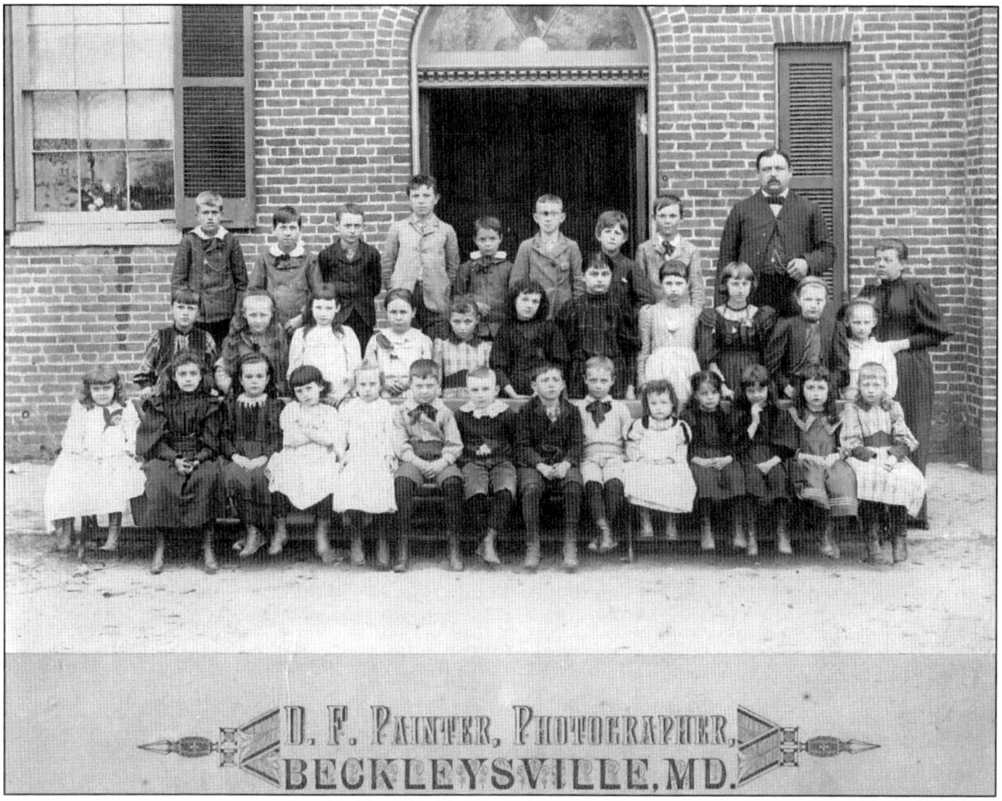

The third and fifth grades in 1896 at the Franklin Elementary School in Franklin Academy are posing for the photographer. In the third row, the fifth boy from left is Percy Gray. Identified in the first row are Bertha C. Buckingham (third from left), Mary Gray (10th from left), Nell Gray (11th from left), and Lucy Gray (12th from left). They were photographed by David F. Painter of Beckleysville, Maryland. (Courtesy of the Reisterstown Room.)

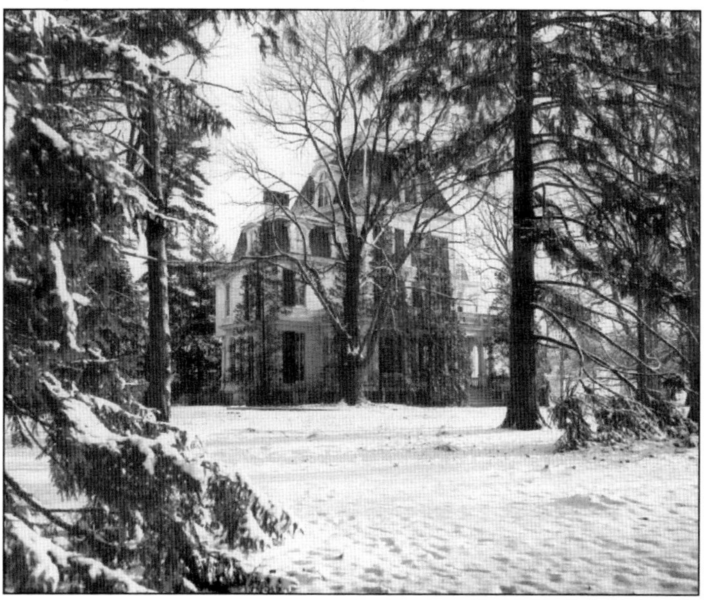
Richleigh on the grounds of the Hannah More Academy campus was originally the home of Dr. Arthur Rich, headmaster of the school and rector of the chapel. His home was later converted to a school. Hannah More (1745–1833) was an Evangelical philanthropist, political writer, playwright, antislavery advocate, and one of the most influential women in her lifetime. (Courtesy of the Reisterstown Room.)

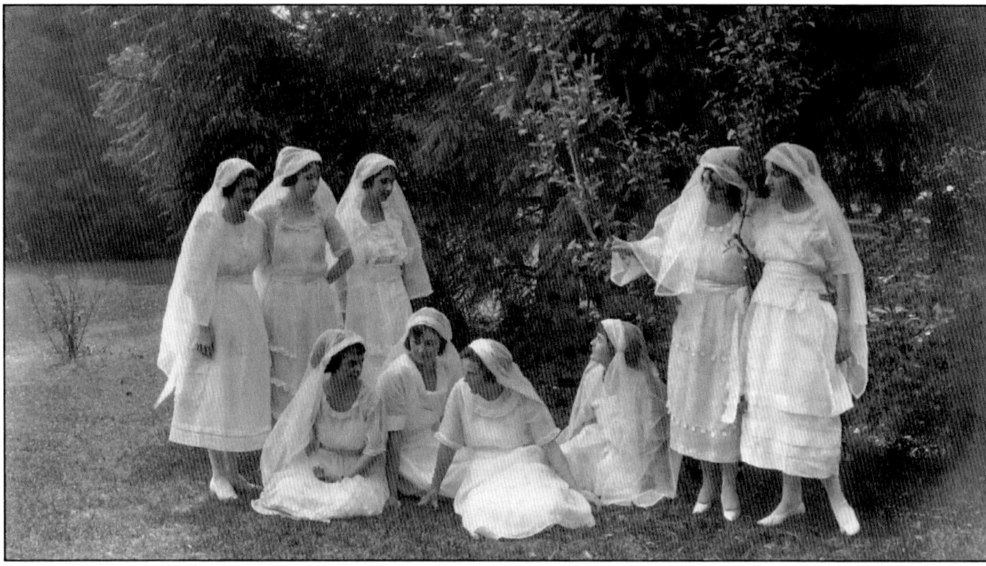

This images shows the 1921 Hannah More Academy graduation. From left to right are Elizabeth Landon Chinn, Mildred Elizabeth Hobbs, Matilda Frances McIlhany, Pauline Virginia Sale, Karolyn Snyder, Anne Louise Taylor, Jean Taylor, Mildred Valliant, and Janet Waters. Hannah More Academy merged with St. Timothy's School in 1974. (Courtesy of the Reisterstown Room.)

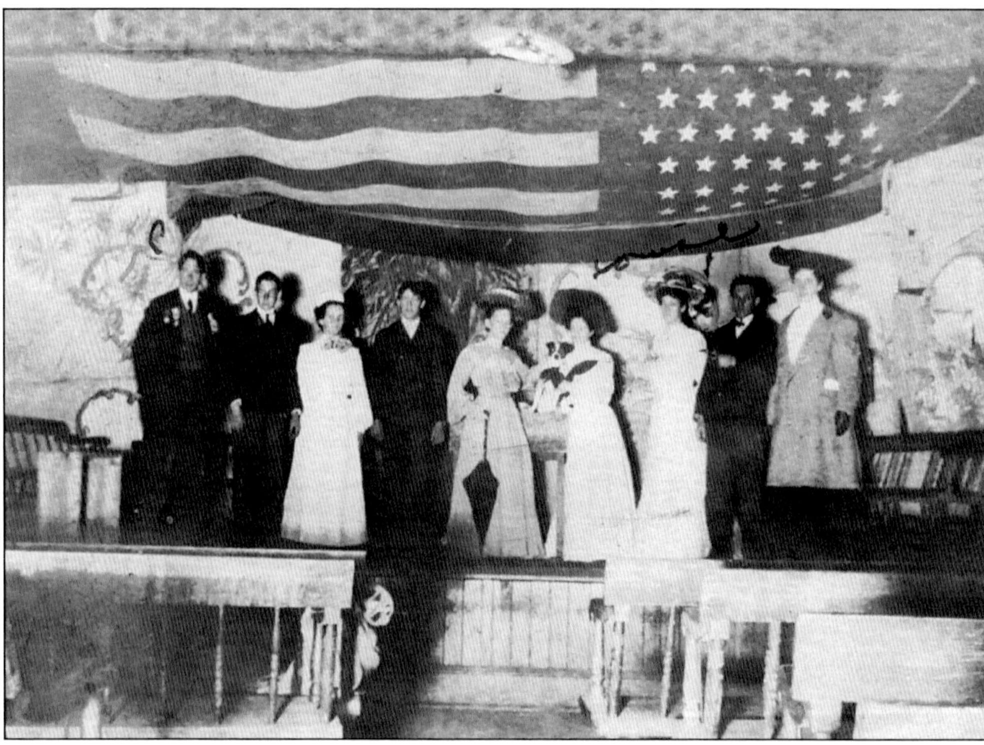

Goodwin Hall is the setting of the play performed by Franklin High School students in this undated photograph. From 1890 until 1896, Franklin High School used the second floor of the hall as a place to hold its commencements. Goodwin Hall was also the original place folks went to see movies before the New Theatre was built in 1935. (Courtesy of the Reisterstown Room.)

Six

PROPER POSES

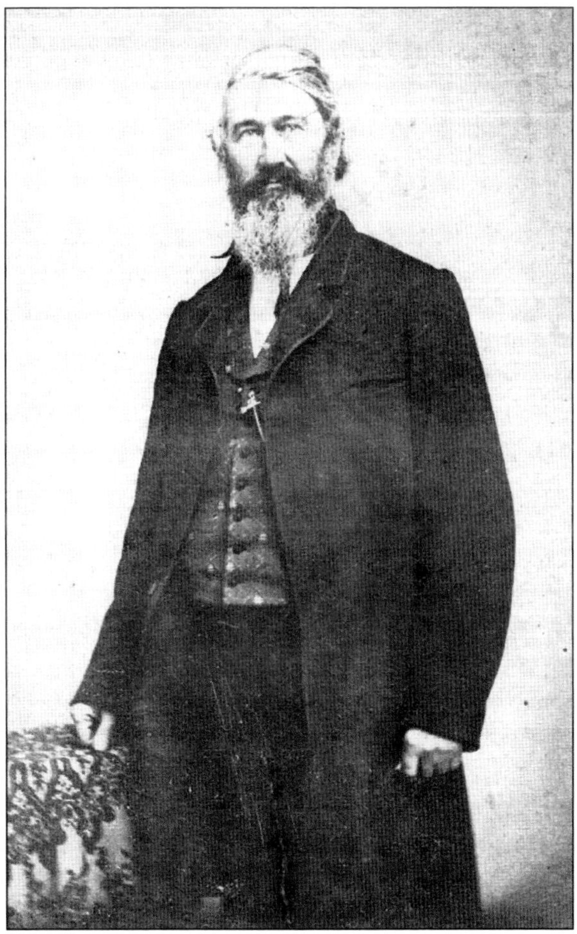

Here is a photograph of local physician Dr. Isaac Newton Dickson on his wedding day, October 27, 1853. He married Lizzie Cockey, mother of Ada Zouck German. William Cowen and Company at No. 85 West Baltimore Street took the photograph. Dr. Dickson's manuscript *The Early Days of Reisterstown and Vicinity* was completed in 1871 and provides a priceless link to the past. (Courtesy of the Reisterstown Room.)

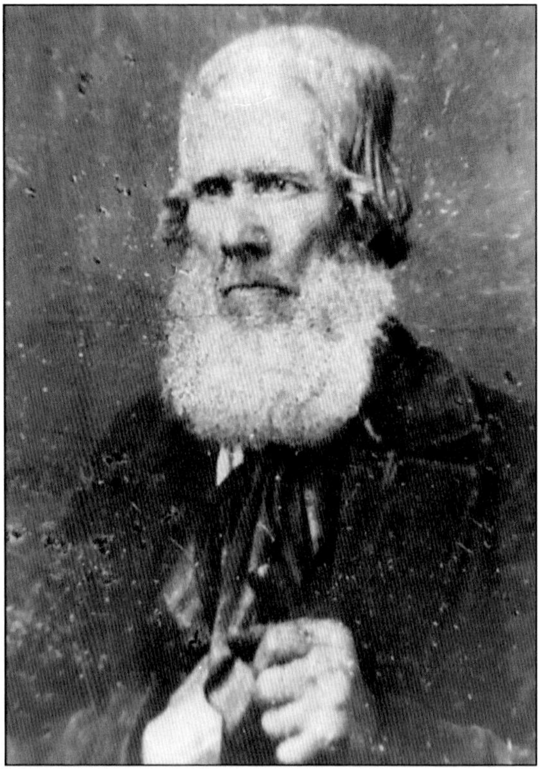

William Russell immigrated to America from County Donegal, Ireland, around 1817. He was born in the town of Raphoe in the province of Ulster in 1765. Russell died at the age of 80 at Shippensburg, Pennsylvania, on June 19, 1845. This picture was found in the Reisterstown Historical Room, and it is believed William Russell was related to the Russell family, one of the leading families of Reisterstown. (Courtesy of the Reisterstown Room.)

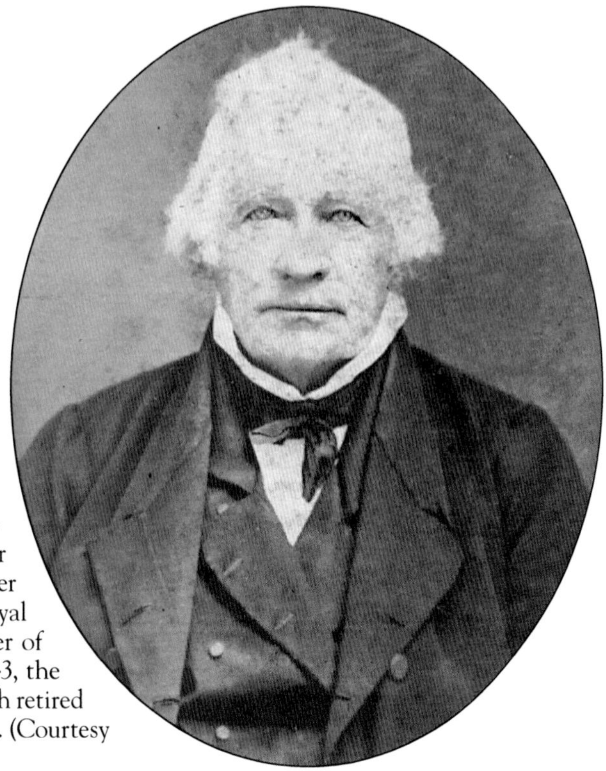

Maj. Harry H. Ducker served in the War of 1812. Later he and his brother Capt. Jeremiah Ducker became partners as merchants. Major Ducker opened the Ducker Tavern, forerunner to the Hitshue Hotel, located where Royal Farms is situated today at the corner of Main and Westminster Roads. In 1843, the two brothers gave up business. Jeremiah retired to his farm. Major Ducker died in 1856. (Courtesy of the Reisterstown Room.)

James Martin Currie and Blanche Curie (his wife) hold their daughter, Martha. They were active members of All Saints Episcopal Church. The Curries owned and operated Currie's Department Store at 237 Main Street between 1890 and 1920. The photograph was taken at Walzl's Imperial Portrait Studios at 205 West Baltimore Street, probably in the 1880s. (Courtesy of the Reisterstown Room.)

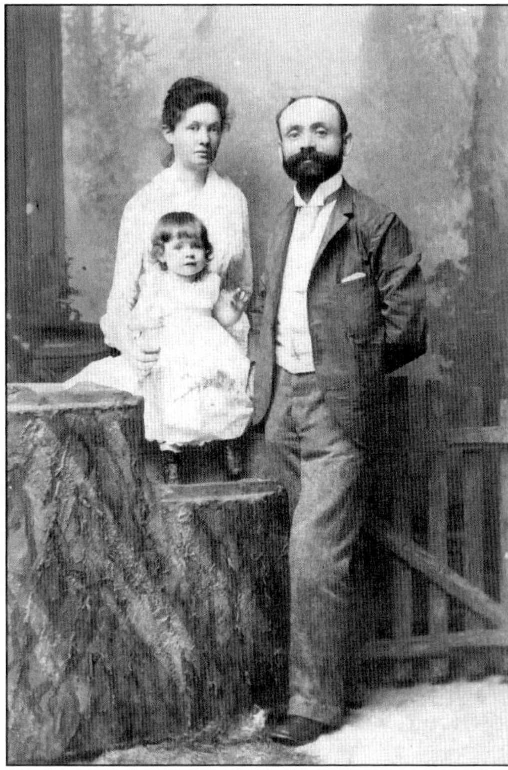

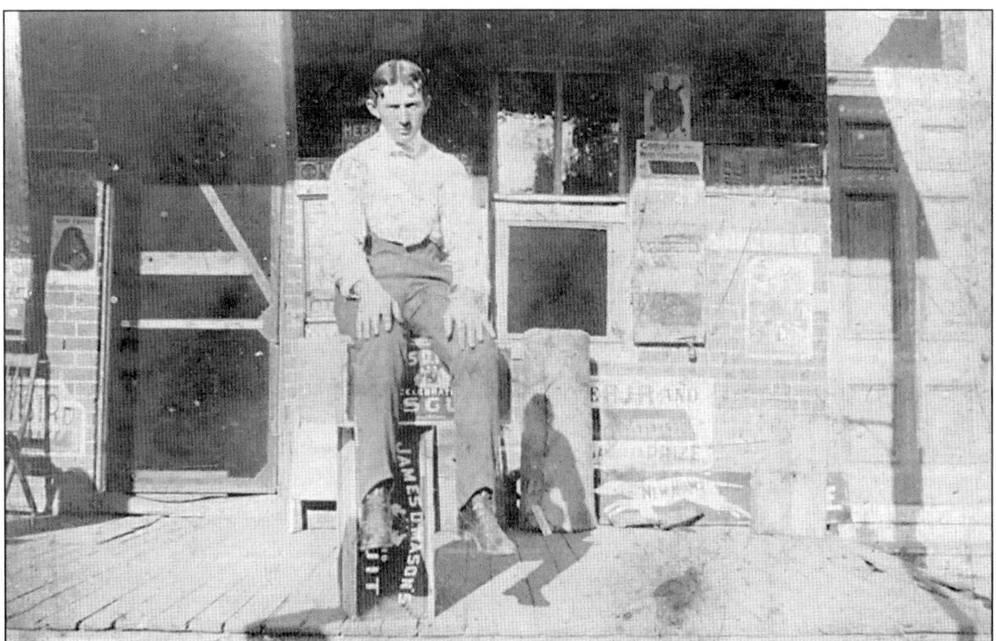

An unidentified boy sits balanced on a stack of crates in this old faded photograph from the late 1800s. The setting is in front of Russell Brother's Store on Main Street. One of the crates the boy is sitting on is from the James D. Mason Bakery on Pratt Street in Baltimore City. The bakery was destroyed by fire on August 4, 1887. (Courtesy of the Reisterstown Room.)

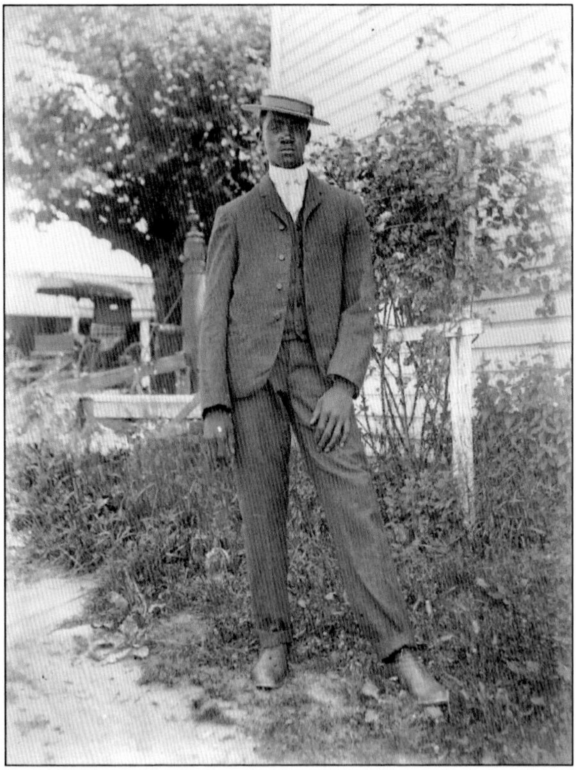

John Franklin Jr. strikes a dignified pose in this July 10, 1904, photograph, taken by Joshua Fitze. According to Louis S. Diggs, author of *Holding on to Their Heritage*, free blacks congregated in a small area of Reisterstown known as Bond Avenue. Reputedly, there was a slave auction block on what was then known as "Bondage Road" (now called Bond Avenue). (Courtesy of the Reisterstown Room.)

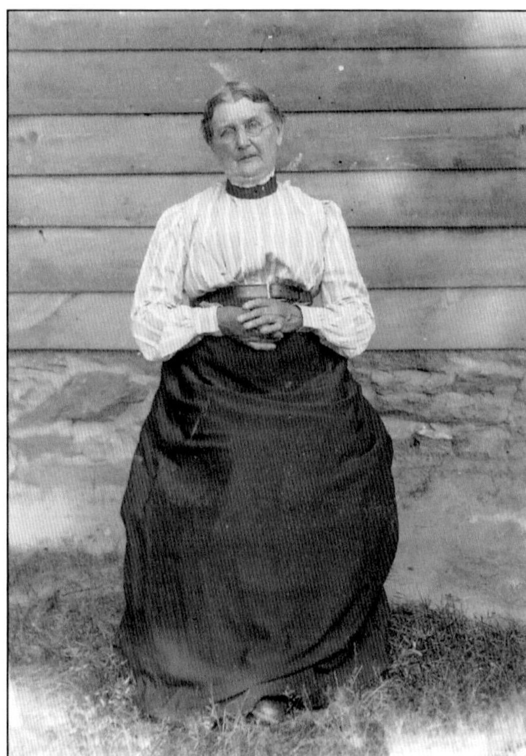

A spectacled Sarah Gore, wife of William Gore Sr., sits patiently for the camera in front of a clapboard building in Reisterstown. She was known as Sarah A. Stocksdail before she married into the Gore family of farmers and millers. The Gores established a mill west of Reisterstown prior to 1796. Joshua Fitze photographed Sarah in August 1904.

James Dorsey is dressed casually in a summer white shirt and pants secured with suspenders, while he smiles posing for the camera at his farm on Cockeys Mill Road in Reisterstown. The photograph was taken on September 27, 1908, by Joshua P. Fitze, with the rolling topography serving as the background for the image. (Courtesy of the Reisterstown Room.)

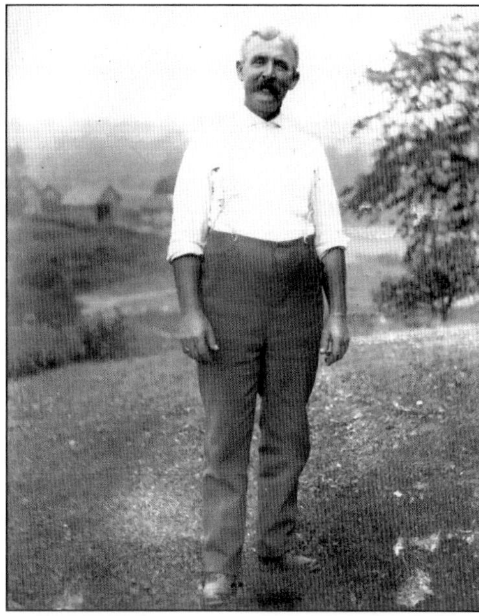

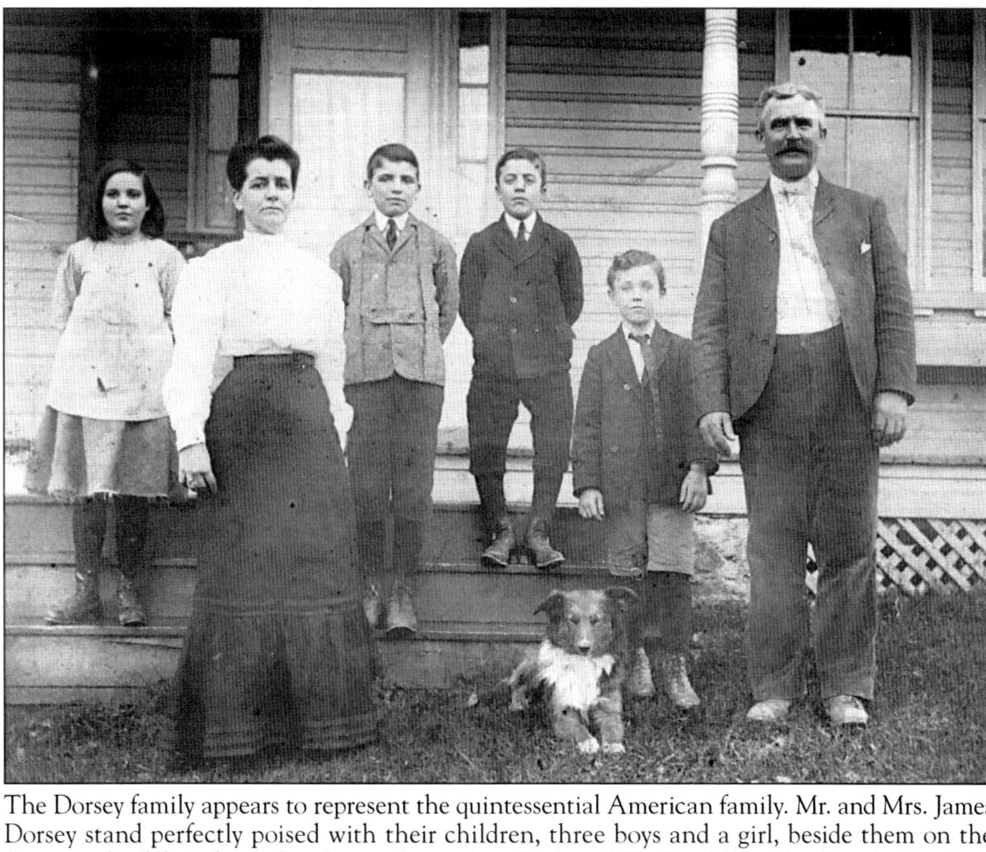

The Dorsey family appears to represent the quintessential American family. Mr. and Mrs. James Dorsey stand perfectly poised with their children, three boys and a girl, beside them on the front porch of their frame farmhouse, located on Cockeys Mill Road. The dog lies obediently at their feet. This faded photograph is undated but probably was taken in 1908. (Courtesy of the Reisterstown Room.)

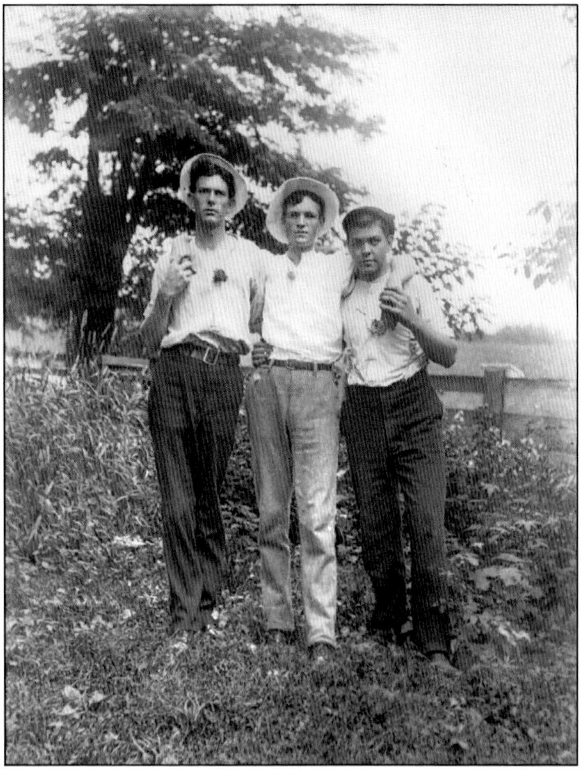

Two brothers and a friend strike a pose in a rural area of Reisterstown. Shown from left to right are William Owens, Harry Owens, and William Lenser. The setting is casual, but the expressions are a tad serious. The image is dated July 30, 1905. Joshua P. Fitze was the photographer. (Courtesy of the Reisterstown Room.)

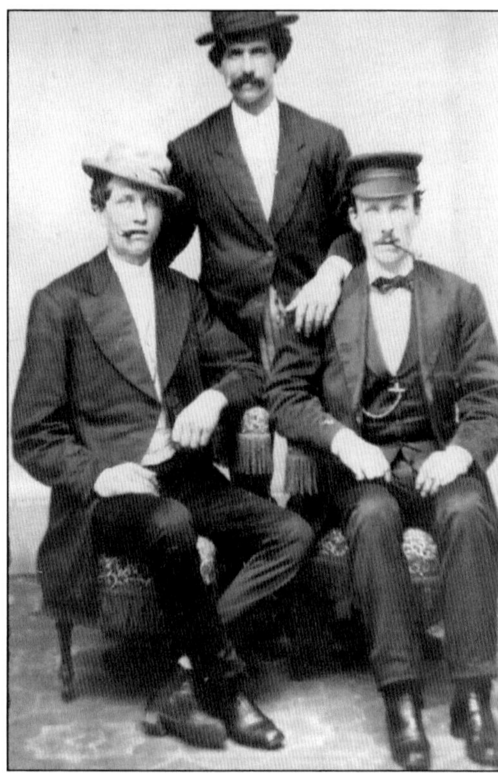

The men strike a staged pose in this image by an unknown photographer. From left to right are Amos Fly, Charles Fly, and Salathiel Fly—most likely brothers. The men are all puffing on cigars, and two are sitting upon floral parlor chairs. The scene is likely from the early 1900s. (Courtesy of the Reisterstown Room.)

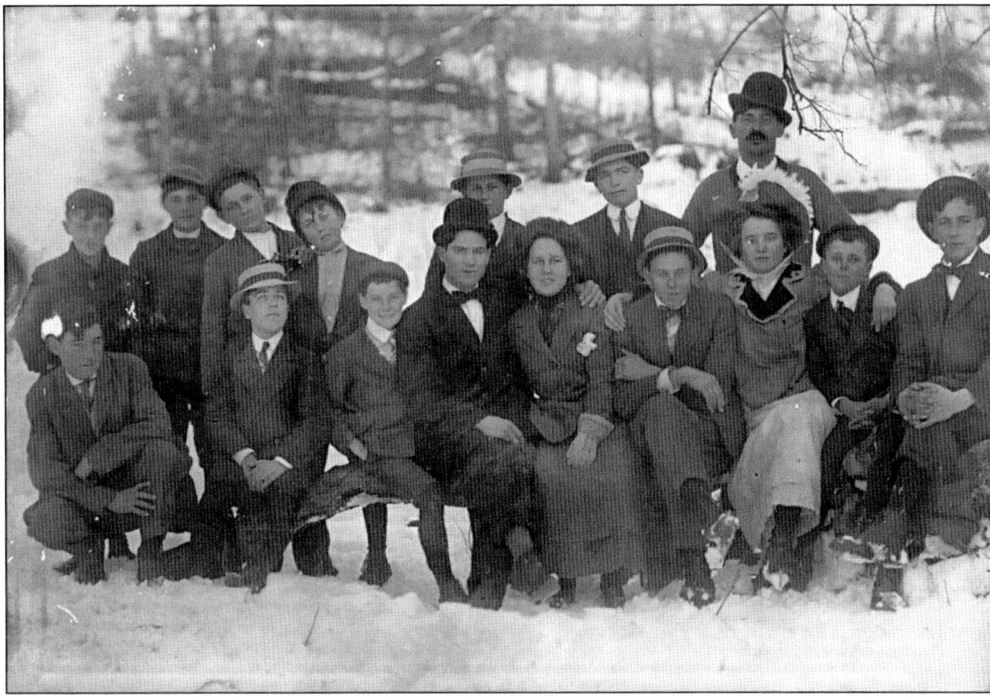

This large group of teens and adults is gathered at the Dorsey farm for some winter merriment. Harry Dorsey is seated second from left in the first row. Interestingly, Harry is the only one in the group who is not looking intently at the camera. The Dorsey farm was located on Cockeys Mill Road. (Courtesy of the Reisterstown Room.)

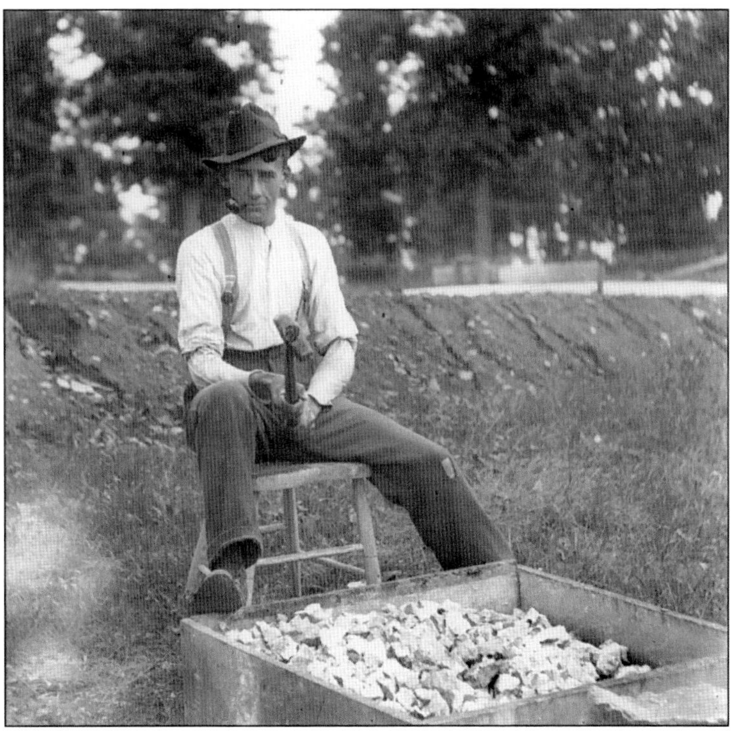

Hilton Gore poses with a wooden box of broken stone at his feet in this plate negative taken by Joshua Fitze on July 20, 1904. He appears to be breaking up stone possibly for a new road. The scene is described as "somewheres in Reisterstown." Gore, wearing a hat and suspenders, seems to enjoy smoking his pipe amidst the tedious task.

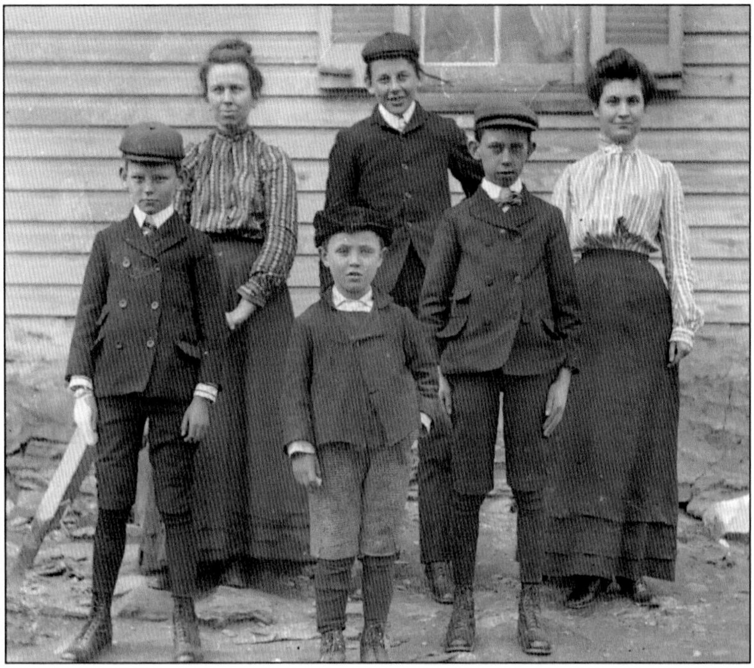

This photograph was taken against the background of a rural farmhouse, possibly the Joshua P. Fitze home. Unidentified members of the Fitze family pose with Laura Greenwood and Herbert Schwartz, caught smiling in the second row. Joshua P. Fitze is identified as the photographer for this undated image. (Courtesy of the Reisterstown Room.)

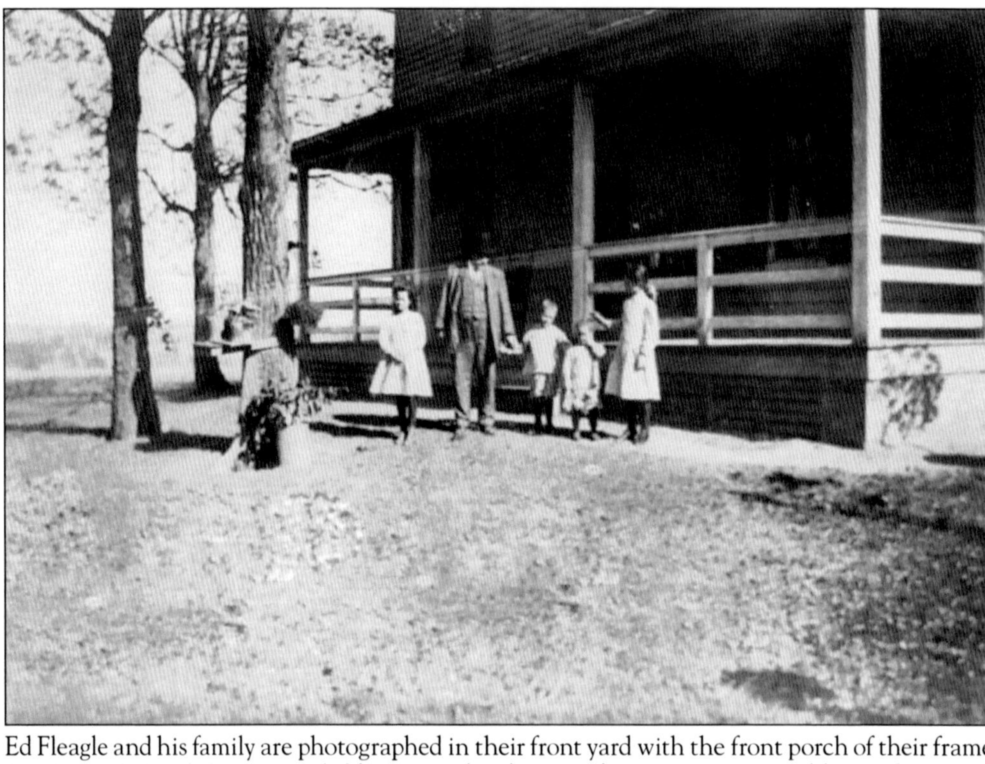

Ed Fleagle and his family are photographed in their front yard with the front porch of their frame farmhouse behind them. His children, two daughters and two sons, surround him. The tree is wrapped in an interesting handmade plant holder. The script on the photograph reads "legendary hired man." The photographer is unidentified, and the date is unknown but appears to be early 1900s. (Courtesy of the Reisterstown Room.)

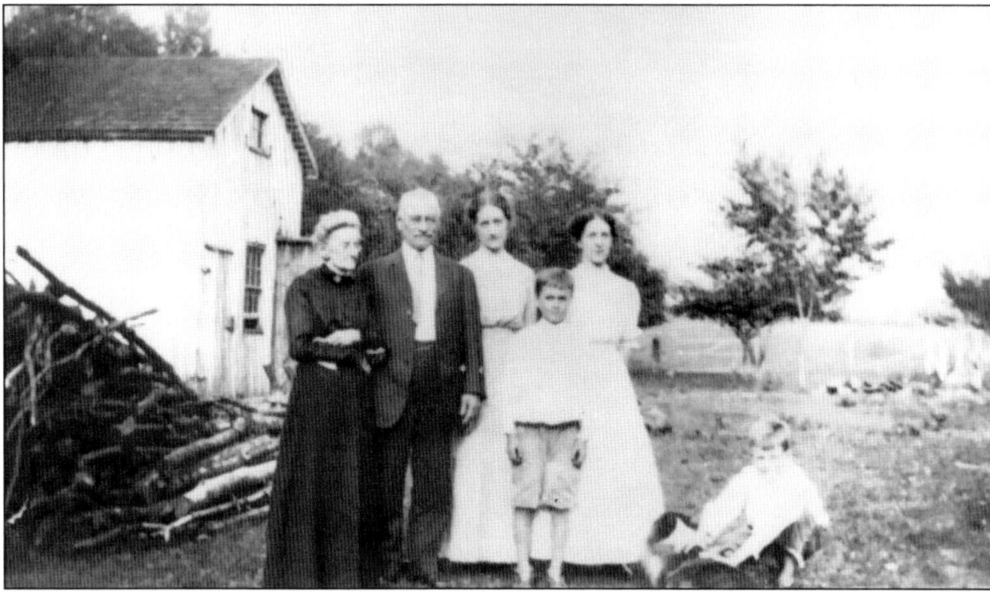

The rural photograph with a woodpile and frame outbuilding in the background shows a group posing for the camera. Standing from left to right are a Dr. and Mrs. Reynolds, Ada Elizabeth Frantz, and Etta Marie Frantz. The young boys in the picture are unidentified. The location is determined to be most likely in Glen Morris, Reisterstown. An unidentified photographer captured the image.

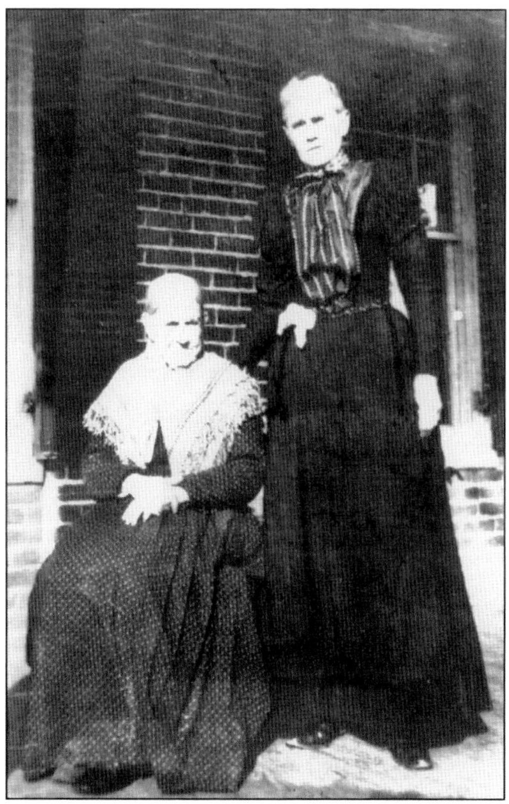

Margaret Wheeler Berryman and her daughter, either Hannah or Vilmina, cast a serious pose for the camera. Margaret was married to Mitchell Berryman in 1834. She died in 1898 and left behind her children George, Vilmina, and Hannah. It is believed that the photograph dates to the 1880s or 1890s. (Courtesy of the Reisterstown Room.)

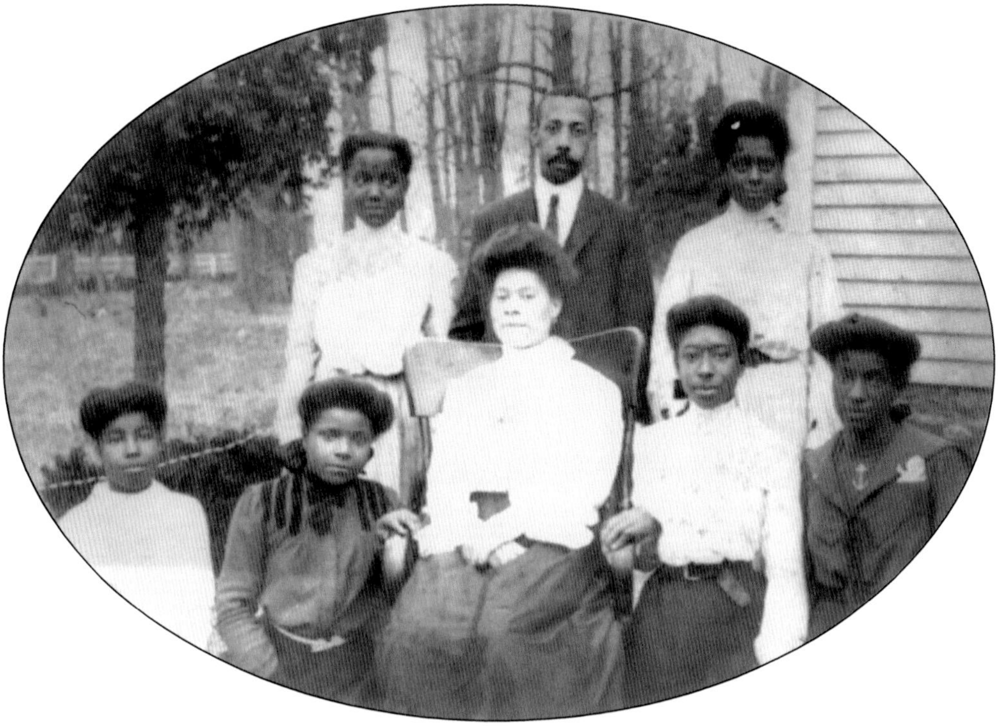

Dr. Alfred M. Bailey (standing, center) was the principal of the school behind St. Luke's Church in the Bond Avenue African American community of Reisterstown. Seen with Dr. Bailey are teacher Annie Granson (seated in chair) and six unidentified female students. The date is not given but is likely the late 19th or early 20th century. (Courtesy of the Reisterstown Room.)

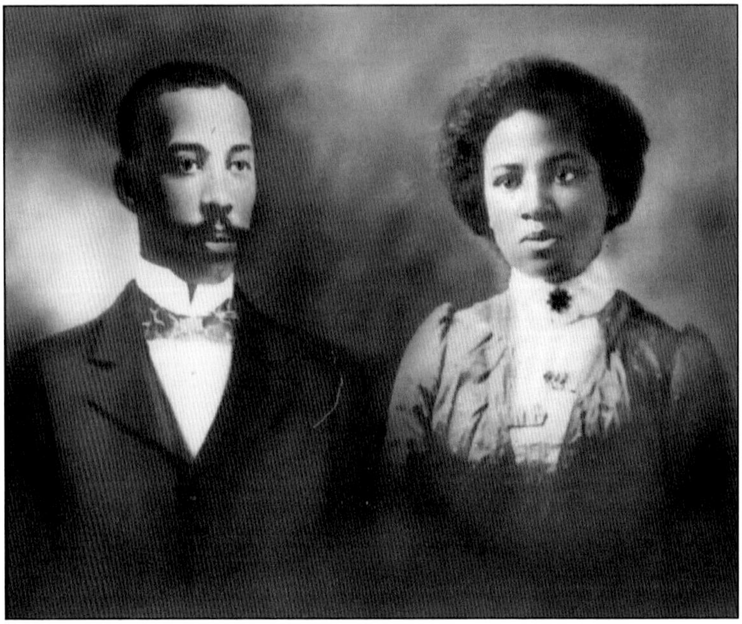

Dr. Alfred M. Bailey and his wife, Ardella H. Tucker Bailey, lived in the St. George area of Reisterstown. Bailey taught in the school behind St. Luke's Church in the Bond Avenue African American community. This striking image dates to the late 19th or early 20th century. (Courtesy of the Reisterstown Room.)

Lottie Gaskins beams at an unidentified photographer while standing on the steps of the Philip B. Welsh house in Glen Morris, Reisterstown, where she worked in the 1920s. Lottie also worked for Ira Wales in Glyndon and for other families as a laundress. Her employer Philip B. Welsh grew award-winning pears and apples, and sold asparagus fern and smilax for use in floral arrangements from his greenhouses.

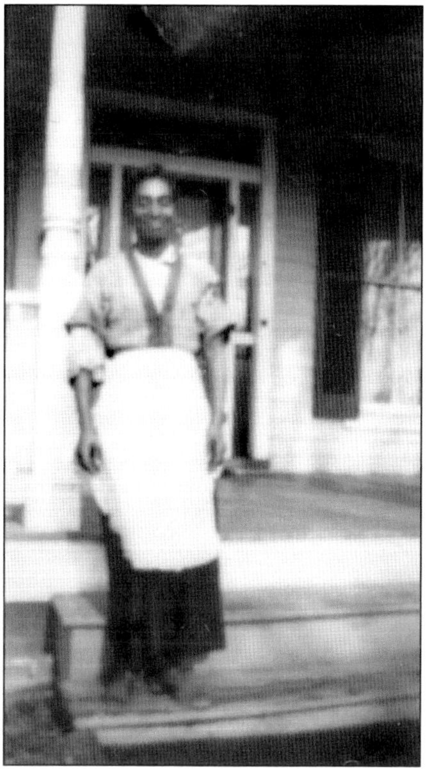

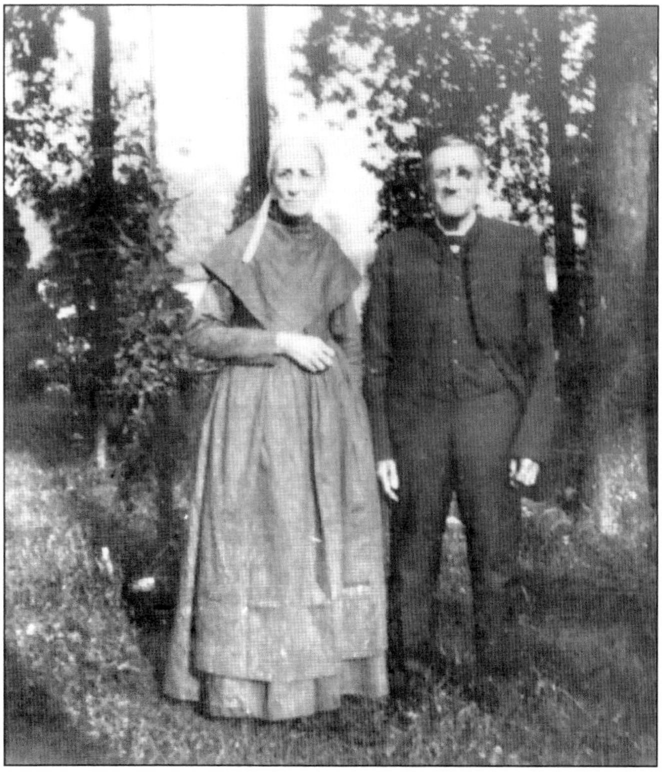

Martha Barr (Funk) Frantz (1845–1931) and Elam Groff Frantz (1840–1923) strike a serious pose for an unidentified photographer. Martha is modestly dressed, wearing a bonnet and linen pinafore. Peeking through the background there appears to be a body of water. The photograph likely dates back to the late 19th or early 20th century. (Courtesy of the Reisterstown Room.)

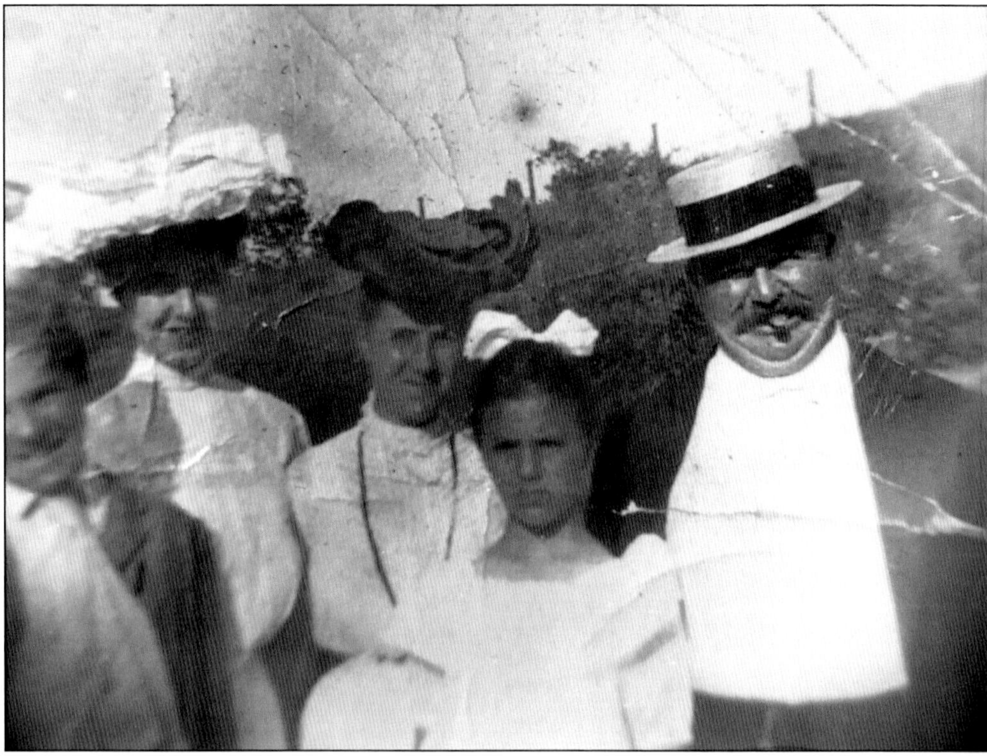

Shown in this photograph, taken in the early 20th century by an unidentified photographer, are members of the Eunice Gray Warner family, although Eunice is not present. Eunice was a member of the David William Gray family who owned "The Elms" estate near Reisterstown. The city purchased the house from the Grays, and it was subsequently demolished to make room for the Liberty Reservoir.

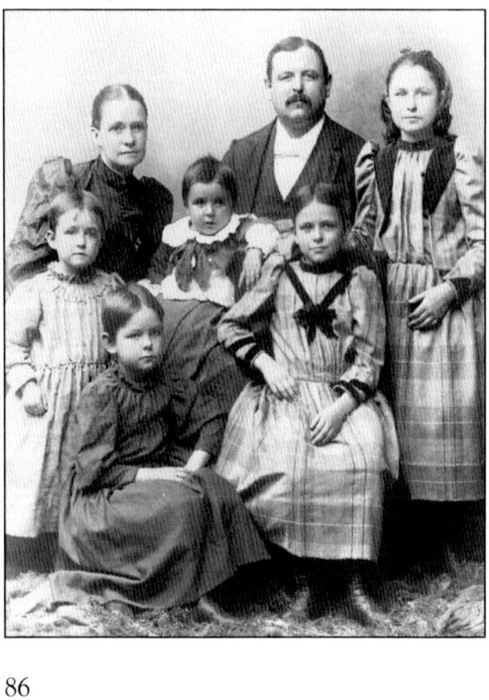

Zachariah "Zacky" C. Ebaugh and family posed for this photograph, taken by London Studio of Baltimore. Professor Ebaugh was the principal of Franklin High School for 22 years. He was beloved for his honesty and kindness, and was known to exact discipline when necessary with a paddle in his office. He was the father of six children, four girls and two boys. The youngest, Dr. Franklin Ebaugh, was not yet born when this picture was taken. (Courtesy of the Reisterstown Room.)

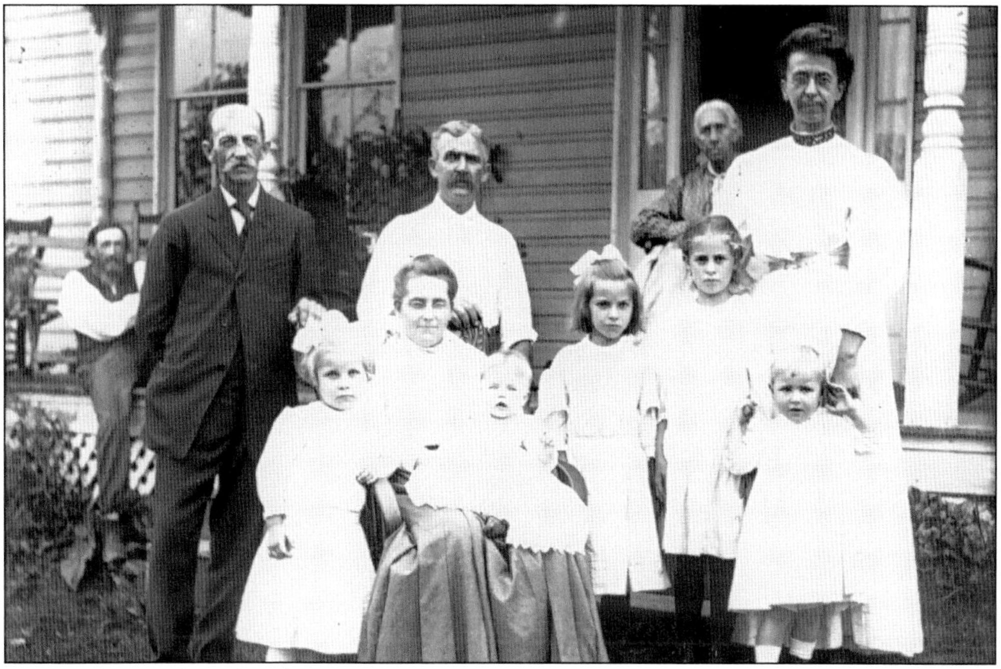

Most of the people in the Shreves family of Reisterstown are not identifiable. Apparently Murray (or Maury) Shreves stands with his wife while surrounded by their children. The bearded older man and the older woman sitting on the porch appear to be hired help. The older woman on the right and the older man in the dark suit are presumably relatives in this posed photograph by Joshua Fitze on September 27, 1908.

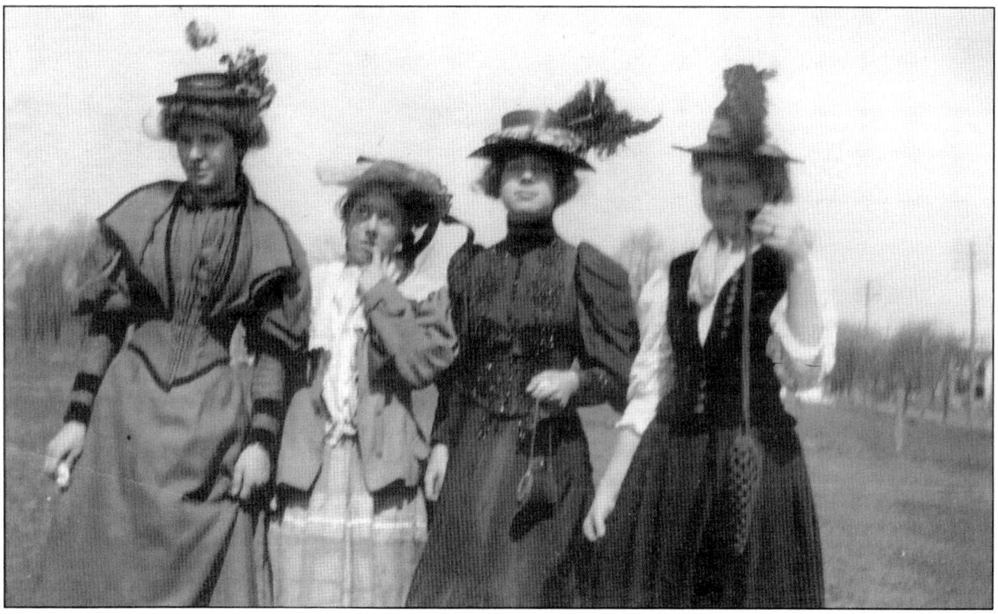

This amusing photograph, dated 1915, was uncovered in a box marked "Goodwin" in the Reisterstown Room. The story behind the photograph is a mystery; however, the women's names were recorded on the back of the photograph. In no particular order, they are Anita O'Keefe, Adelaide Roschen (spelling uncertain), Lorena Cook, and Aurelia Smith. (Courtesy of the Reisterstown Room.)

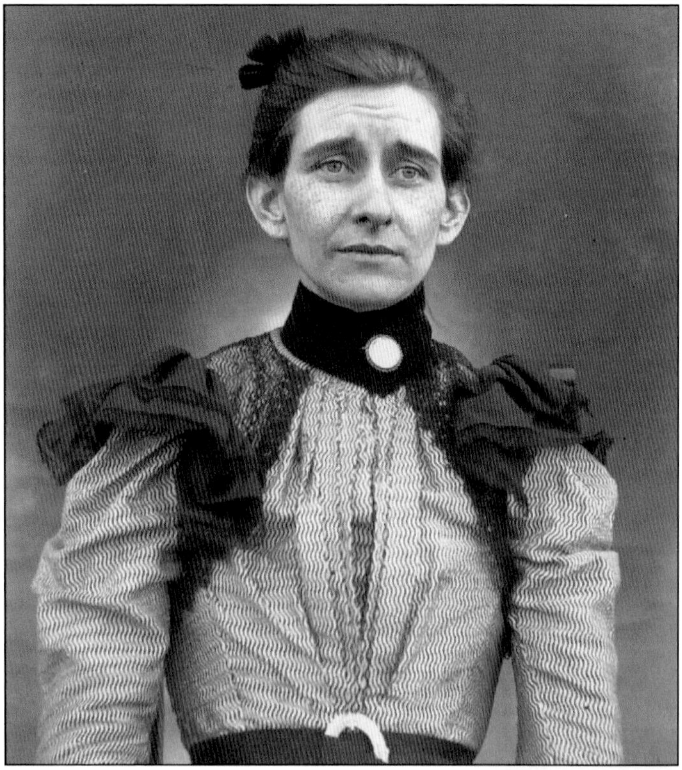

Ada "Addie" Zillah Cook (1869–1923) of Reisterstown posed for this image by Reisterstown photographer Joshua Fitze in April 1902. Addie was baptized on August 15, 1869, by George Zimmerman at the Grace Methodist Church South that was formed in response to disagreements over slavery and state rights following the Civil War. (Courtesy of the Reisterstown Room.)

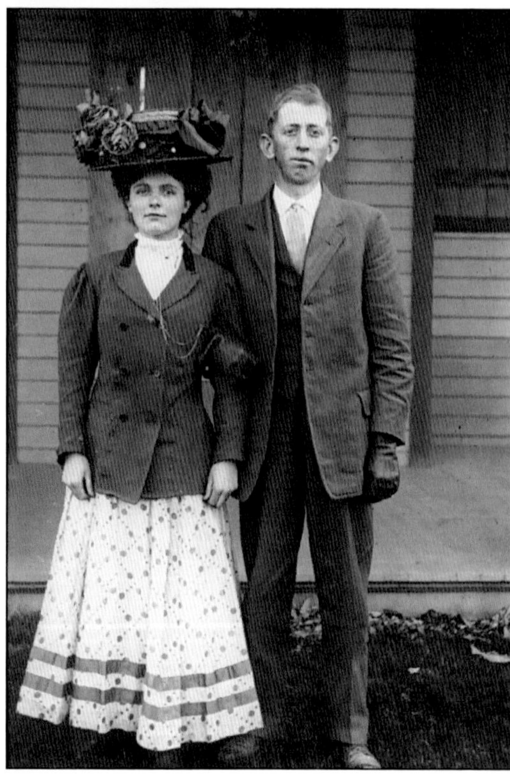

This classic period photograph was taken on April 11, 1909. The photographer is not identified. Pierce Martin and his sister Ada are the couple in the image, clearly dressed for the occasion. Notice the broad hat and full feminine hairstyle on Ada that was characteristic of the times. (Courtesy of the Reisterstown Room.)

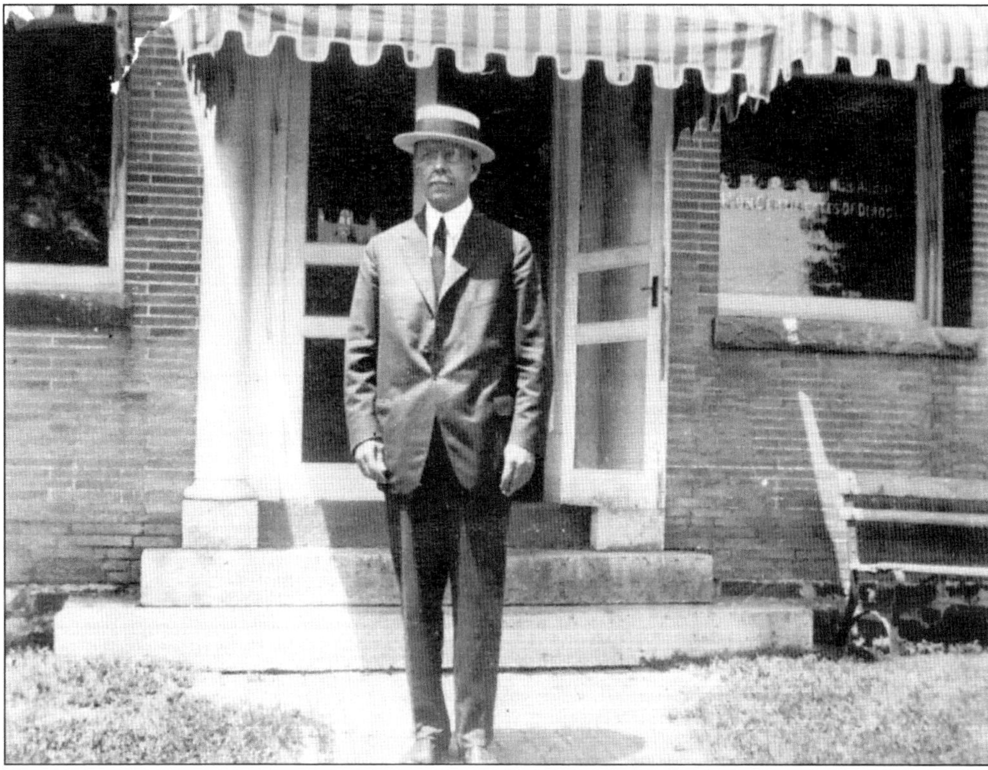

Frank H. Zouck is shown here in the 1920s at the Reisterstown Savings Bank on Main Street, where he was president from 1901 to 1950. Zouck was born in Beckleysville in 1866 to Henry and Mary Alice Zouck. He resided at 337 Main Street, although he once owned Meadow Park Farm. Frank served as chairman of the state roads commission in 1912 and again in 1917 for eight years. He died in 1950 and is remembered for his service to the community.

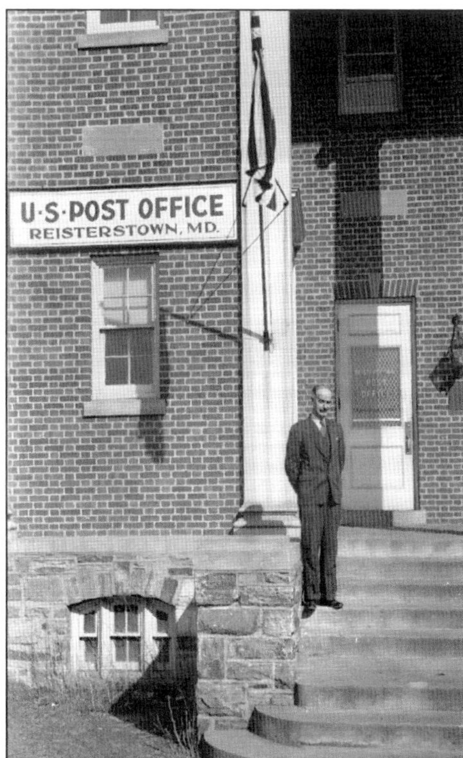

Postmaster William H. L. Slade stands on the steps of the Reisterstown Post Office, located at 85 Main Street at the time of the photograph. Slade was postmaster from 1934 to 1960, and he was the grandson of William A. Slade, who was postmaster from 1893 until 1897. William graduated from Franklin High School in 1916. Louise Bland Goodwin took this photograph in 1941.

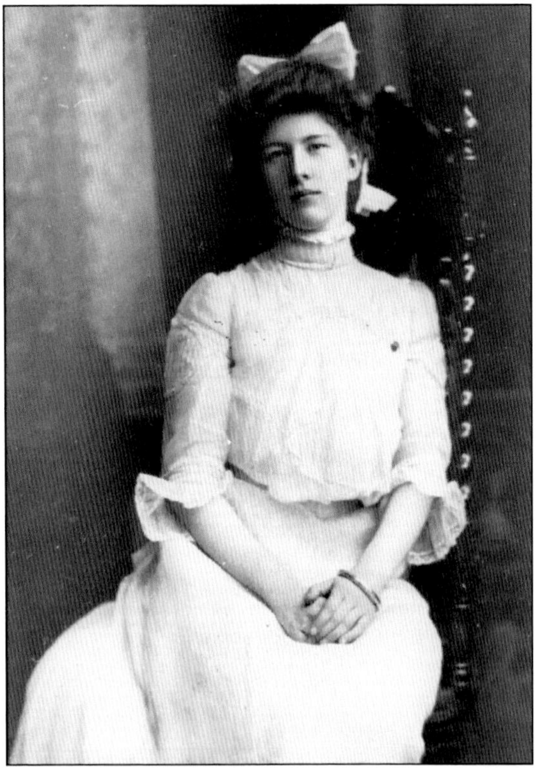

Susannah Kephart Wightman (1884–1926) was a member of the Kephart family who owned Walnut Grove Farm. She married William Stevenson on October 4, 1910, at her mother's home. Her sister Belle Wightman held her bouquet while the wedding ring was being put on. She was the mother of Susannah S. Baldwin and grandmother of John W. Baldwin. (Courtesy of the Reisterstown Room.)

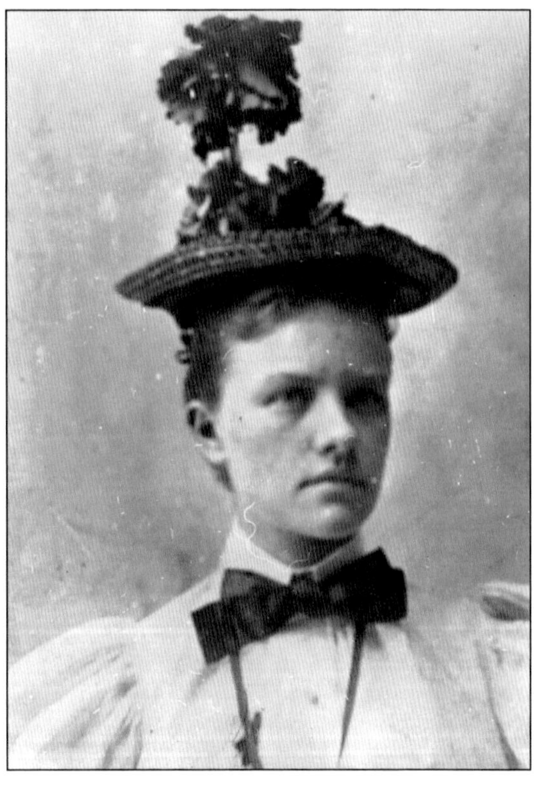

The back of this undated photograph bears the inscription "Bella Ruth Wightman." She was likely the sister of Susannah Kephart Wightman, pictured above. Bella is wearing a vintage hat adorned with feathers. (Courtesy of the Reisterstown Room.)

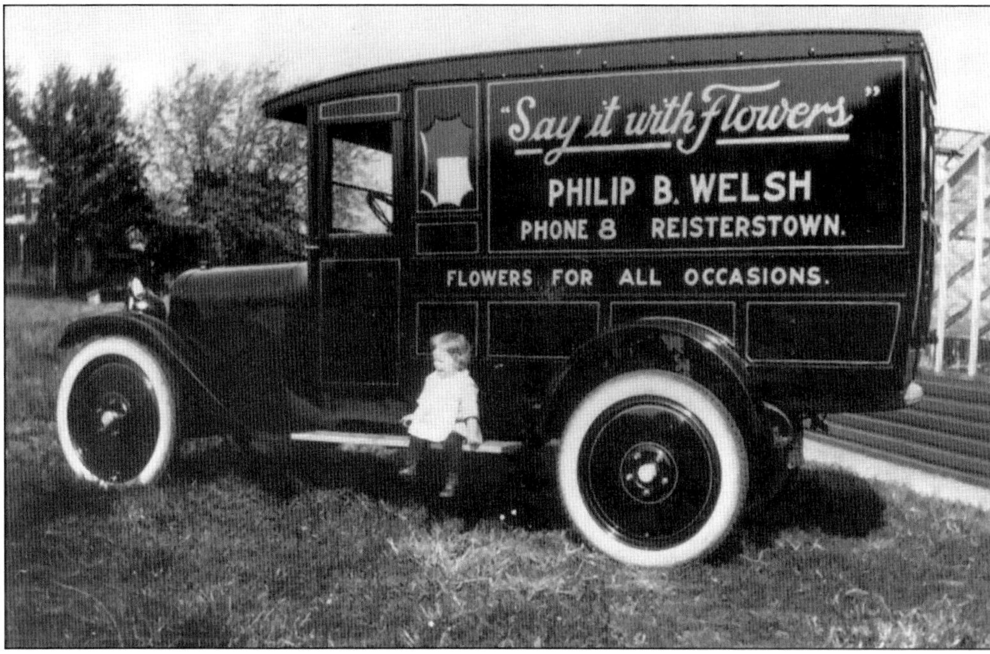

Adorable Helen Louise Geist, daughter of Arthur and Helen Marie Geist (née Welsh), sits on the stepping board of Philip B. Welsh's flower delivery truck. Welsh owned the estate known as Glen Morris. His business supplied flowers for all occasions, and his slogan was "Say it With Flowers." The photograph dates back to 1903. (Courtesy of the Reisterstown Room.)

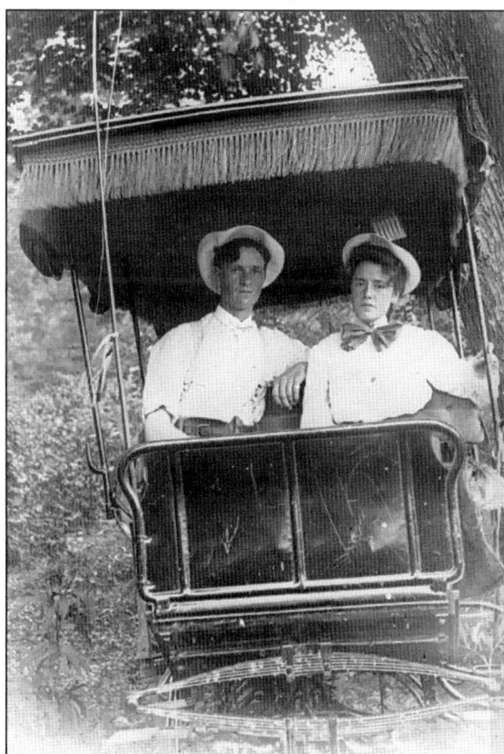

Bertha Rawlings and her future husband, William F. Owens, are identified in this photograph, taken on July 4, 1905. It was in 1905 that a new building was erected for Franklin High School, leaving the Old Academy building to be used for an elementary school. The gentleman and his lady appear to be posing in a prop for the patriotic occasion. (Courtesy of the Reisterstown Room.)

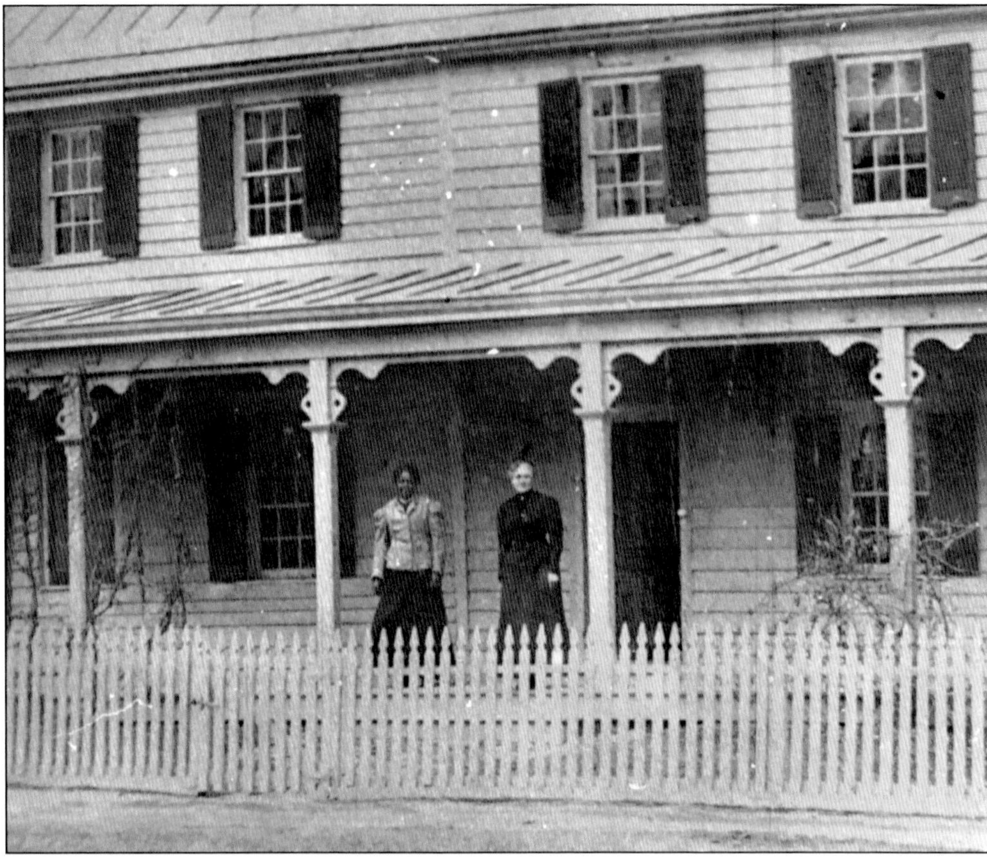

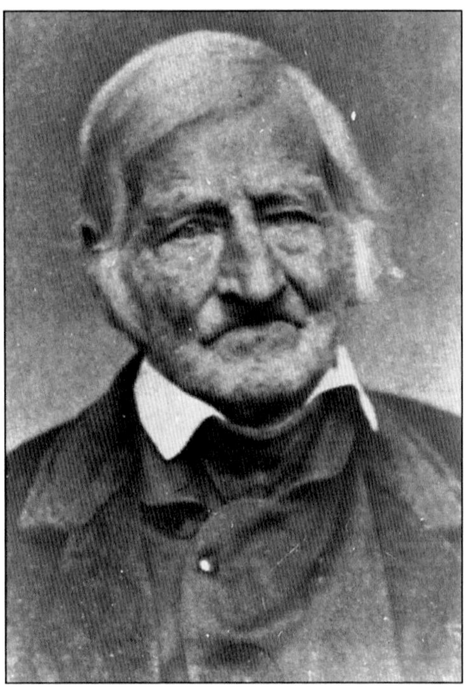

Rebecca J. Stocksdale, known by locals as "Miss Jane," stands at right on her front porch at 234 Main Street with an unidentified woman. John Reister Sr. built the log house covered by clapboard in the late 1700s. After being used as a tavern for years, the structure was converted into a home in 1808. Local lore suggests "friendly" ghosts visit the house. (Courtesy of the Reisterstown Room.)

Philip Reister Jr. (1781–1870), grandson of John Reister, married Maria Larsh in 1834 at the ripe age of 53. They lived for a time at the brick house at 14 Main Street. Although the couple had no children, they were fond of their many nieces and nephews. He was a merchant, a farmer, and at one time owned an inn. His sister was Susan Whalen (see page 93). (Courtesy of the Reisterstown Room.)

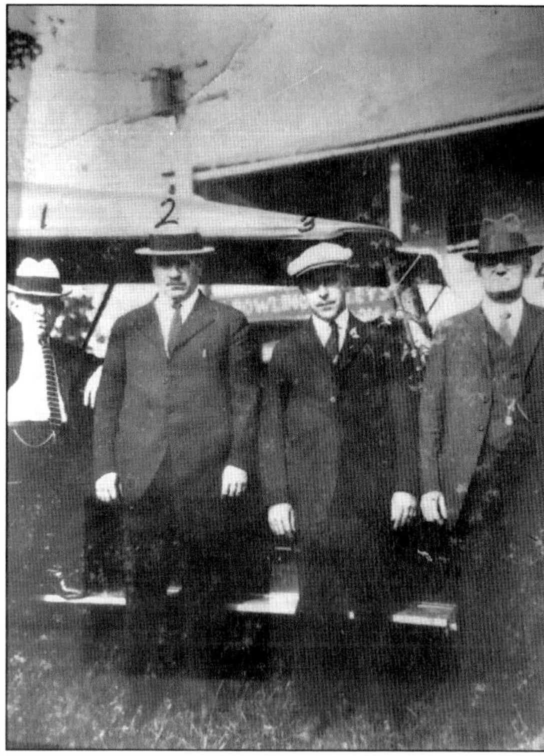

This group photograph shows prominent Reisterstown businessmen posing before a sign that reads "Bowling Alley." The men, identified in no particular order, are J. F. Eline, J. W. Wolf, G. Walter Tovell, and Samuel Yingling, all of Reisterstown. This outdoor photograph is undated. (Courtesy of the Reisterstown Room.)

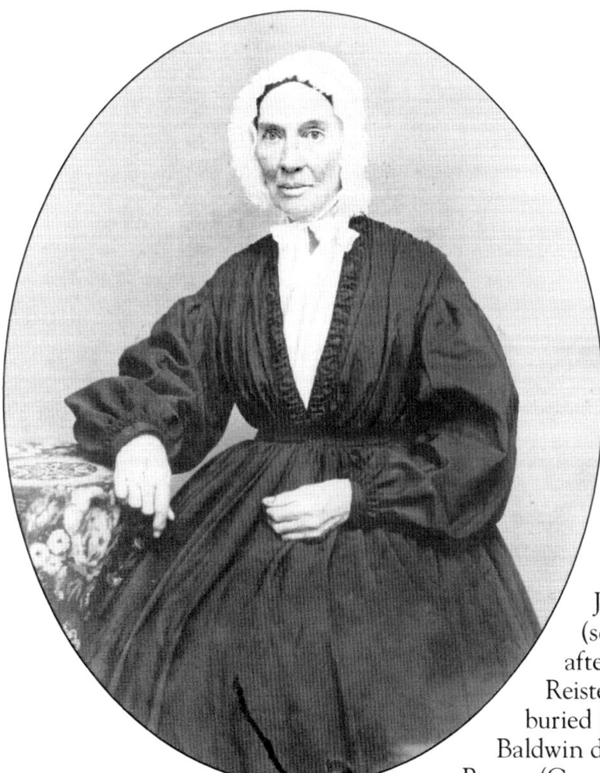

The framed portrait is of Susan Reister Whalen (1792–1882), granddaughter of John Reister and sister of Philip Reister Jr. (see page 92). Susan was born 16 days after the sudden death of her father, Philip Reister. Both she and her brother Philip Jr. are buried in the Old Lutheran Cemetery. Susan Baldwin donated the image to the Reisterstown Room. (Courtesy of the Reisterstown Room.)

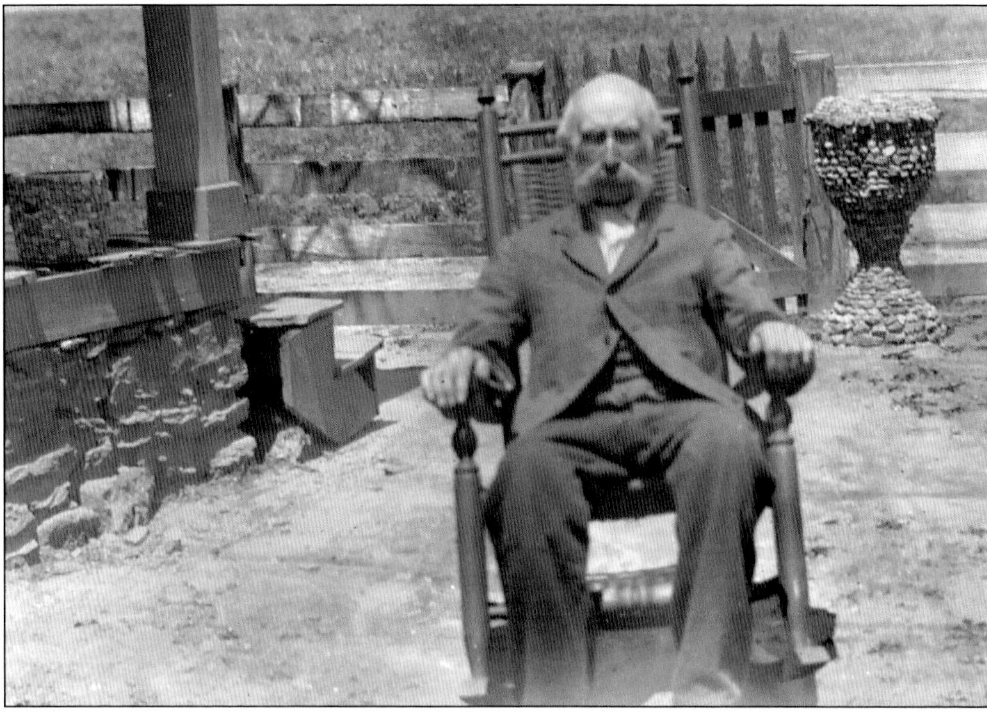

Joshua P. Fitze is photographed here at an advanced age. Fitze was renowned in the area for taking professional photographs, many of which are included in this book. He is particularly remembered for taking school pictures. His home is also featured in this book. Look closely and the viewer will recognize the fence, porch, and picket gate in the details of both photographs. (Courtesy of the Reisterstown Room.)

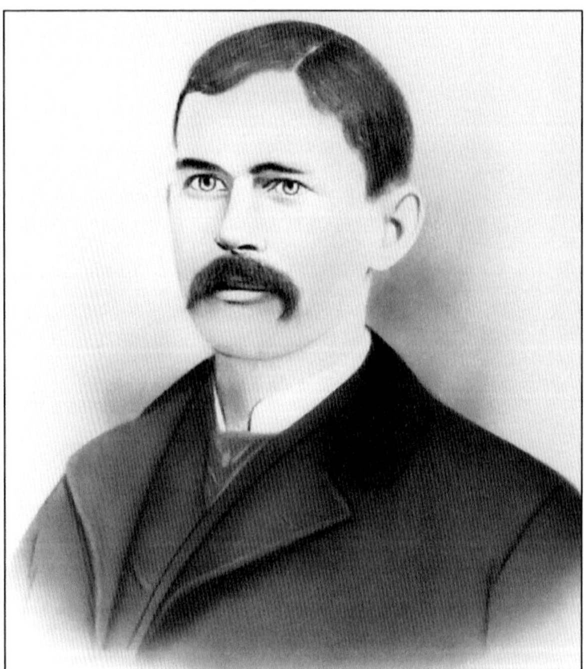

Henry "Harry" Clay Reister (1850–1896) was the only son of Adam and Elizabeth Reister. Like his father and grandfather, Harry was a saddler by trade. He operated a feed and harness store at 411 Light Street. Harry purchased a tavern in 1890 at 2100 Hanover Street that his widow operated after his early death. (Courtesy of the Reisterstown Room.)

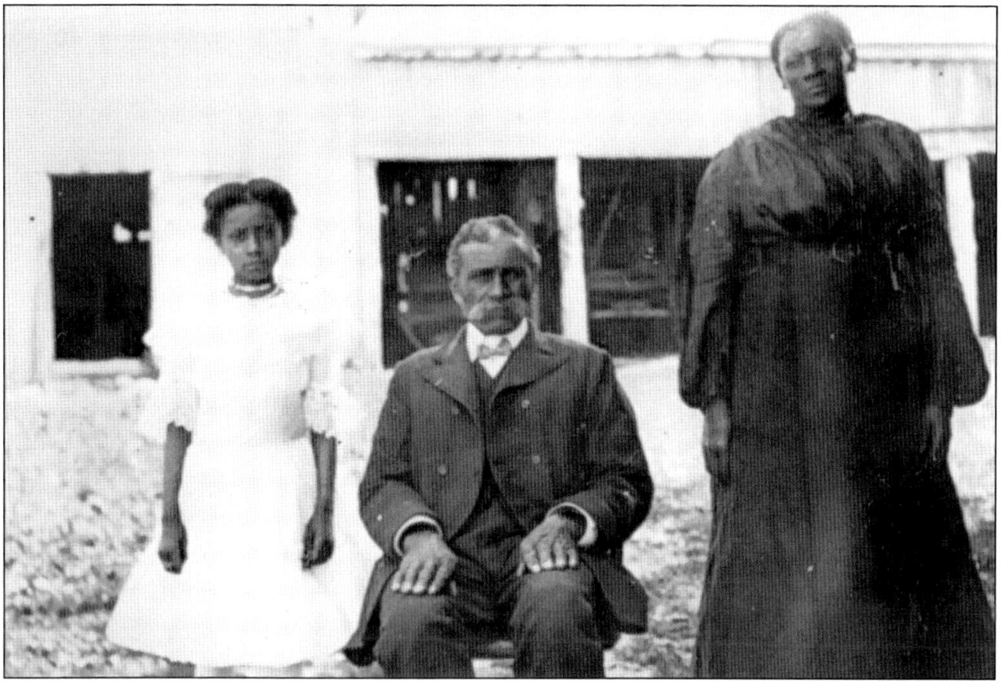

Mr. and Mrs. John Franklin and their daughter resided on Cockeys Mill Road in Reisterstown. Cockeys Mill Road was originally a Native American trail and was first named Academy Lane. This 1904 photograph is from the Louis S. Diggs Photographic Collection. (Courtesy of the Reisterstown Room.)

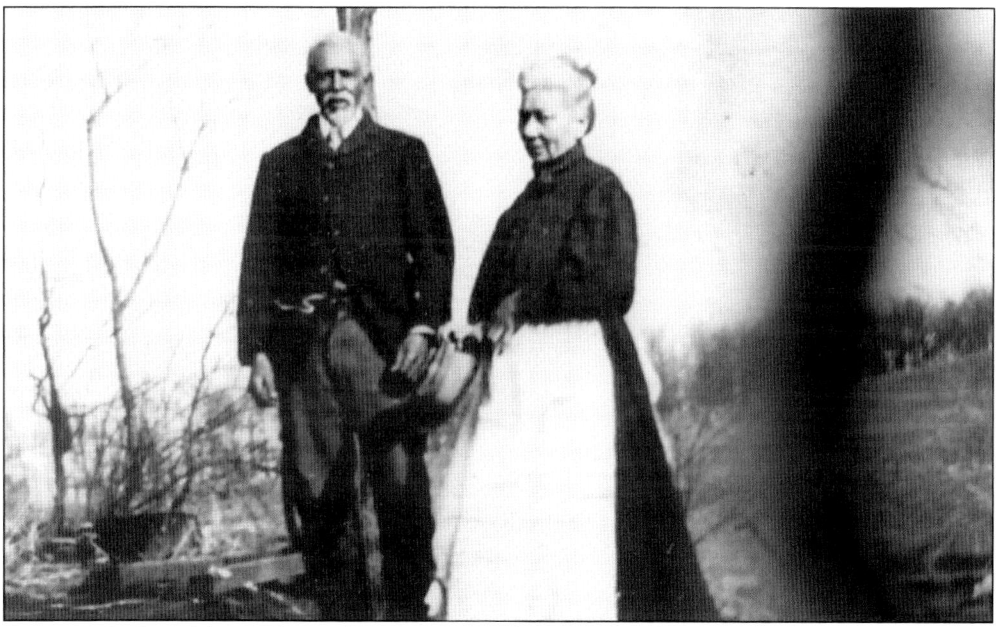

George Mack and his wife, Molly, are captured posing for the camera on their property in Reisterstown. They owned their own land since the days of slavery, and their descendants still call the same plot home. The photograph dates from the mid-1800s and is from the Louis S. Diggs Photographic Collection. (Courtesy of the Reisterstown Room.)

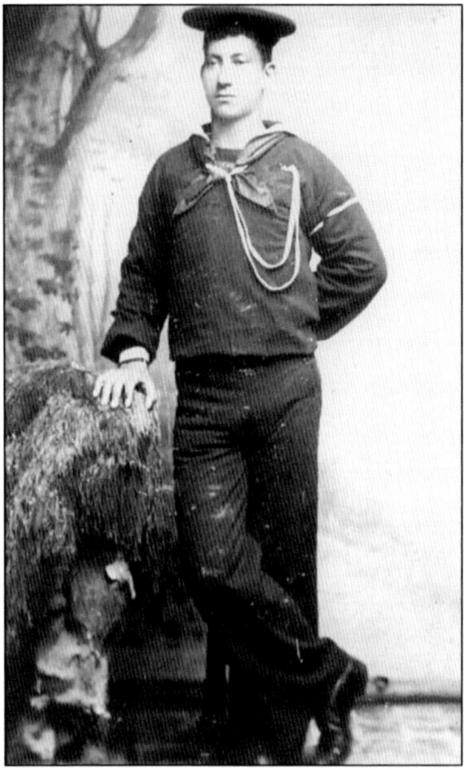

James Welch was the brother of John Thomas Welch. He was born on July 18, 1874, and died on March 13, 1955. James lived on Bond Avenue and is buried in the cemetery of St. Luke's United Methodist Church. The photograph dates to the late 1800s and is from the Louis S. Diggs Photographic Collection. (Courtesy of the Reisterstown Room.)

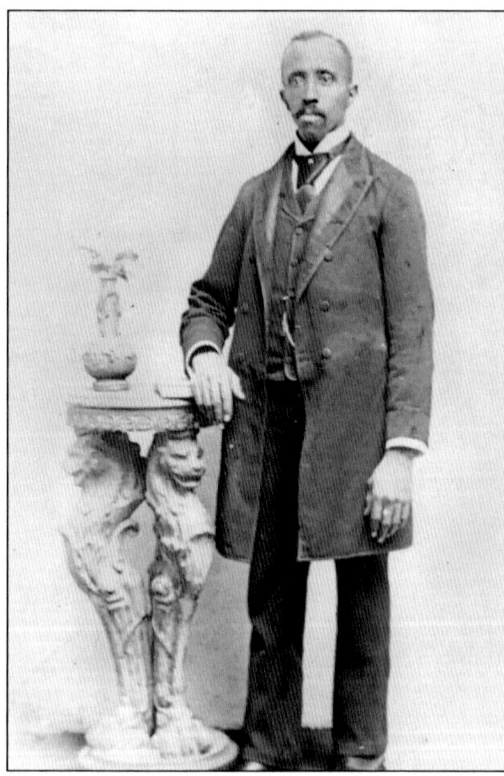

John Robinson is shown in this 1894 photograph from the Louis S. Diggs Photographic Collection. John was born in Piney Grove in Boring, Maryland, but spent some of his life on Bond Avenue in Reisterstown. In the early days, the African American communities of Bond Avenue and Piney Grove Road were close-knit. (Courtesy of the Reisterstown Room.)

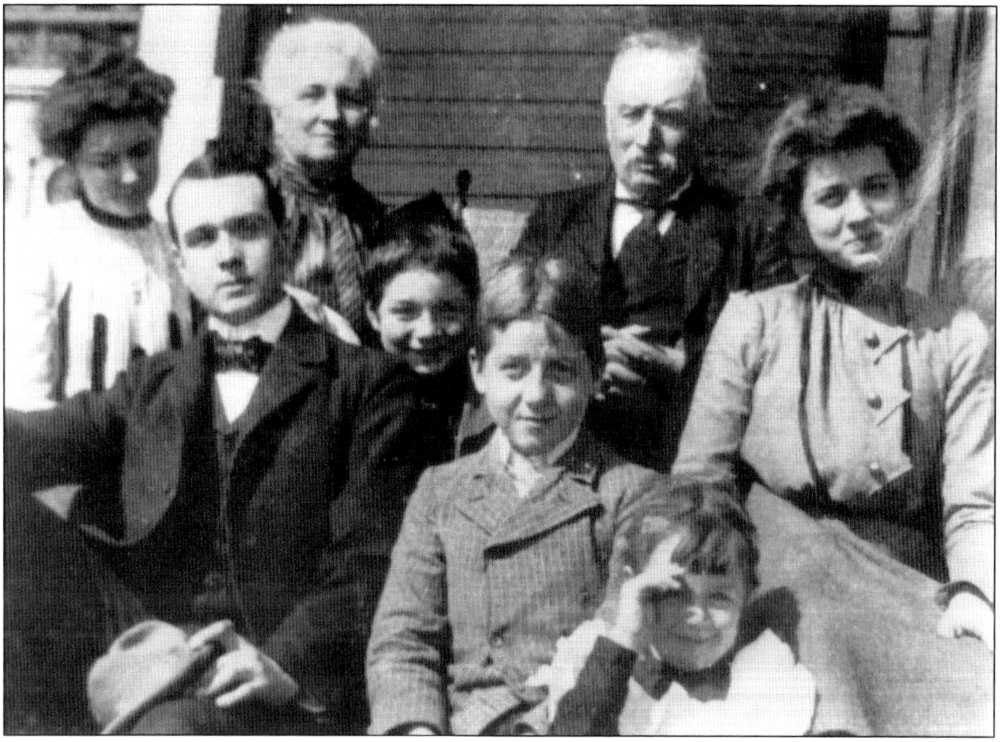

The Campbell family is seen posing together (above) in an image that appears to contain three generations of the family. Individual names of the family members are not known. An unidentified photographer took the picture of the Campbell boys (below) on a child's buckboard wagon in October 1927. The writing on the back of the old photograph is illegible but appears to name one of the boys David or Daniel. The dog is identified as Fluff, and "Miss Extra" could refer to the goat. The markings on the wagon in the photograph indicate that the Climax Wagon Company manufactured it. (Both, courtesy of the Reisterstown Room.)

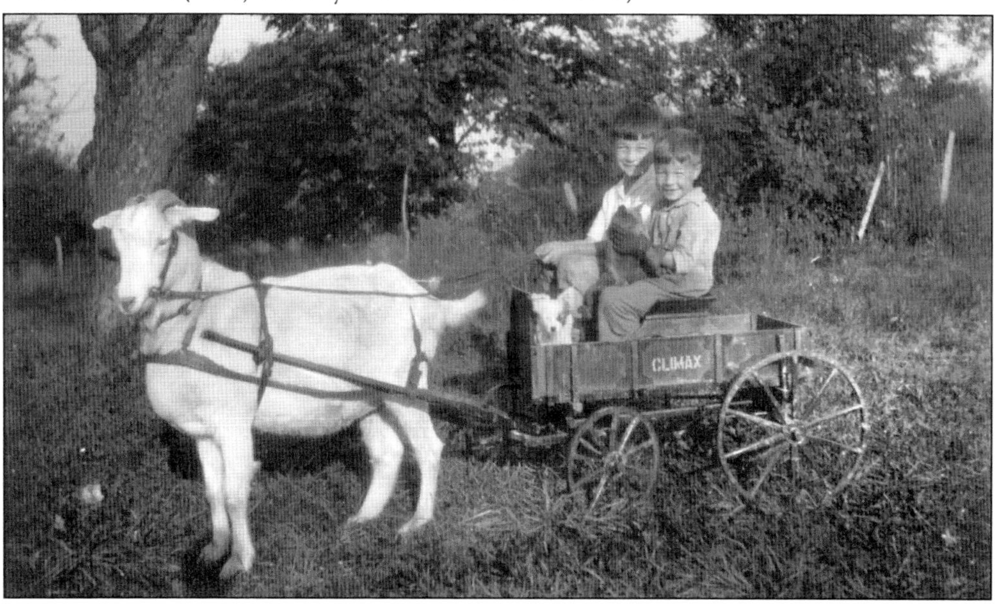

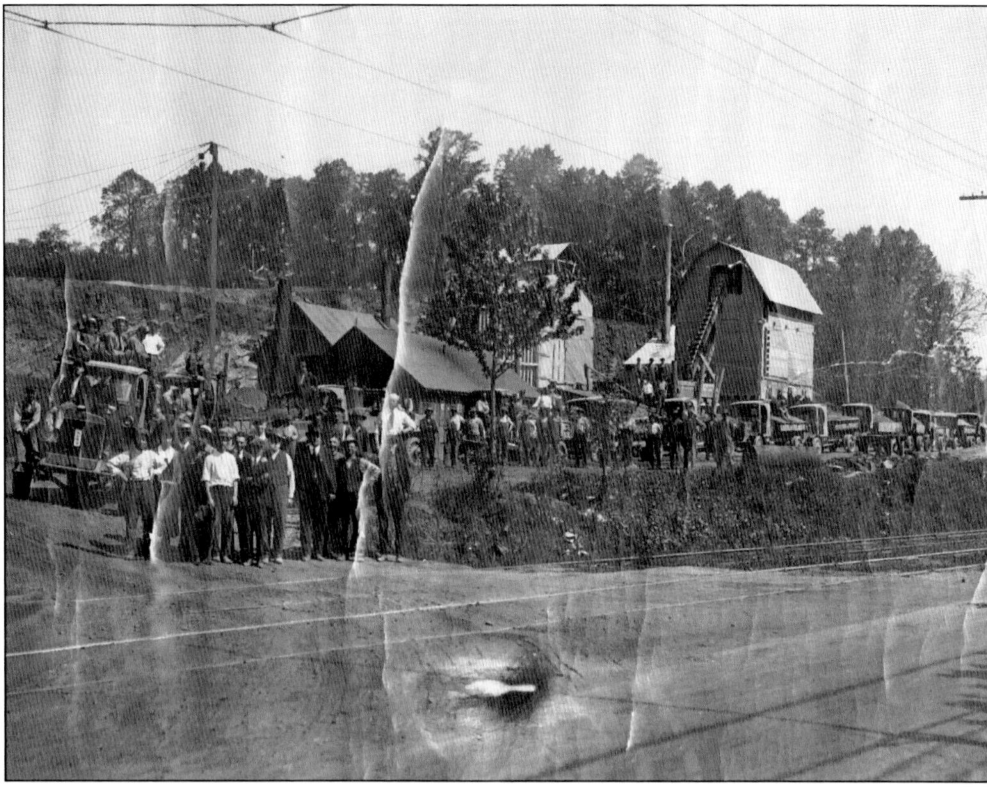

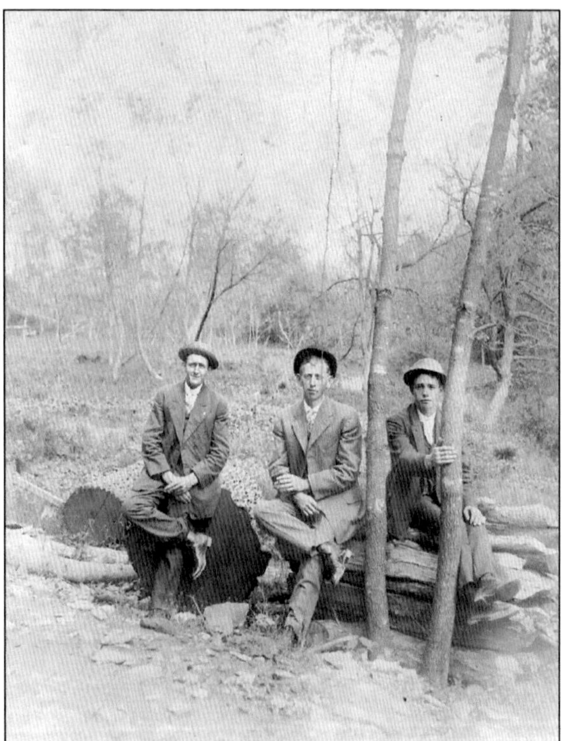

The Flint Mill of Glen Morris in Reisterstown is photographed on the west side of Old Hanover Road, across from present-day Reisterstown Lumber. It was an important industry in Reisterstown for many years, until the mill burned to the ground in 1925. Workers and management are congregated in this unusual and rare image. (Courtesy of the Reisterstown Room.)

Three young Reisterstown men pose for the camera while sitting on some large logs cut down in a woodland scene. The setting appears to take place in the fall, as the leaves are off the trees. Pierce Martin sits in the center flanked by Walter Merkel and Al Walters on either side. (Courtesy of the Reisterstown Room.)

Seven

PLEASURABLE PURSUITS

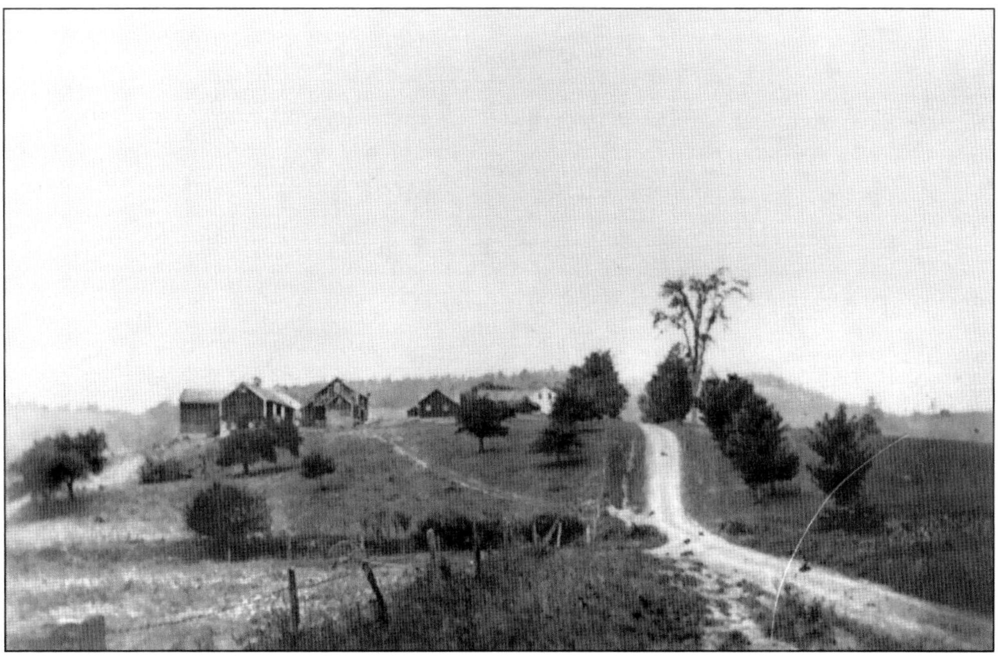

This beautiful panoramic image of an unidentified road in Reisterstown was discovered hidden away in the Reisterstown Room. The photograph is believed to originate from the 1930s or earlier. It is typical of the Reisterstown countryside, which sits high above sea level, offering the best of health and scenery. (Courtesy of the Reisterstown Room.)

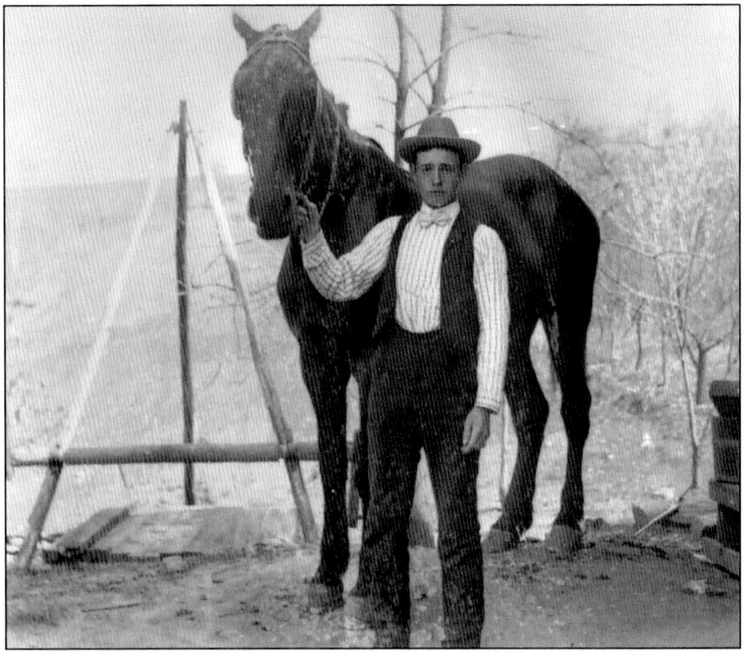

A young groom, William Inman Walters, poses with his horse in front of a hog-slaughtering tripod. Walters appears dressed for the occasion, wearing a striped shirt with bow tie, suspenders, vest, and hat. Joshua Fitze took the glass-plate negative image of his patient subjects, a lengthy process, somewhere in the Reisterstown area on April 23, 1905. (Courtesy of the Reisterstown Room.)

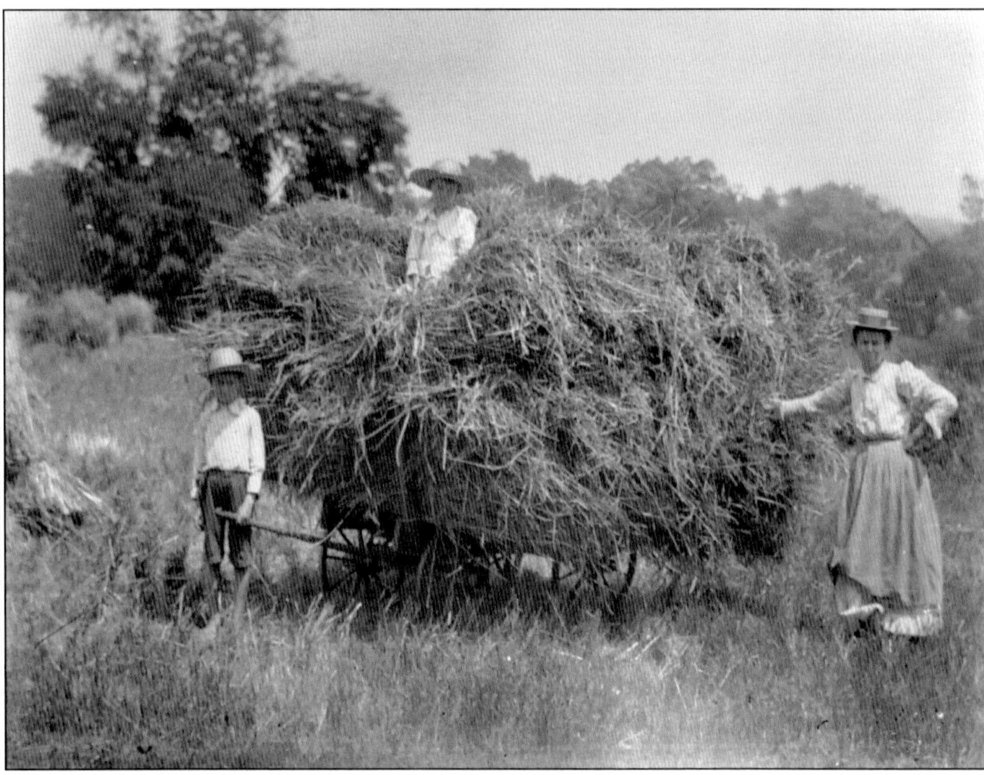

Joshua Fitze captured this nostalgic farm picture in the early 1900s. The harvest scene shows a woman at right standing beside a fully loaded, but small, four-wheeled hay cart; one young boy stands between the traces, and another child perches in the hay on the cart. Everyone is wearing hats for protection from the sun.

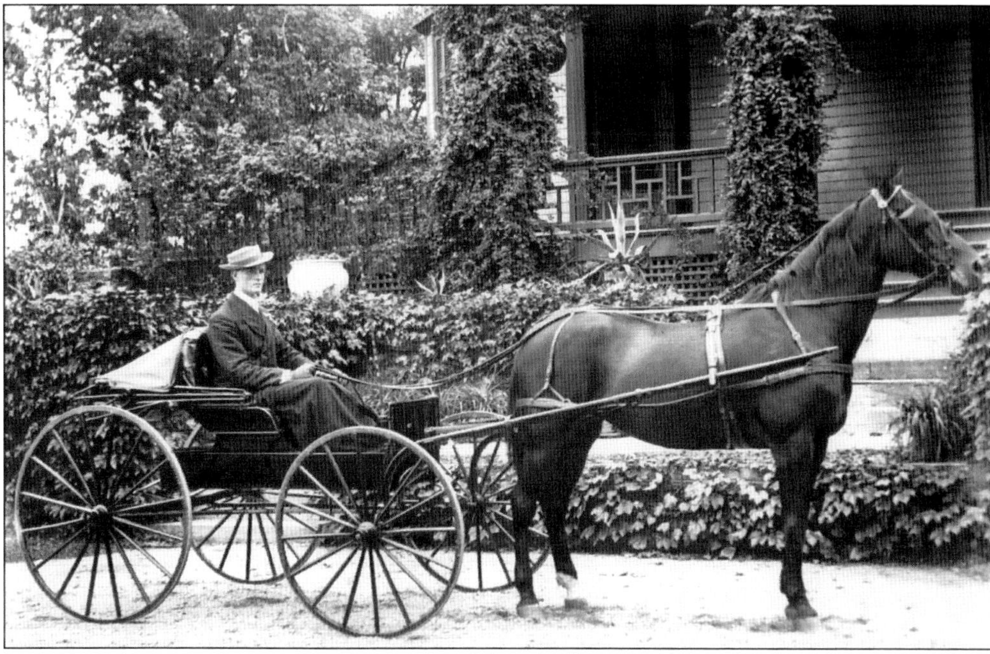

William F. Owens poses splendidly in his finest in this photograph, taken on April 8, 1906, at Brentwood, the Keyser estate on Cockeys Mill Road. William Keyser bought the old Norris estate (the "Mount") in 1886 for a summer residence and erected a new home where the old one had burned. He renamed the 160-acre property "Brentwood" in honor of his mother, Mary Brent Keyser. (Courtesy of the Reisterstown Room.)

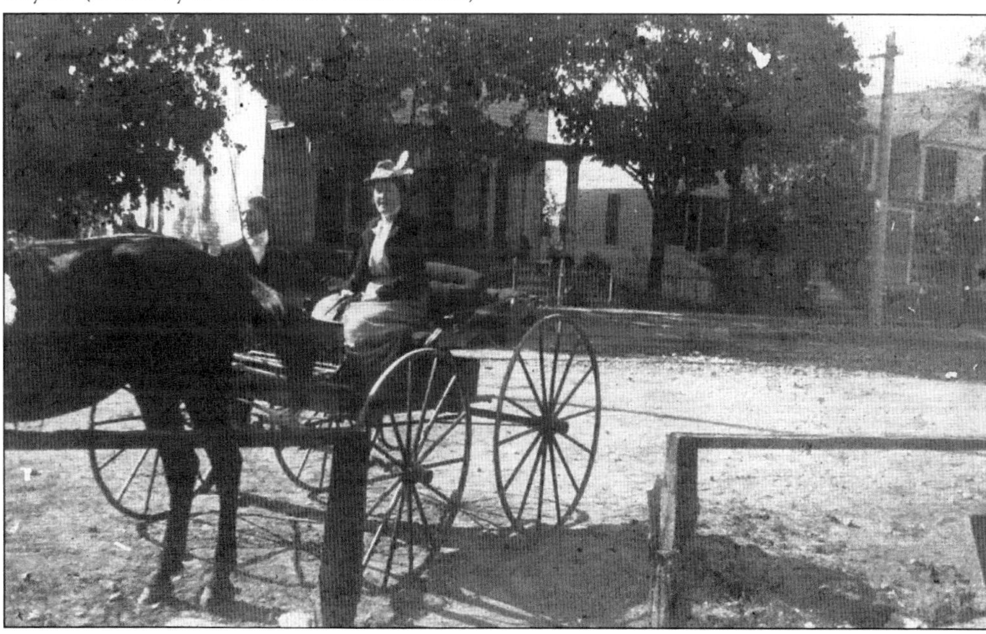

An unidentified man appears to stand beside a one-horse buggy with a woman sitting atop posing for the camera. The couple is dressed in their finery. The back of the photograph appears to say "Eline's Colemare." The picture was taken at the corner of Main Street and Reisterstown Road. (Courtesy of the Reisterstown Room.)

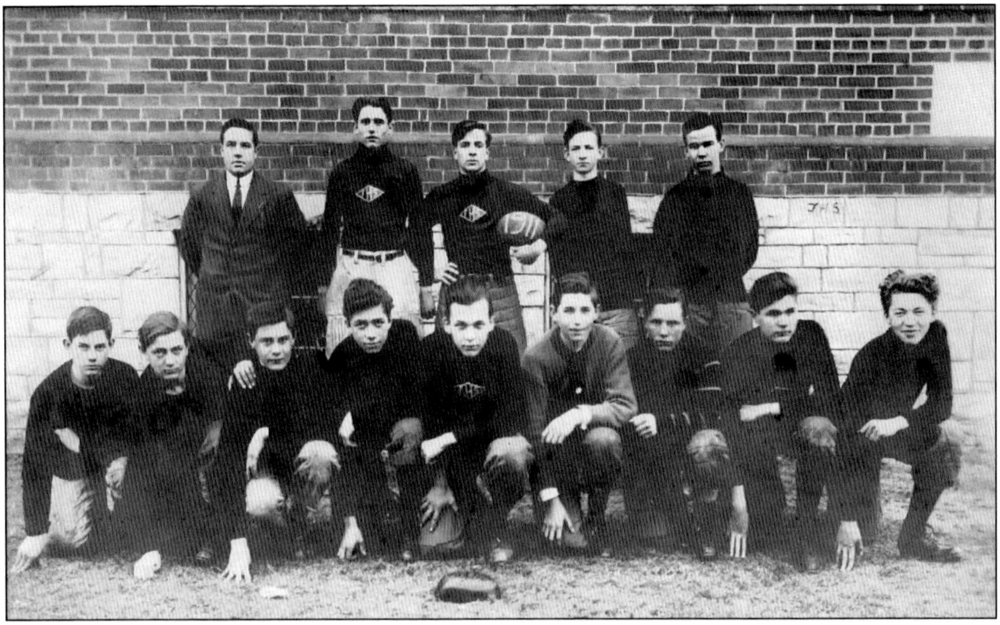

The Franklin High School football team poses in 1911 with coach ? Ward (standing, far left). The playears are, from left to right, (first row) Geist (right end), Sisk (right end), McKenny (right tackle), Gopes (right guard), Bowdre (guard), Frank (left guard), Richmond (left guard), Shaw (left tackle), and Bailey (left end); (second row) Marshal (SHB), Ruff (fullback), McLean (quarterback), and Waters (RHB). (Courtesy of the Reisterstown Room.)

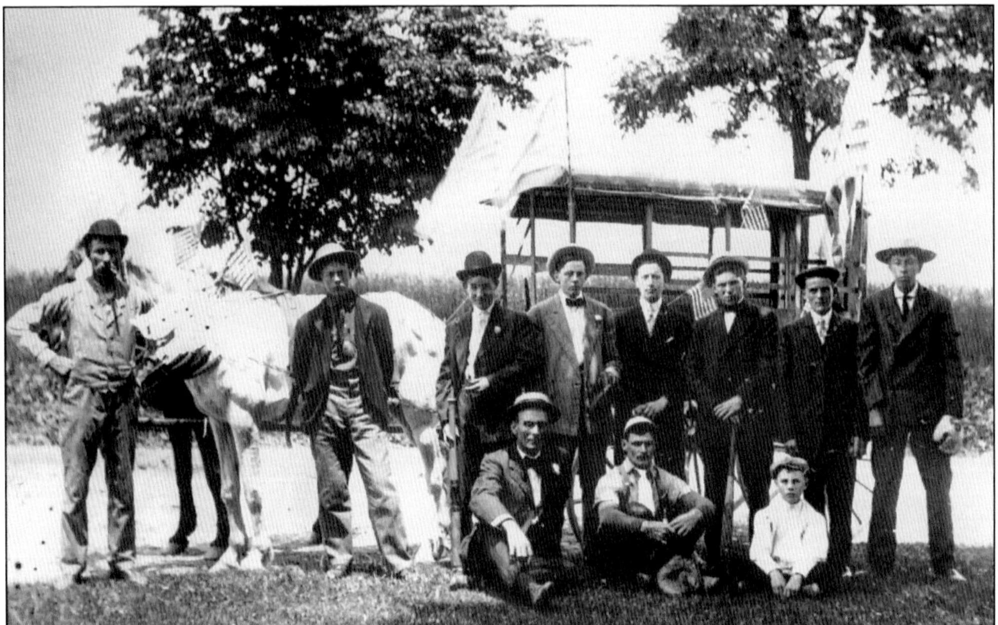

Unidentified members of the West Point baseball team of Cockeys Mill Road pose with their coach on July 4, 1907. The team members are shown out of uniform next to their two-horse covered bus. Renowned Reisterstown photographer Joshua Fitze captured the image. (Courtesy of the Reisterstown Room.)

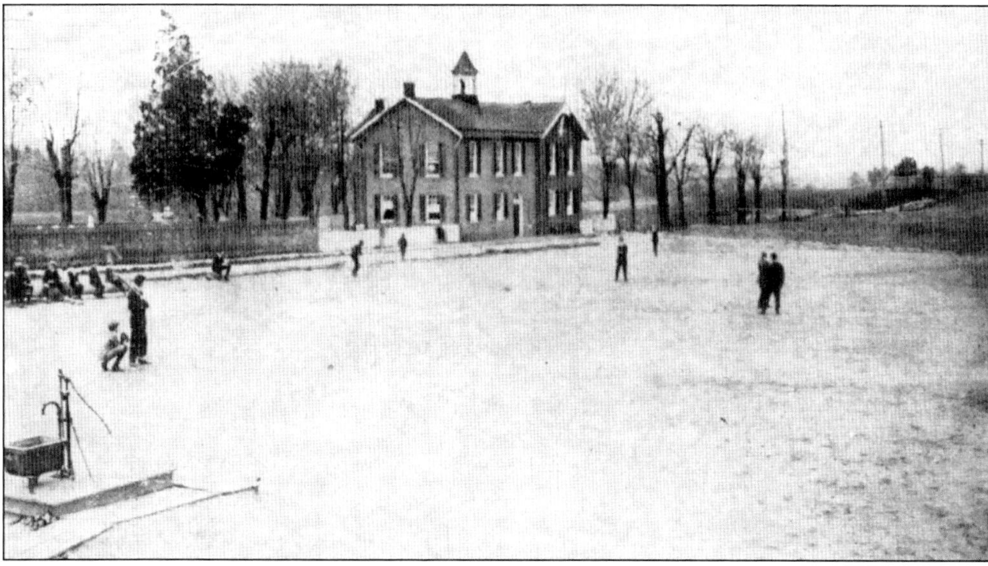

The athletic field of the new Franklin High School was located on the grounds of what is now Franklin Middle School. At the time Reister settled here in 1758, two families of Native Americans remained; one lived at Bank's Spring, not far from Franklin Middle School grounds (shown). The Old Franklin Academy is seen in the distance, and the Old Lutheran Cemetery is surrounded by a wall at center left. (Courtesy of the Reisterstown Room.)

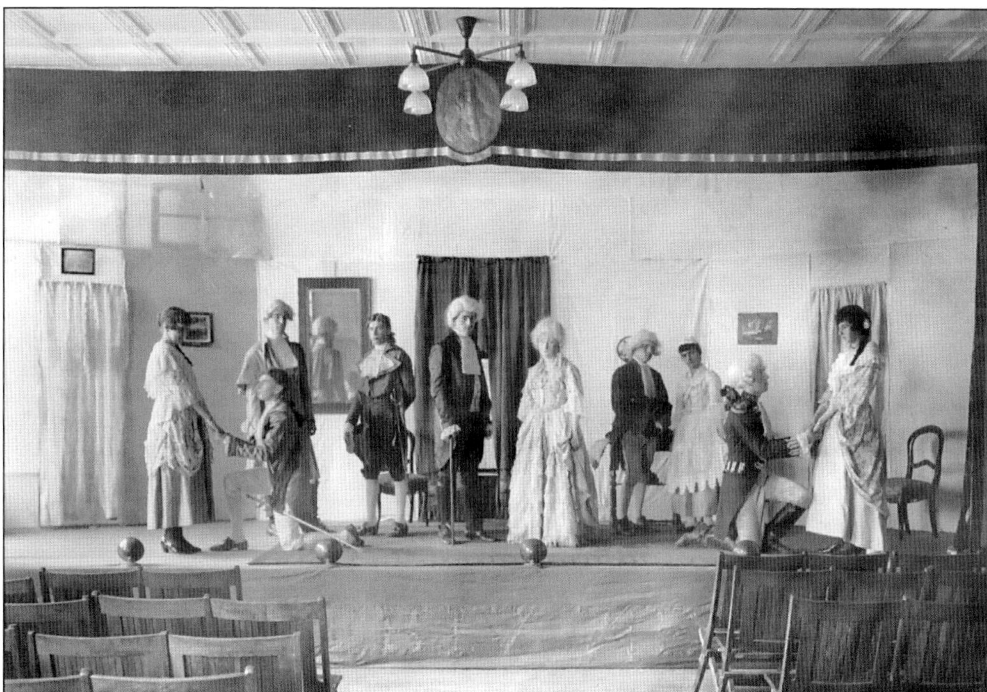

Among the students pictured here are Margaret Leight, Ethel Uhler, Pleasance Sollers, Helen Arnold, Raymond Hyson, Clarence Fischer, Carl Effers, and John Smith. Students appear to be practicing for a play at Franklin High School. They are dressed in period costumes possibly depicting the Revolutionary War. (Courtesy of the Reisterstown Room.)

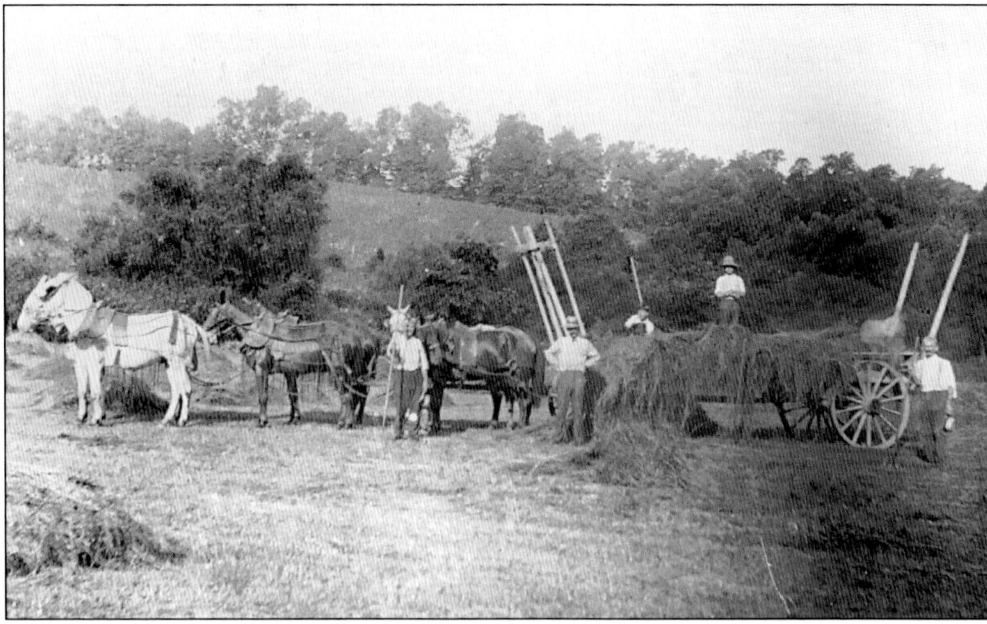

This image by Joshua Fitze, taken in July 1908, shows men and boys posing with a six-horse team. The team with the partially loaded hay wagon was photographed on Cockeys Mill Road at the James Dorsey farm. After allowing the hay to air-dry for several days, the horse-drawn wagon would be brought along each of the hay piles, where workers would manually fork the pile onto the wagon.

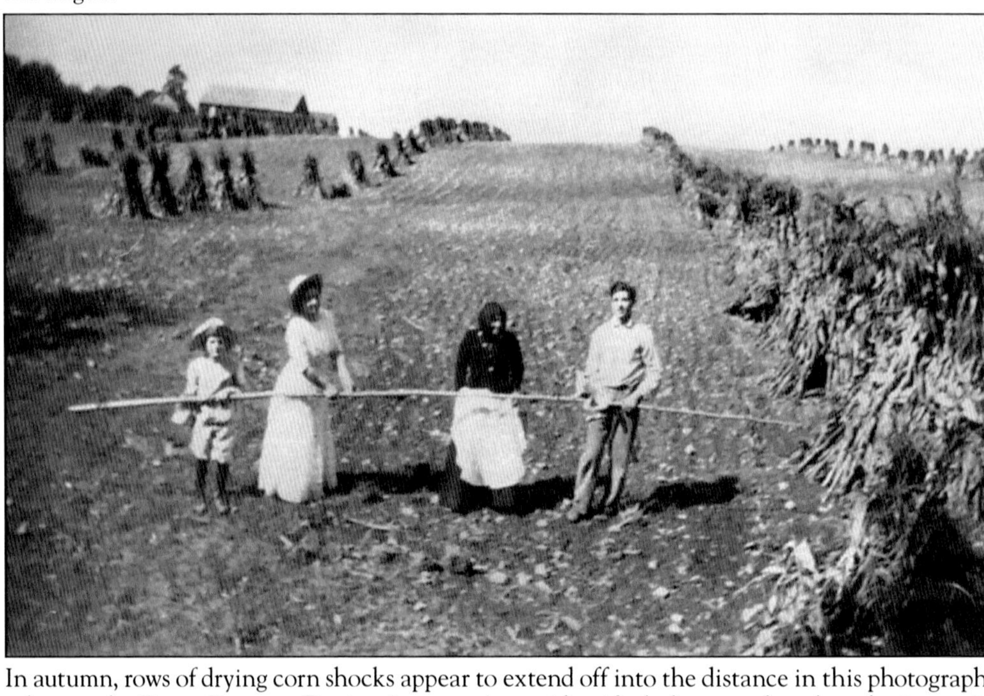

In autumn, rows of drying corn shocks appear to extend off into the distance in this photograph, taken at the Reese Farm on Bonita Avenue. An unidentified photographer shot the image in 1910. Holding onto the chestnut-threshing pole are, from left to right, Donald Reese, Margaret Reese, Mary Horm, and Clement Reese. (Courtesy of the Reisterstown Room.)

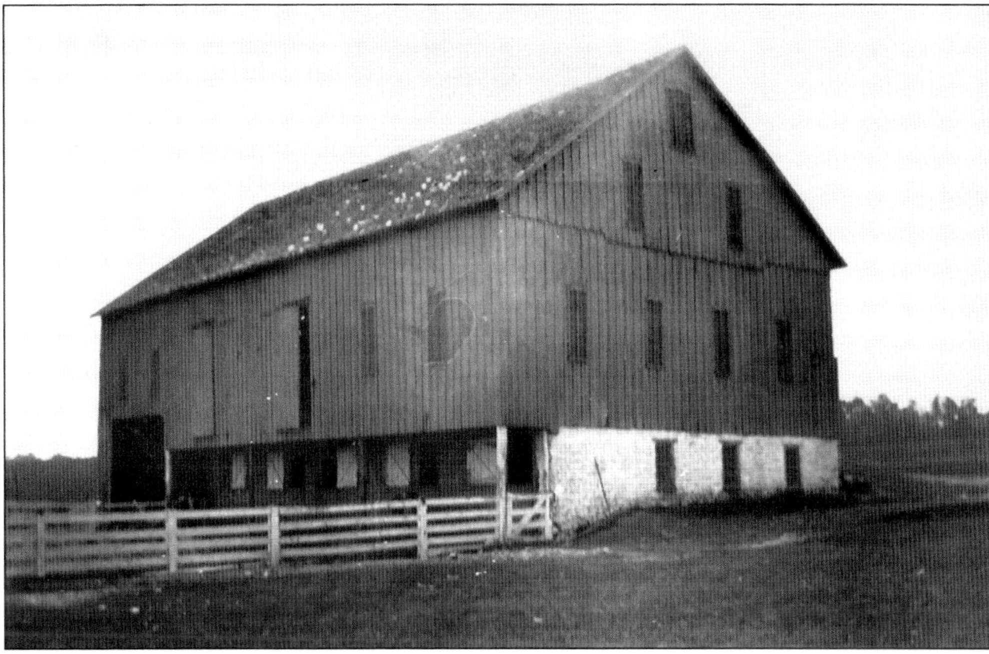

Shown is an old bank barn located at the Batsous Forest Farm. The barn's lower level housed animals, and the upper level was used for threshing hay and storage. Notice the second floor is cantilevered over the first to allow protection or shelter for the animals in bad weather. The hillside entrance to the second level made it easy to access the wagons loaded with hay. (Courtesy of the Reisterstown Room.)

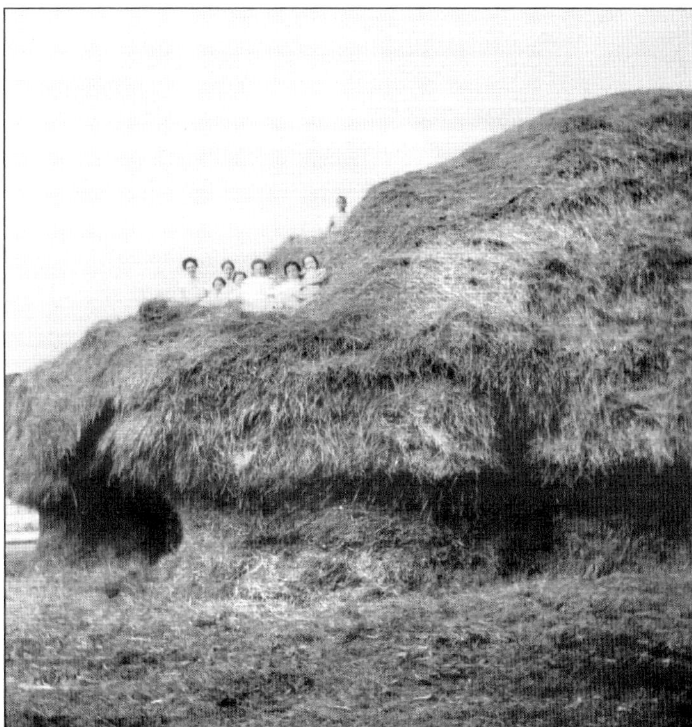

A bevy of unidentified women in cool summer whites enjoy relaxing on a mound of stacked hay at the Frantz-Reter Farm, which was located on Park Heights and Walnut Avenues. The farm was known as the "Batsous Forest Farm." An unidentified photographer captured the moment. (Courtesy of Reisterstown Room.)

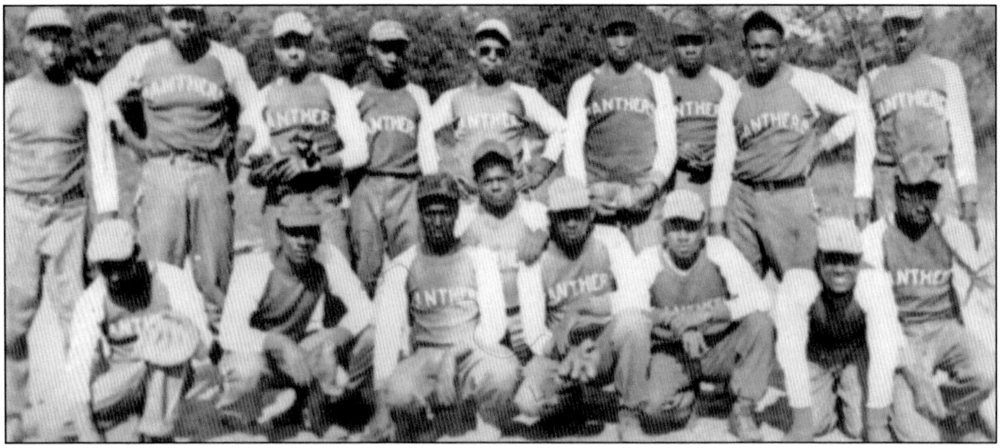

The 1949 Panthers from the Reisterstown African American community and other black enclaves pose for the camera. From left to right are (first row) Wyatt Madden, Benson Jackson, Jimmy Payne, Albert Figgs, George Mack, Clayborn Ghee, Benjamin Madden, and Elmer Dorsey; (second row) Eli Johnson, S. Leo Jones (manager), Rufus Dorsey, Harvey Wright, Albert Madden, Bernard Jordan, Robert Berry, Andrew Dett Jr., and Otho Dutton. (Courtesy of Annie Milligan.)

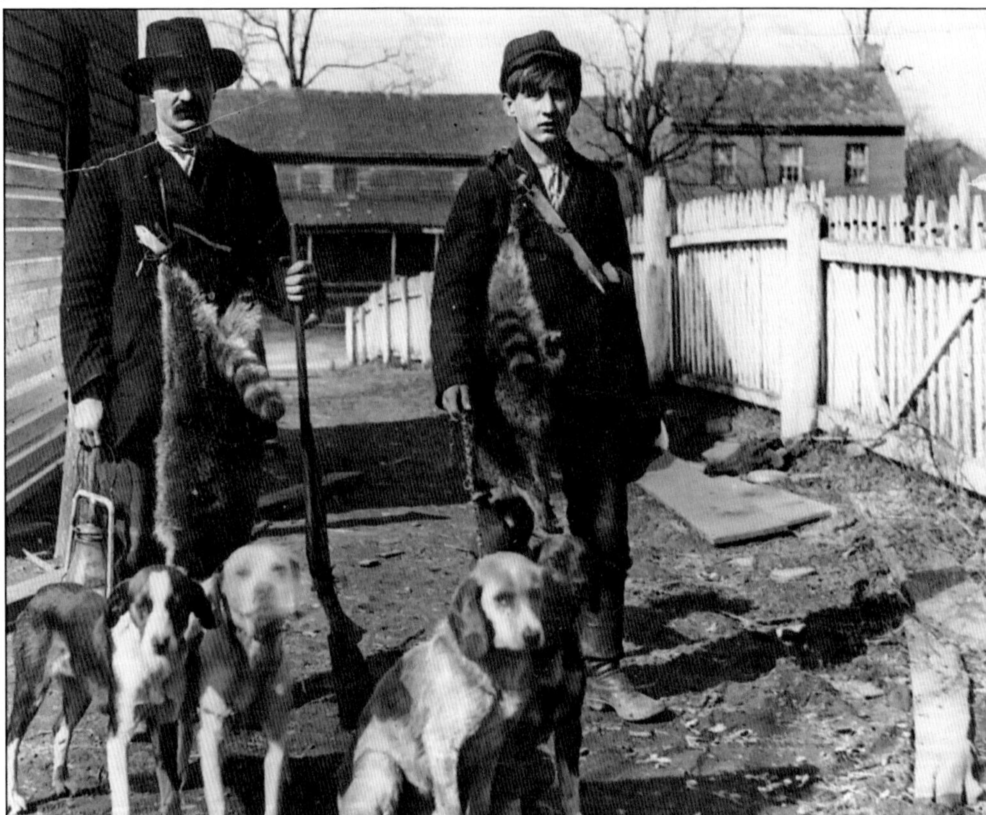

Brady Mann and an unidentified friend had been coon hunting with their dogs. Note that each one has a raccoon slung over their shoulder and a lantern in tow. The photograph was taken on March 21, 1907. (Courtesy of the Reisterstown Room.)

Eight

Gracious Living

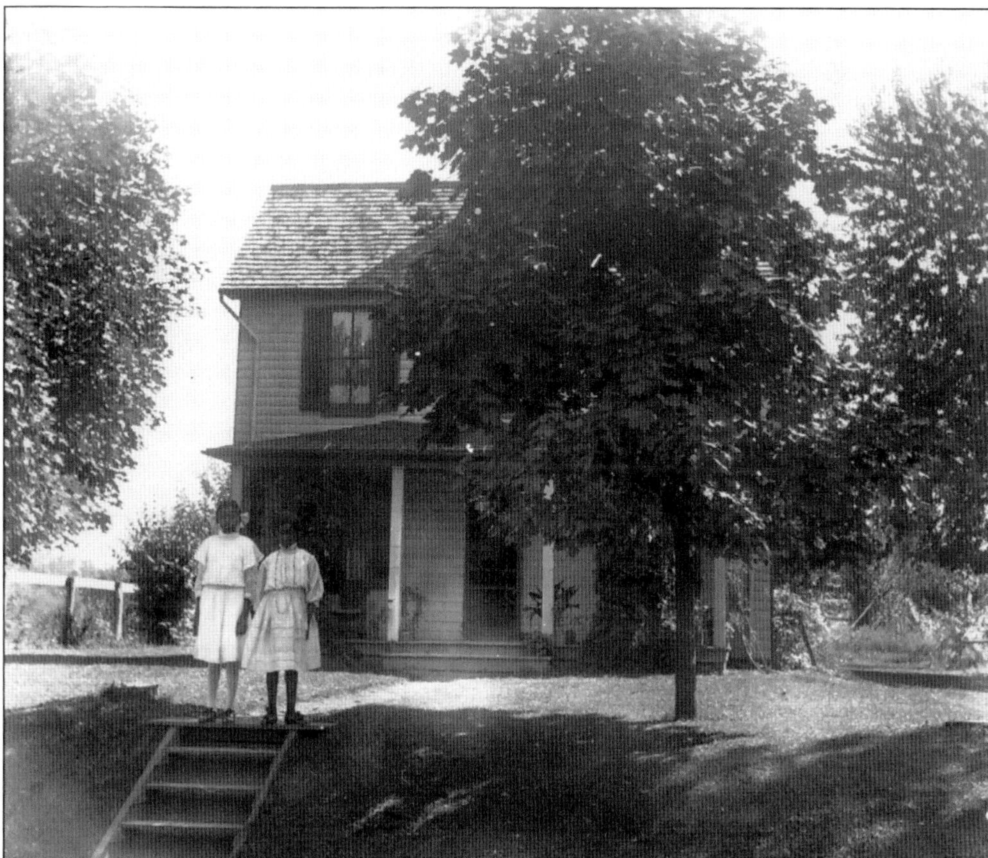

Two unidentified young girls strike a pretty pose all dressed up in their Sunday best and standing in front of the home of John Franklin. The picturesque farmhouse was located on the Cockeys Mill Road (formerly Academy Lane) in Reisterstown. Joshua Fitze snapped the c. 1904 photograph.

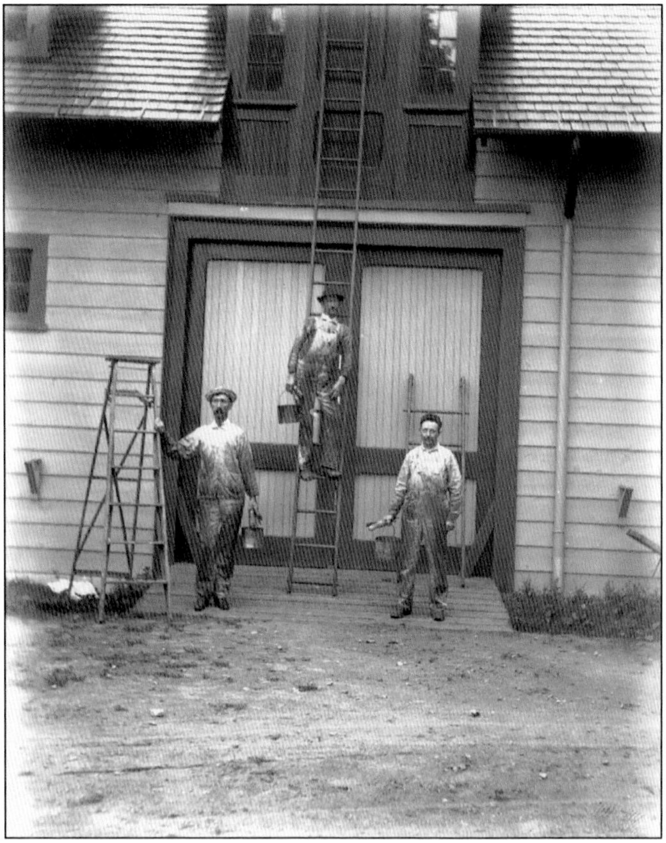

Three unidentified painters in overalls are perfectly posed with their ladders, brushes, and buckets. Photographer Joshua Fitze snapped the image on June 22, 1904. The painters were working at the stables at Brentwood, the Keyser estate, located on Cockeys Mill Road.

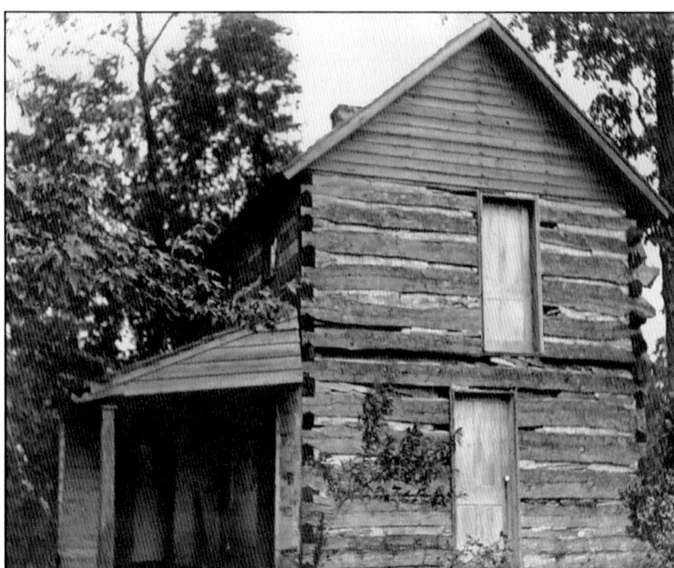

Joshua Fitze photographed this two-story log house on May 25, 1902, and labeled his glass negative "Old Cook Homestead." The house appears in the 1877 Atlas of Baltimore County. It was probably located south of Nicodemus Road near Cooks Branch. The Cook family has deep roots in Reisterstown. Prof. A. S. Cook was superintendent of the Baltimore County schools in 1911. (Courtesy of the Reisterstown Room.)

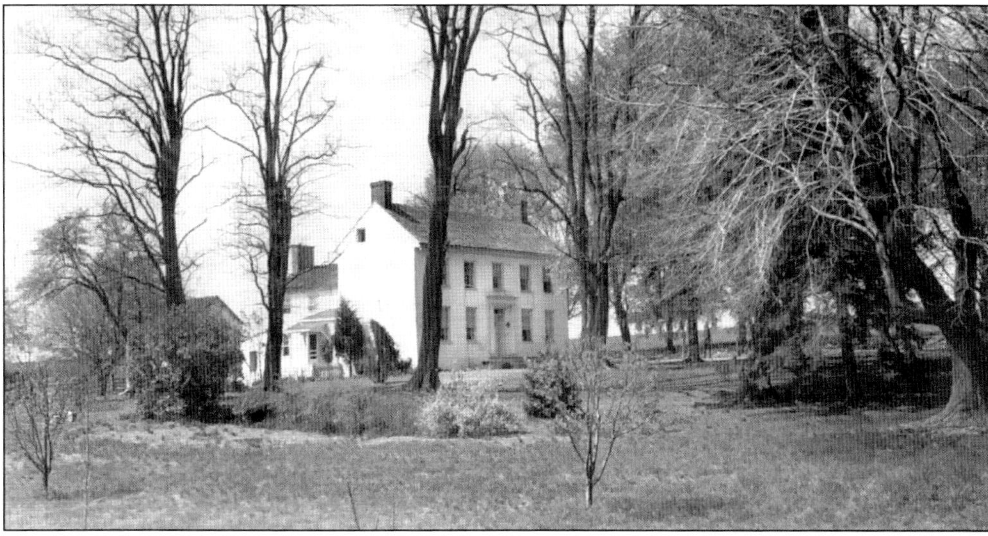

The estate known as Chatsworth, shown here in 1941, was built around 1830 by Daniel Bower Banks (1786–1875) on the original land grant known as Spring Garden. Banks was the grandson of one of the original Reisterstown innkeepers, Daniel Bower. He built his home on almost 600 acres of mostly unimproved land west of the turnpike. During the Civil War, many Confederate soldiers sought shelter at Chatsworth. (Courtesy of the Reisterstown Room.)

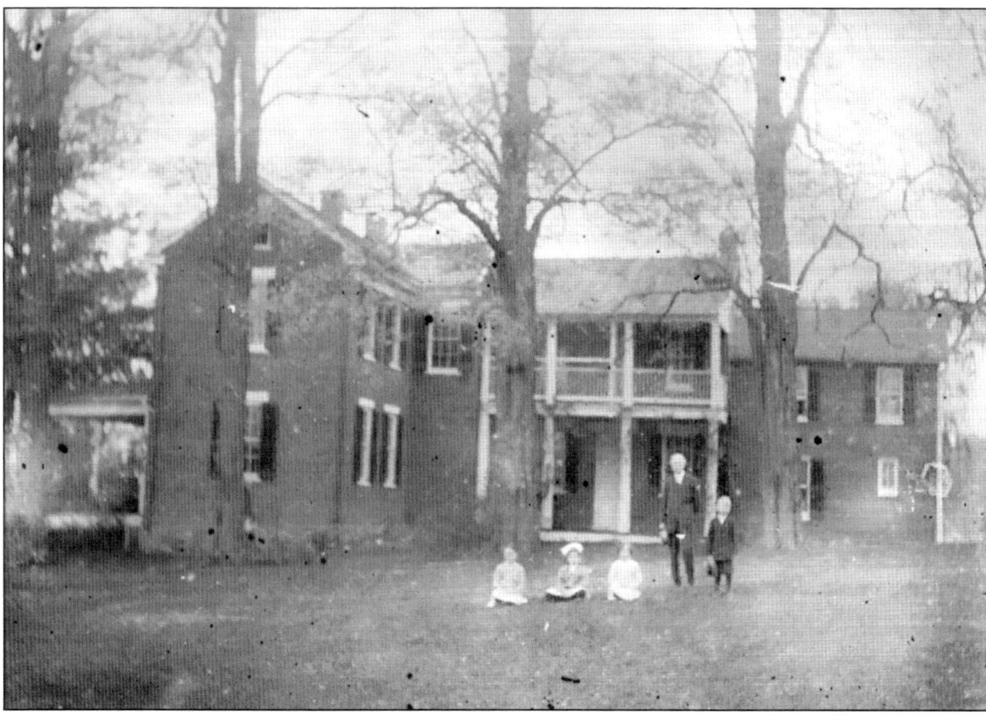

Walnut Grove was a 300-acre estate owned by Thomas Moale of Greenspring Valley. George Peter Kephart, Hannah Reister's husband, was the second owner of the estate. Kephart sold Marshall Harden the property, and he sold it to a Major Shirley, who changed the name to Chartley Park, after his ancestral home in Staffordshire, England. Today Walnut Grove has been transformed into the Chartley development. (Courtesy of the Reisterstown Room.)

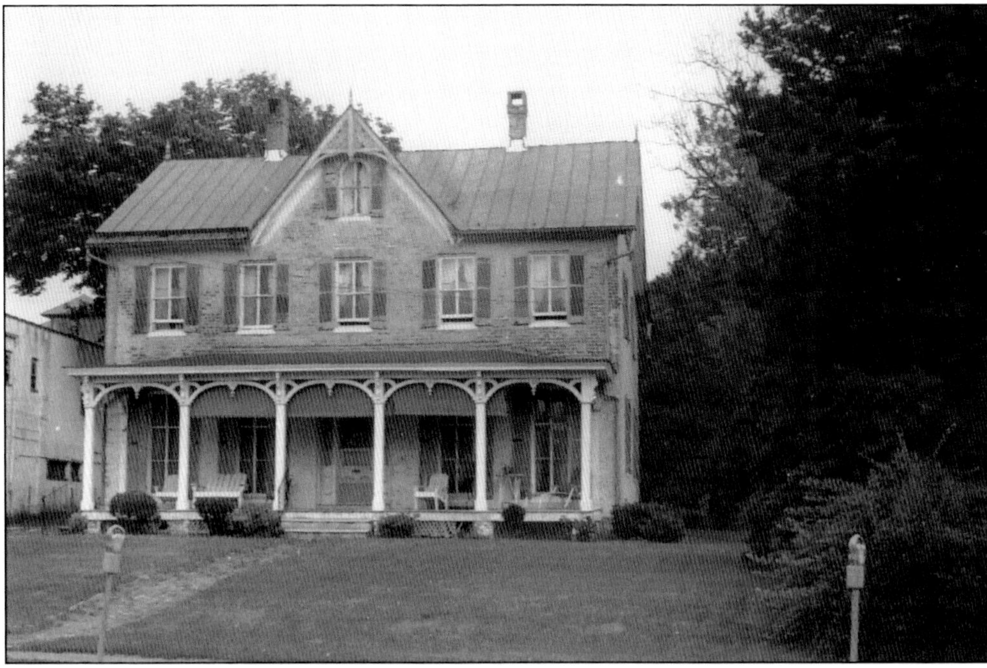

The former home of Reister Russell (1842–1922), located at 19 Hanover Road, is shown in this photograph. Russell, co-owner of Russell Brothers' Store, built the picturesque house on land he leased from John Hitshue for $30 a year starting in 1857. After constructing his home, he finally purchased the property in 1878 for the sum of $500. (Courtesy of the Reisterstown Room.)

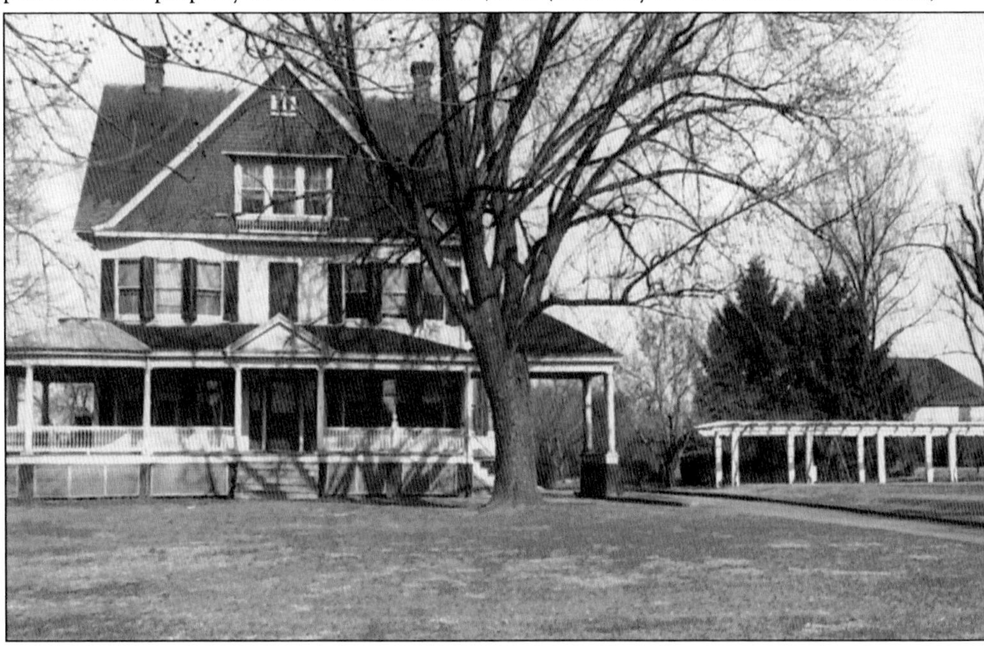

This graceful Victorian frame dwelling at 337 Main Street belonged to Frank H. Zouck. Bob Caron built the house for Zouck in 1901. It featured seven bedrooms, a reception hall, a library, a butler pantry, several fireplaces, and a five-room servants' quarters. Zouck was a former president of the Reisterstown Savings Bank. (Courtesy of the Reisterstown Room.)

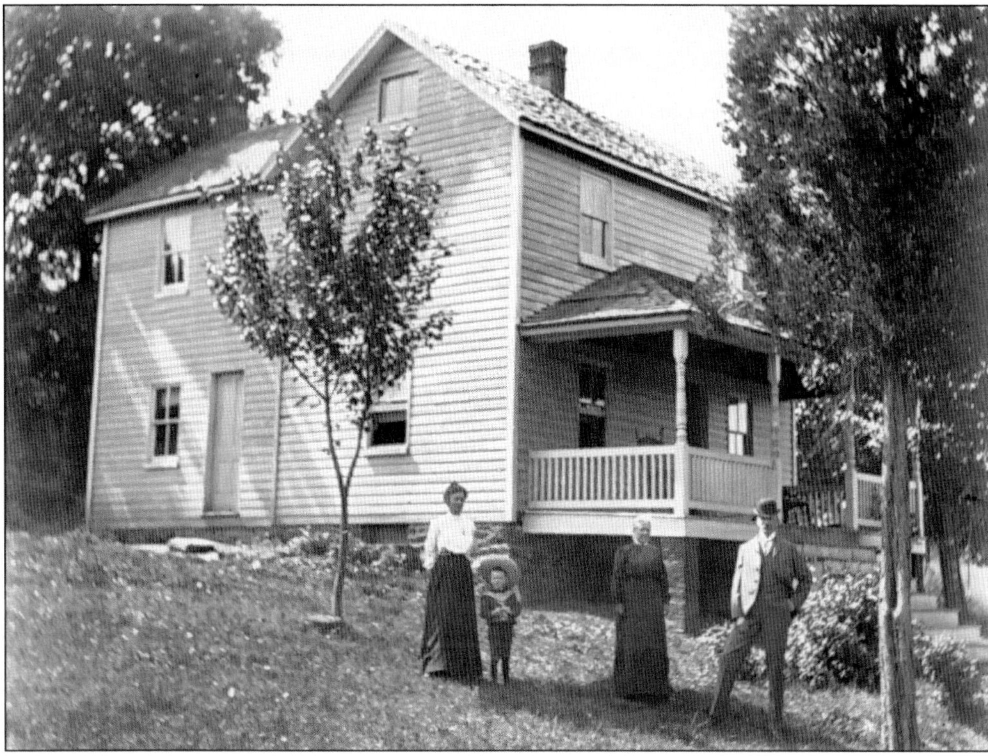

H. H. Gore's two-story frame home with a covered front porch and addition looks the picture of rural tranquility. Mr. and Mrs. Gore are seen posing with their young son, who is dressed up in a sailor suit and wide-brimmed hat. Sarah A. Gore, née Stocksdail, married to William Gore, is also present. Joshua Fitze photographed this Reisterstown scene on July 10, 1904.

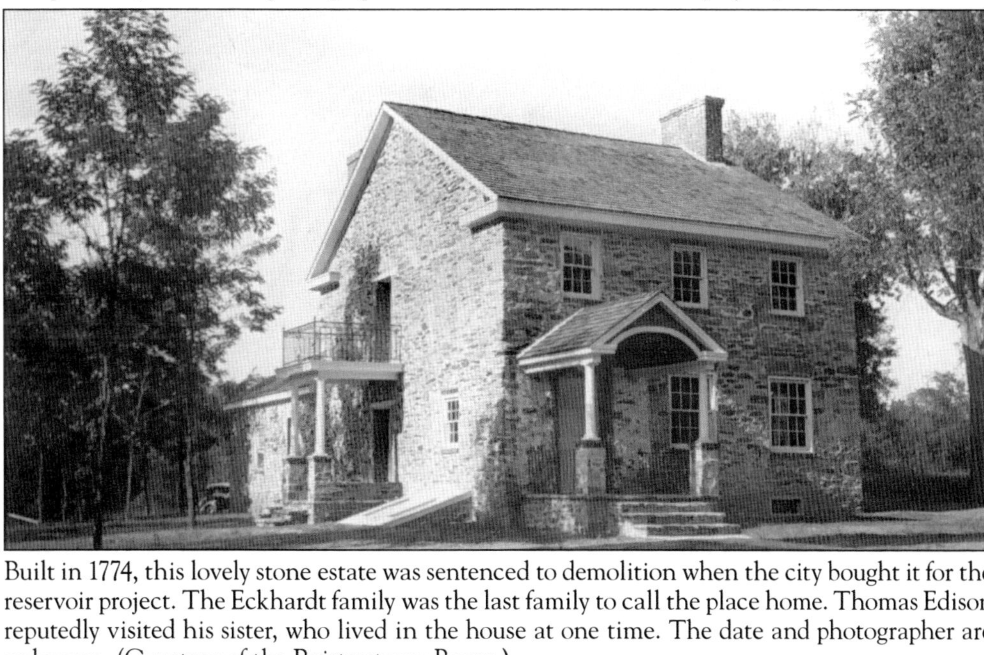

Built in 1774, this lovely stone estate was sentenced to demolition when the city bought it for the reservoir project. The Eckhardt family was the last family to call the place home. Thomas Edison reputedly visited his sister, who lived in the house at one time. The date and photographer are unknown. (Courtesy of the Reisterstown Room.)

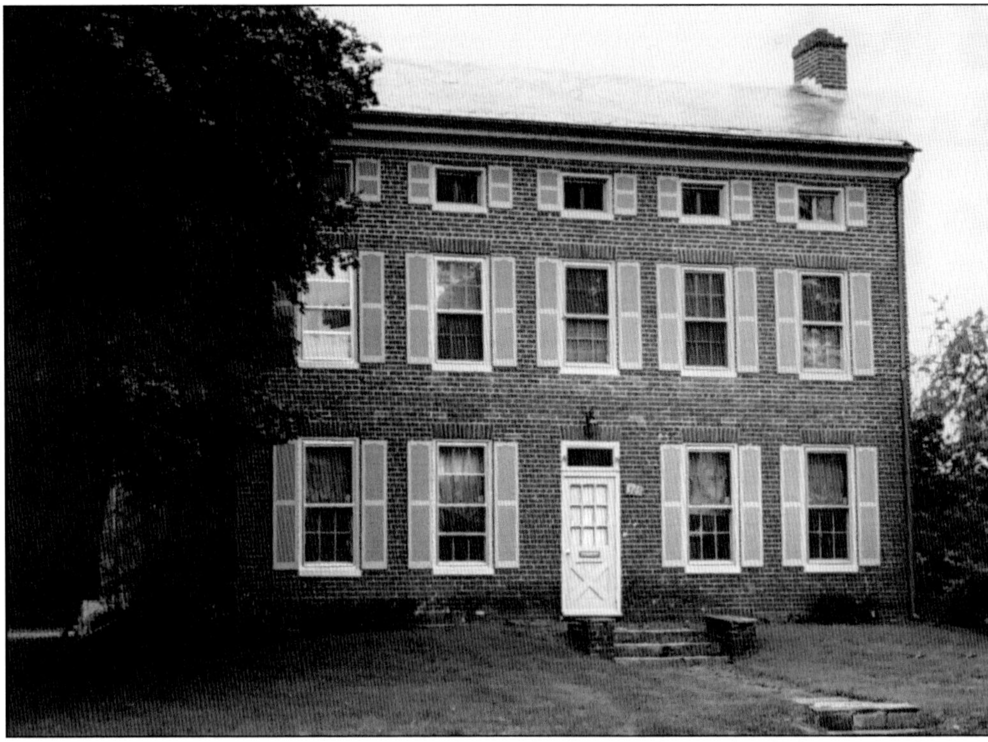

The house at 365 East Main Street was built, or rebuilt, around 1861 by Philip Reister Owings. In 1869, Dr. Isaac Newton Dickson wrote in his manuscript *The Early Days of Reisterstown and Vicinity* that John Reister Sr. "retired to that part of the land whereon Mr. Philip Reister Owings now resides." (Courtesy of the Reisterstown Room.)

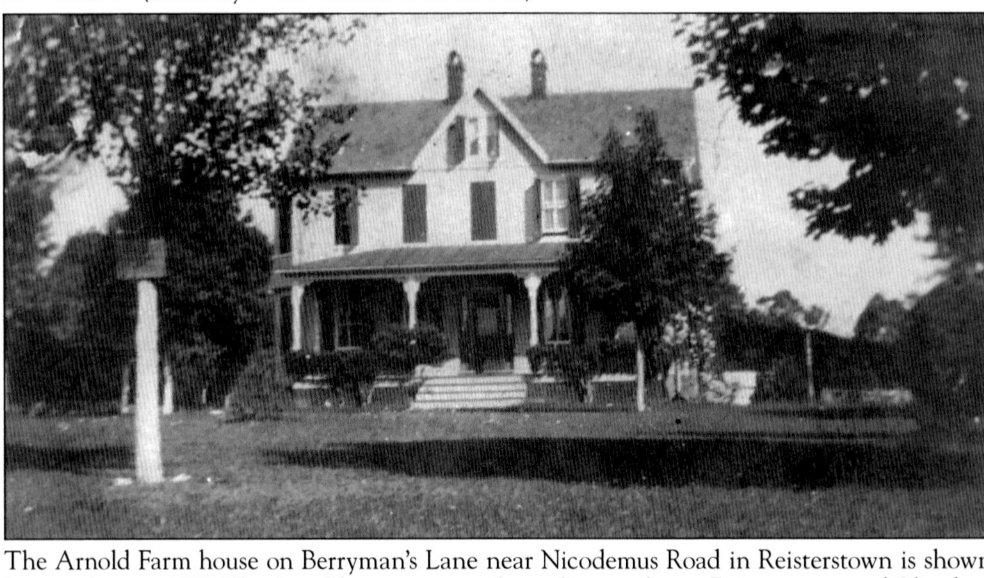

The Arnold Farm house on Berryman's Lane near Nicodemus Road in Reisterstown is shown here in the year 1919. The Arnolds were among the earliest settlers to Reisterstown and Glyndon. Around 1873, David Arnold erected the second house built in Glyndon. His 16-year-old son left home to join Gen. Stonewall Jackson's regiment as a scout during the Civil War. (Courtesy of the Reisterstown Room.)

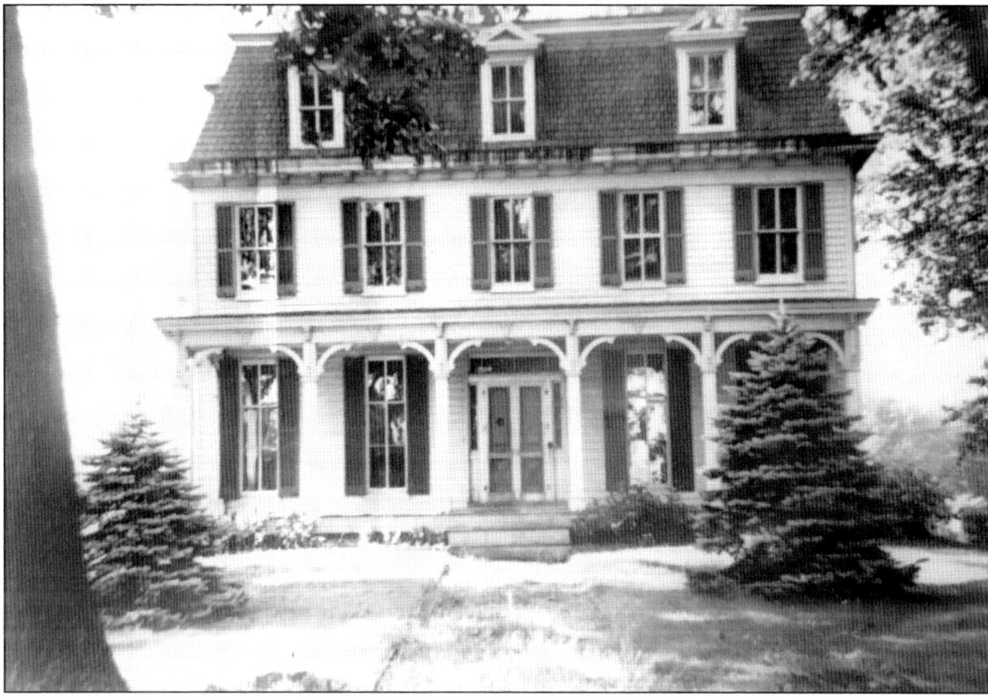

Richleigh was the frame and clapboard home of Rev. Dr. Arthur Rich, headmaster of the Hannah More Academy and rector of St. Michael's Chapel. The mansard-roofed home was built in 1873. It served subsequently as an administrative center of the Hannah More School. Louise Bland Goodwin photographed the home, located at 12025 Reisterstown Road, in 1941.

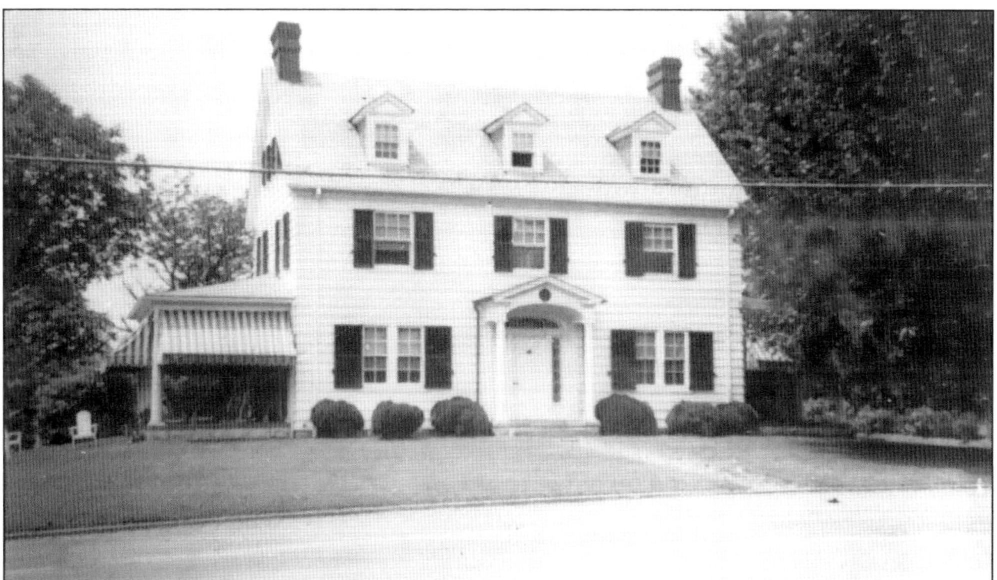

This well-maintained home was the residence of Reisterstown builder G. Walter Tovell. Tovell constructed the now demolished Reisterstown Elementary School. He also erected Fullerton and Halethorpe Fire Stations in 1920, and the Essex, Dundalk, and Pikesville Fire Stations in 1921. Louise Bland Goodwin took this photograph in 1941.

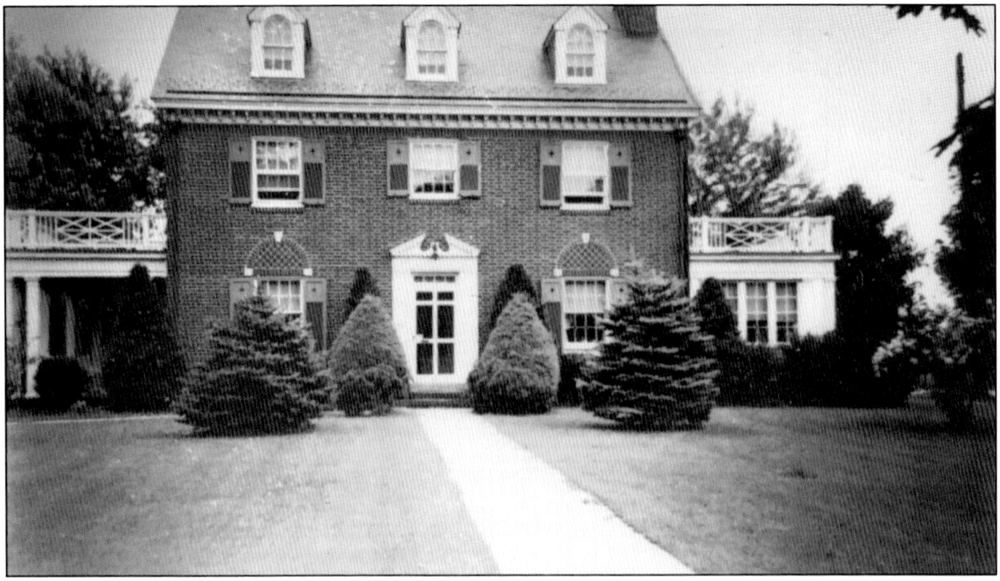

Mr. and Mrs. Charles Eyler once lived in this gracious brick residence, located at 415 Main Street. Mrs. Eyler was a former vice principal of Franklin High School. Today the property is listed in the inventory of the Maryland Historical Trust. In 1941, Louise Bland Goodwin photographed the home. (Courtesy of the Reisterstown Room.)

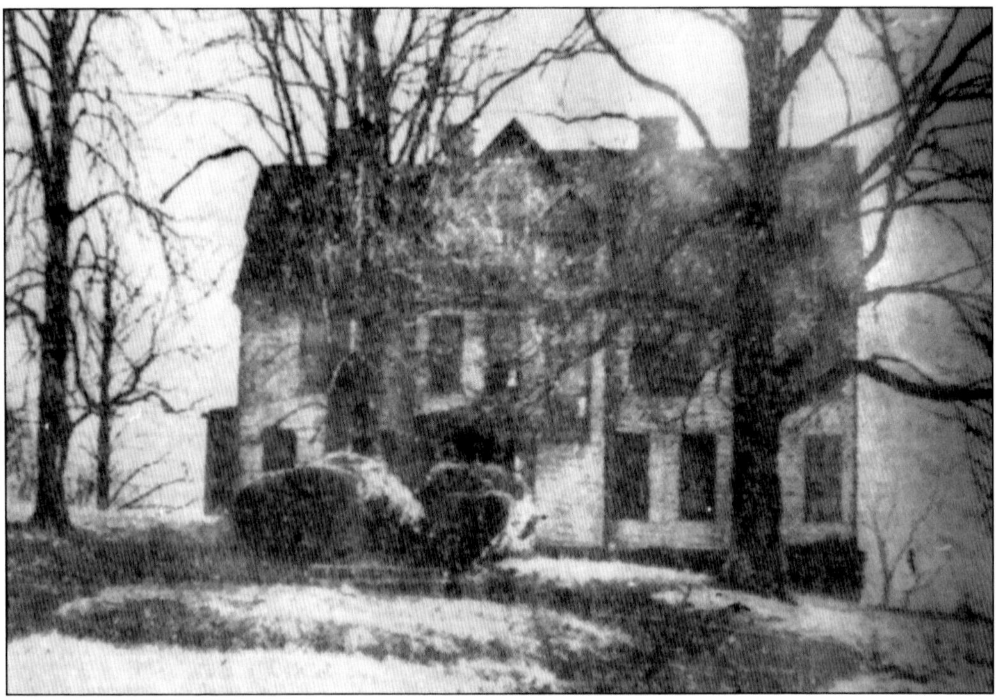

Brookland on Cockeys Mill Road was the home of Col. William Norris, chief of the signal corps, Confederate States Army. Norris and a navy friend, Lt. Reed Werden, married sisters they had met at a naval ball in Valparaiso, Chile. Werden became an admiral in the Union navy. Norris never forgave his old friend. The home was photographed in 1941 by Louise Bland Goodwin. It burned in 1946.

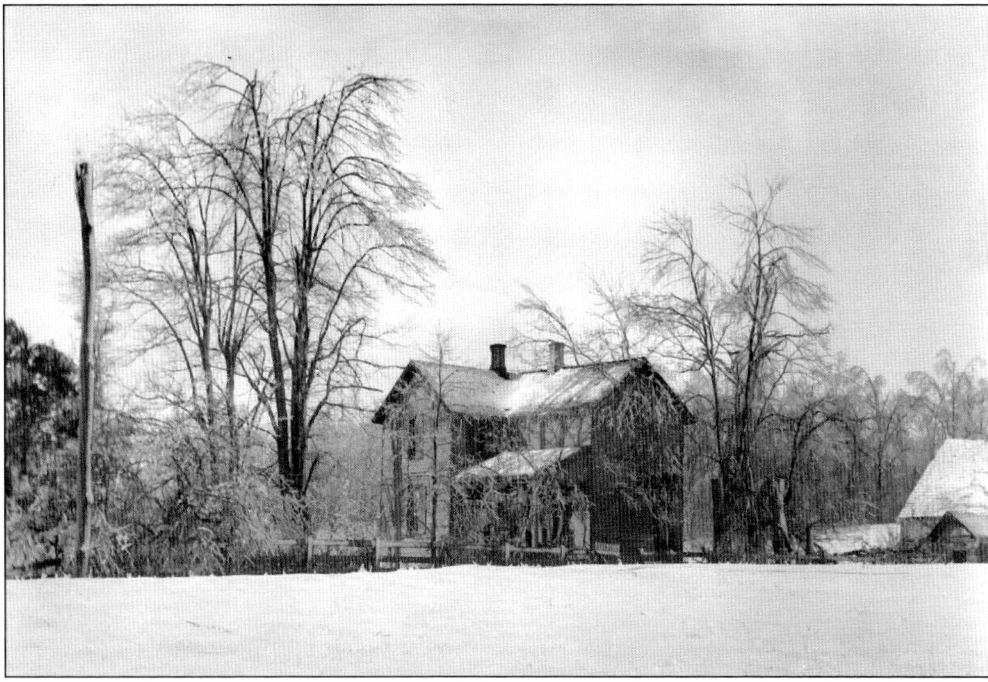

This winter farmstead has been identified as likely the historic Fitze home, shown covered with a dusting of snow in this *c.* 1902 image. Joshua Fitze was a renowned photographer whose family lived in the Reisterstown area. Without his efforts, much of the history of Reisterstown and surrounding Baltimore County would have gone unrecorded. (Courtesy of the Reisterstown Room.)

The estate known as the Elms, once having a distinguished history, is shown here having degraded into a squatters' dwelling. From 1835 until 1850, the estate was the home of Francis Scott Key Jr., the son of Francis Scott Key, the author of the U.S. national anthem and frequent visitor to the Elms. John Beall originally built the mansion around 1775–1780, calling it "Beall's Venture." The property near Reisterstown was razed in 1954 to make way for the Liberty Reservoir.

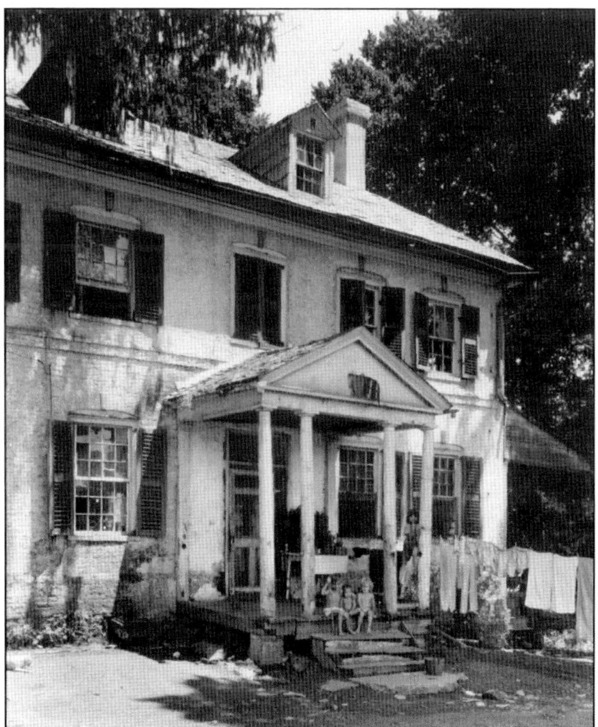

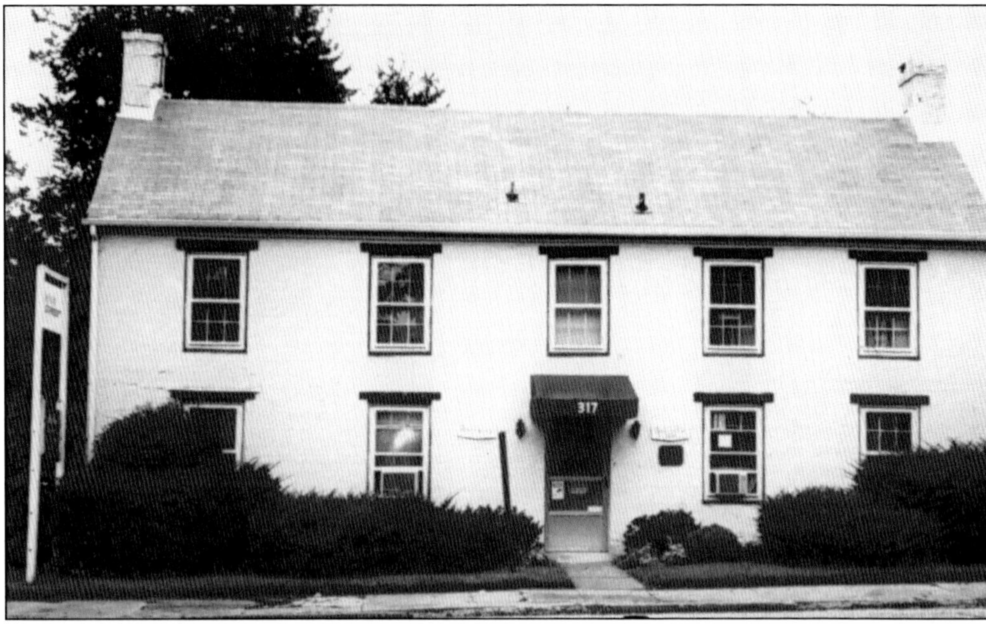

The historic house at 317 Main Street has a log cabin at its core. Sitting on property that John Reister deeded his son John II in 1793, the home has changed hands many times since then. Hannah Reister took possession in 1845 and enlarged the house and added a brick veneer. It is sometimes known as the Pouder-Susemihl house in recognition of two unrelated but more recent owners. (Courtesy of the Reisterstown Room.)

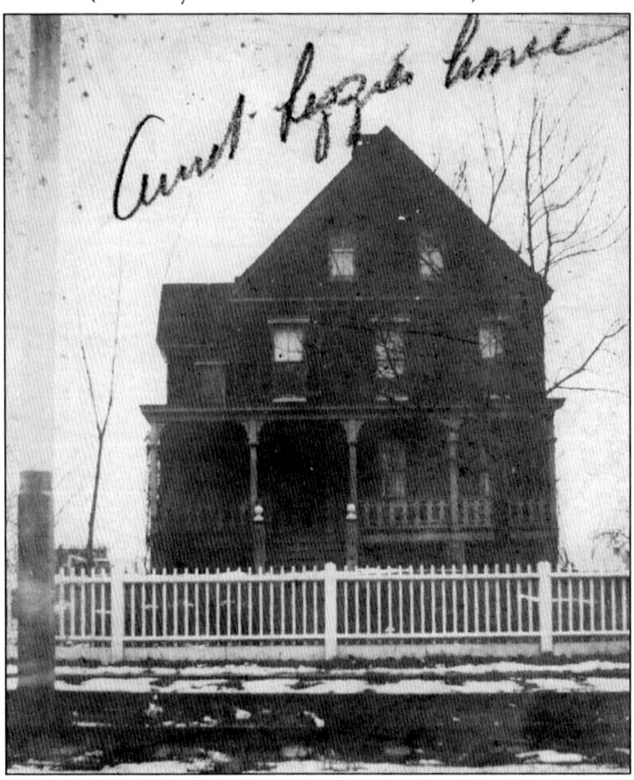

The Lizzie Russell house with a decorative fence is shown in the photograph at left before it burned down. Her brother Reister Russell lived next door at 19 Hanover Road. After the home burned, a Dr. Landau's house was built in its place. The photographer and date are unknown. (Courtesy of the Reisterstown Room.)

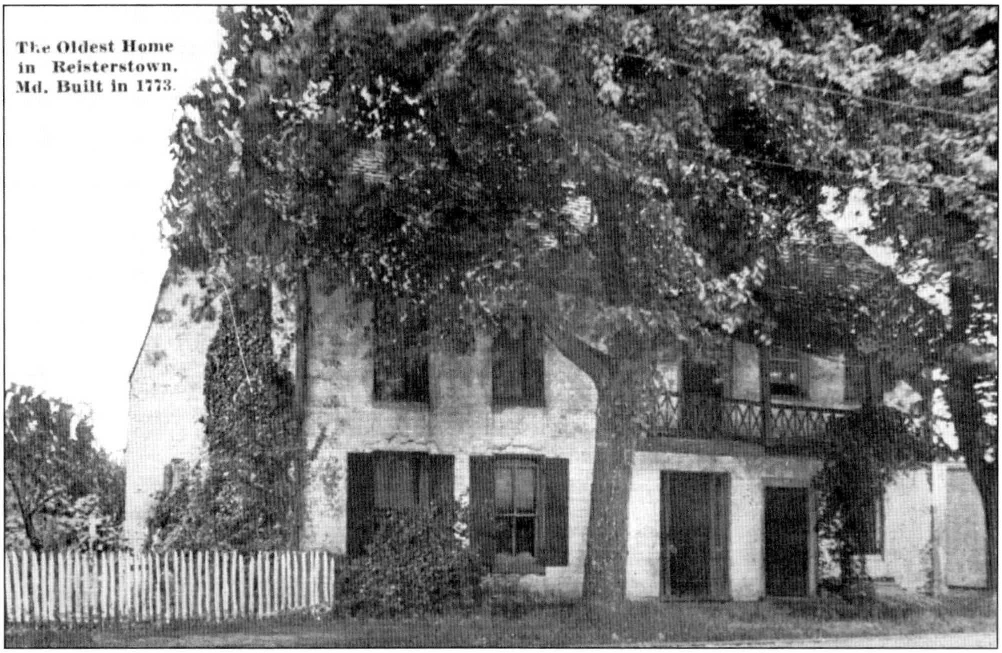

This postcard shows one of the oldest houses in Reisterstown, located at 410 Main Street. It is a brick house covered over by stucco that was built in 1773 by Jacob Bren. A large brickyard and tannery were located behind it. At one time, the Henry Weist family lived there. Weist was a son-in-law of John Reister Sr. Later known as the Berryman house, it was sold in the 1940s. (Courtesy of the Reisterstown Room.)

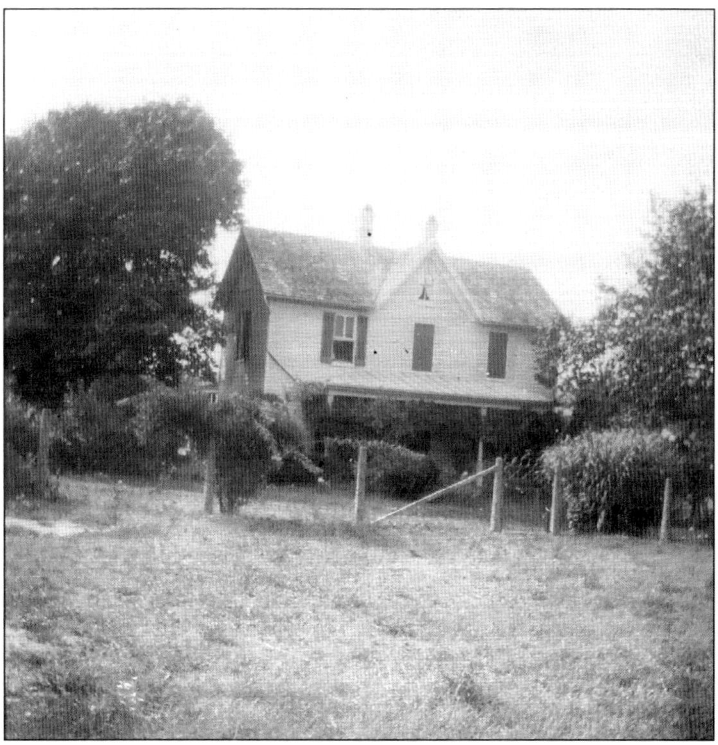

Featured is a classic old American farmhouse with a covered front porch and center fireplace, strategically located to keep the chimney warm. This inviting country home was part of the Frantz-Reter Farm, located on Park Heights and Walnut Avenues. The farm was also known as the Batsous Forest Farm. (Courtesy of Reisterstown Room.)

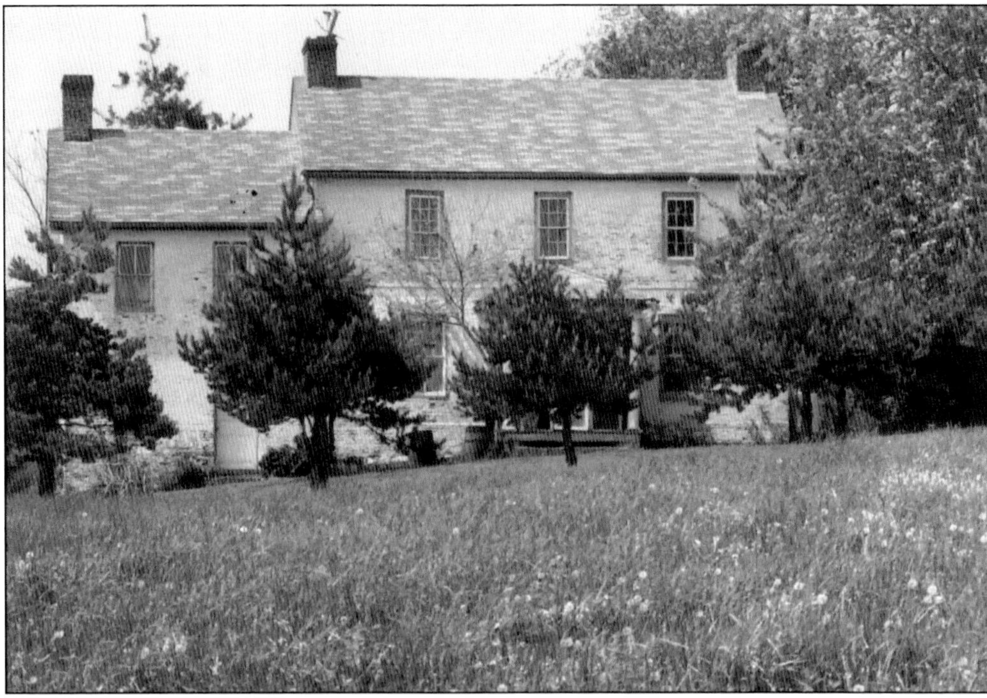

The photograph of the Andrew Banks house shows how the property looked on West Chatsworth Avenue near the fire department. (Courtesy of the Reisterstown Room.)

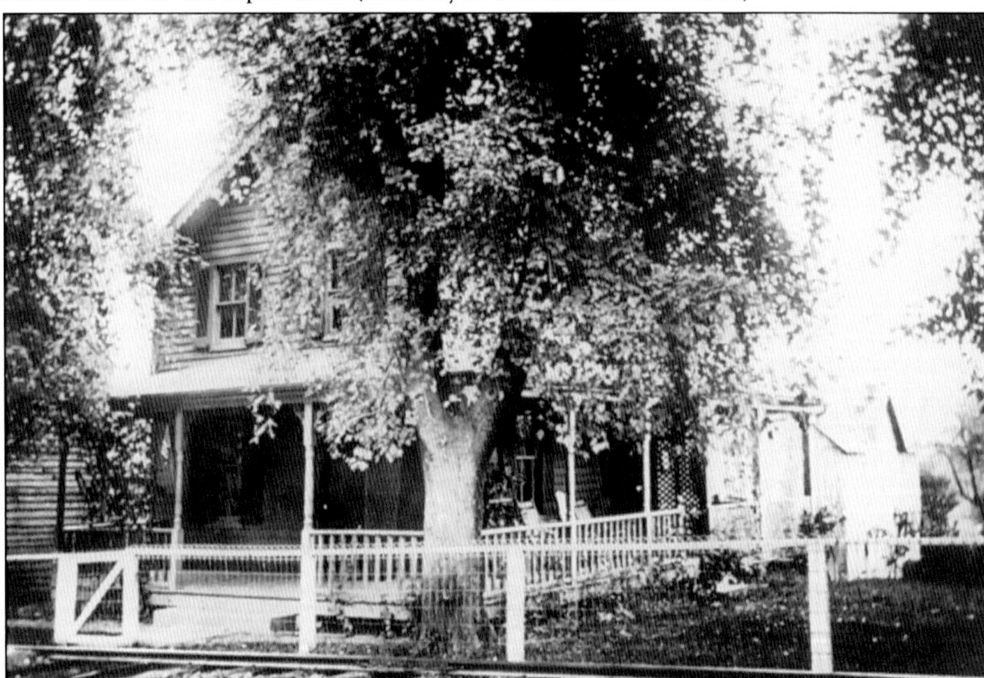

The home of Dr. Alfred M. Bailey and his wife, Ardella, was located in the area known as St. George near Bond Avenue in Reisterstown. The 1930s image is from the Louis S. Diggs Photographic Collection. (Courtesy of the Reisterstown Room.)

Nine

Thanks Be to God

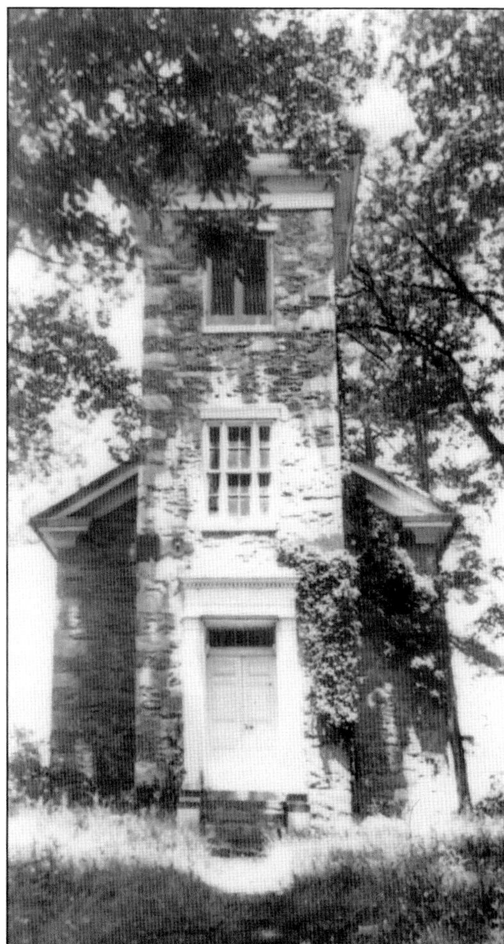

Louise Bland Goodwin snapped this photograph of the impressive entrance to the chapel at Montrose Mansion in 1941. The photograph captures the full frontal view of the one-story fieldstone chapel, which was completed in 1855. The Greek Revival structure features a three-story entrance and a bell tower at its south end. (Courtesy of the Reisterstown Room.)

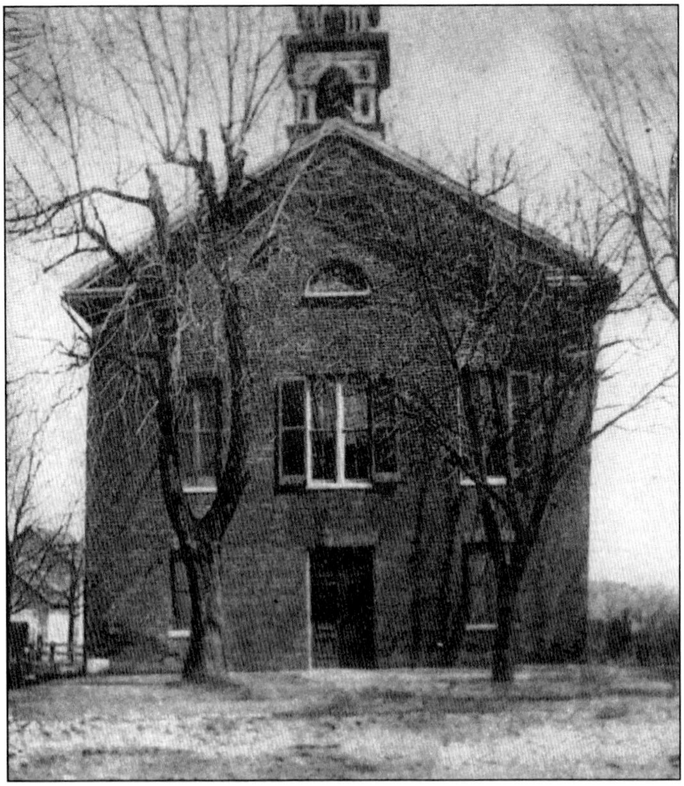

Trinity Lutheran Church was built and dedicated on January 13, 1867. The church began when John Reister deeded one-quarter acre of land in 1764 for a cemetery, school, and small log church to be used by all denominations. After the log church was torn down in 1854, members held services in private homes until 1855, when Trinity was accepted as a congregation in the Maryland Synod. (Courtesy of the Reisterstown Room.)

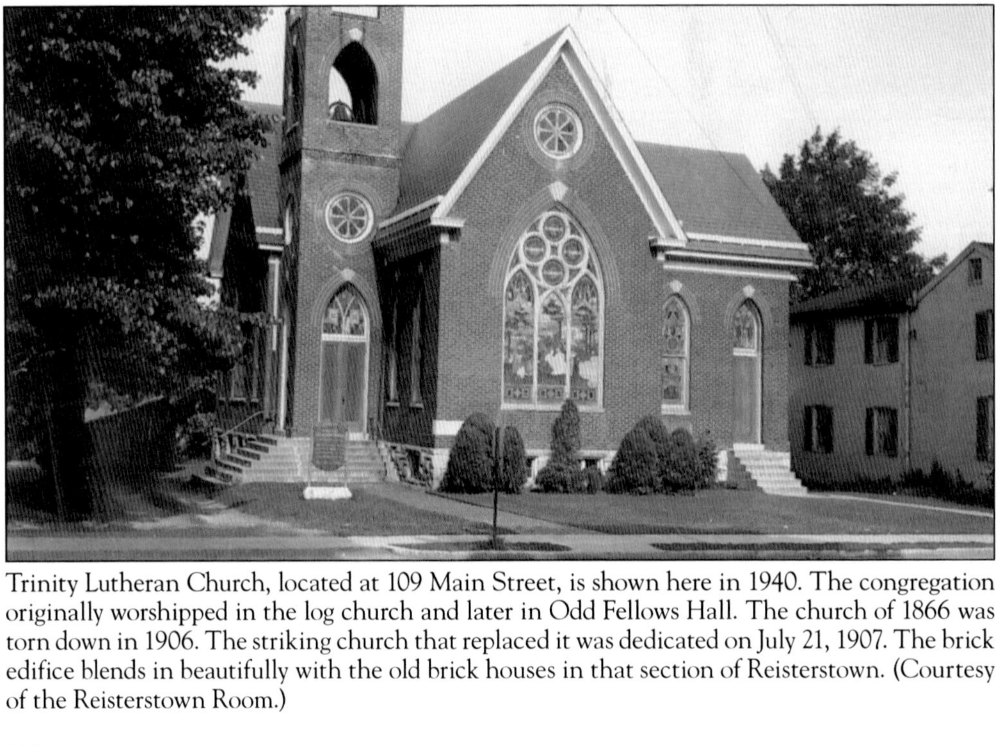

Trinity Lutheran Church, located at 109 Main Street, is shown here in 1940. The congregation originally worshipped in the log church and later in Odd Fellows Hall. The church of 1866 was torn down in 1906. The striking church that replaced it was dedicated on July 21, 1907. The brick edifice blends in beautifully with the old brick houses in that section of Reisterstown. (Courtesy of the Reisterstown Room.)

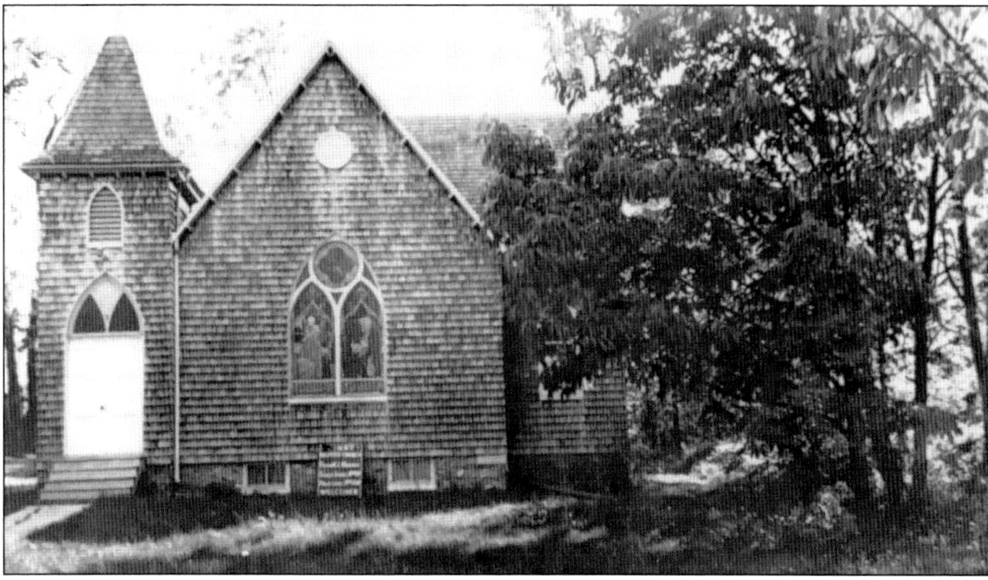

The Reisterstown Baptist Church originally held meetings in halls in the area. They congregation built its first church in 1909 on Main Street near Berryman's Lane. Eventually the church structure was sold to the Seventh Day Adventist Church. The photograph shows the original shingled Baptist church as photographed by Louise Bland Goodwin in 1941.

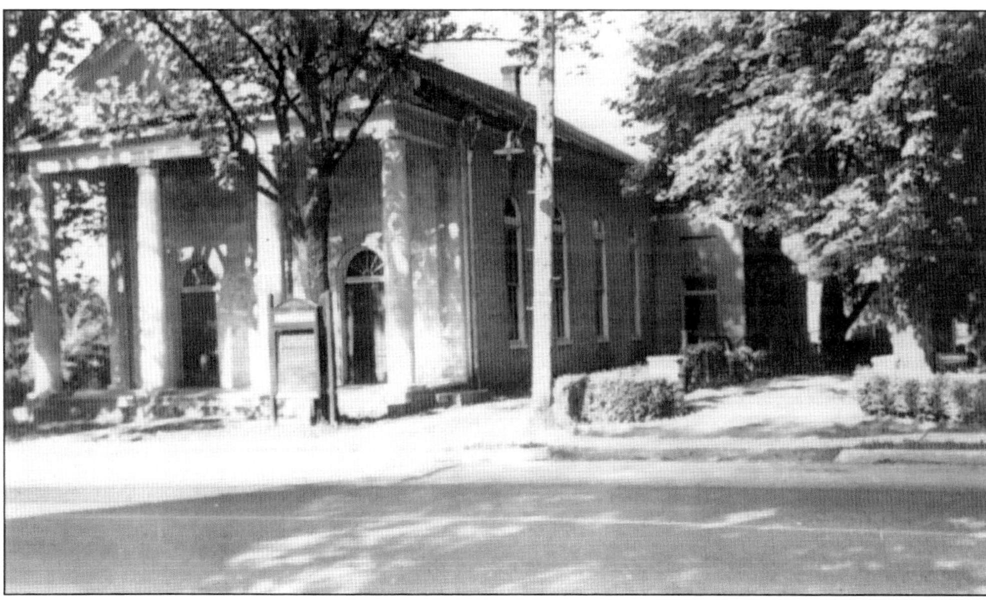

Grace Methodist Church South was built in 1866–1868 after some members of Asbury Methodist Church withdrew because of a dispute over slavery and state rights that grew out of the Civil War. In 1883, the congregation adopted the name Grace Methodist Episcopal Church. In 1941, the congregation reconciled with the Asbury Chapel across the street. Louise Bland Goodwin photographed the Greek Revival–style structure in 1941.

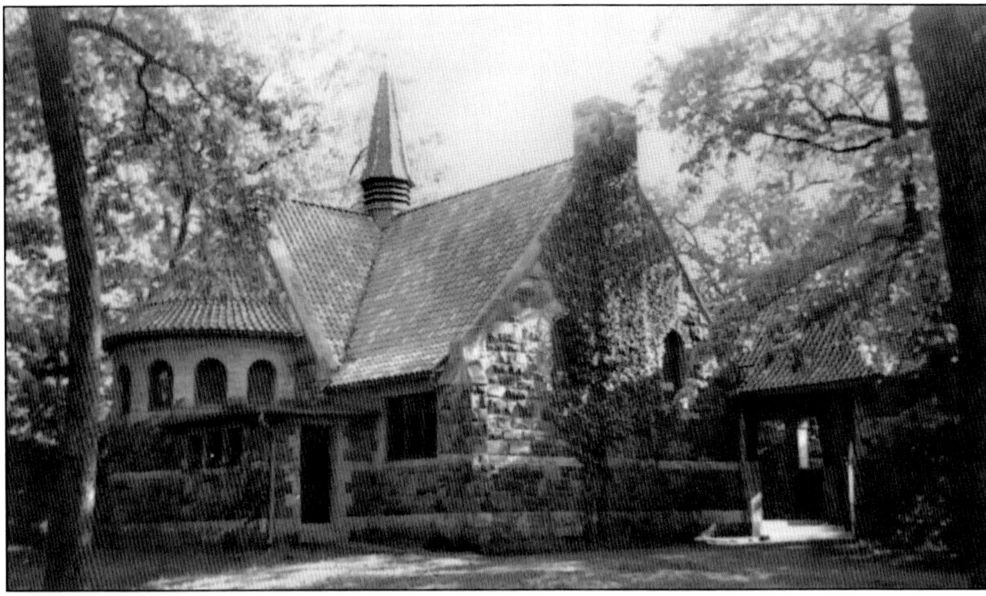

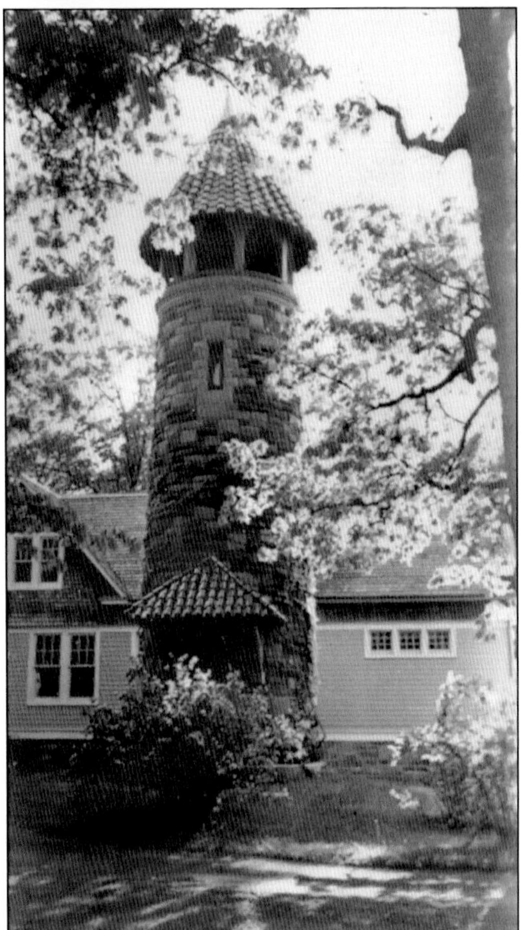

The side facade and baptistery of All Saints Episcopal Church, located at 203 East Chatsworth Avenue, is shown above. The church with rock-faced green stone was built in 1890 and was modeled after an English church at Magnolia, near Manchester by the Sea, according to inventory records of the Maryland Historical Trust. William Keyser, benefactor of the church, donated the money for the church and erected the memorial tower (shown at left) in memory of his mother, Elizabeth Wyman Keyser. In 1882, the vestry of St. Michael's Chapel purchased 10 acres on Bond Avenue to be used for All Saints Chapel and a cemetery. It was in this chapel that the Episcopalians worshipped until 1890. All Saints Episcopal Church is a classic example of the Romanesque Revival architectural style. Louise Bland Goodwin took both photographs in 1941. (Both, courtesy of the Reisterstown Room.)

Sacred Heart Roman Catholic Church, located on Sacred Heart Lane, was built in 1873. Louise Bland Goodwin took this photograph in 1941. The stone for the Gothic church came from Worthington Quarry at the foot of Dark Hollow Hill. The church is frequently referred to as the Reisterstown Church, since Glyndon did not exist at the time the church.

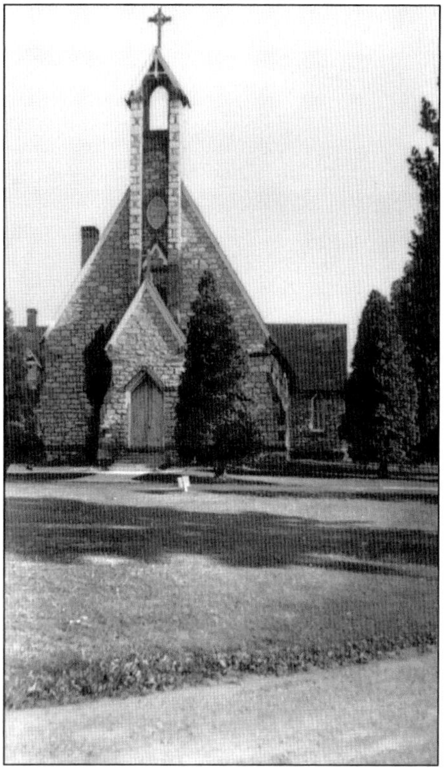

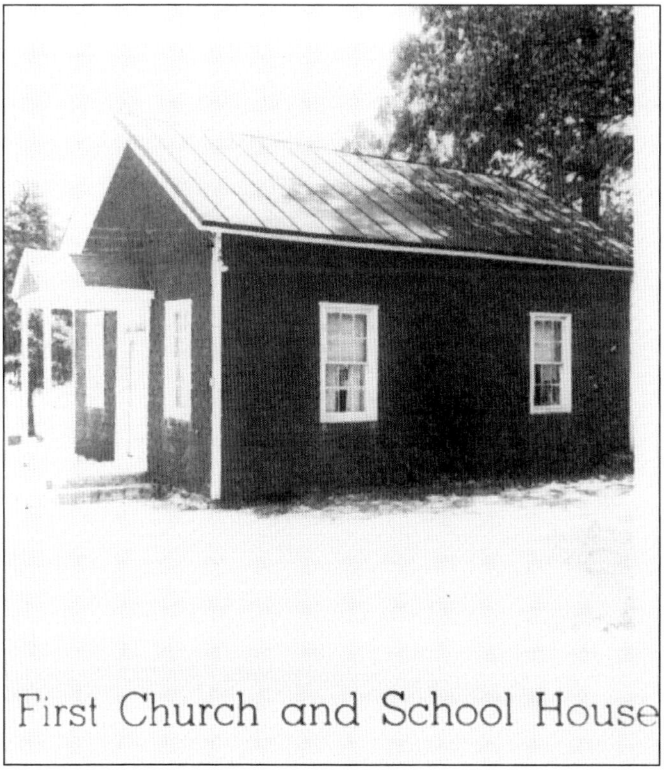

At a historical meeting recorded in a book of the Asbury Chapel (now known as Reisterstown United Methodist Church), 43 African American slaves were granted their request to hold class meetings in the year 1843. Out of this meeting two churches arose, Piney Grove Methodist of Boring and St. Luke Methodist of Reisterstown (shown at left). The photograph shows the original church and school during the 1850s. (Courtesy of the Reisterstown Room.)

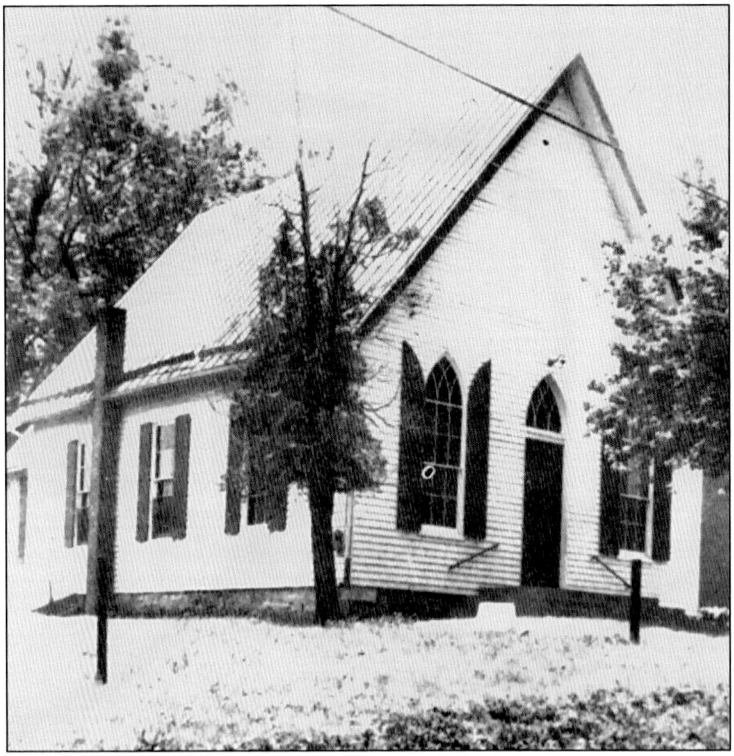

St. Luke Methodist Church is shown in the photograph at left as it appeared around 1960. The church was built in the Gothic Revival style in 1880 and was placed in front of an existing school building. Two structures are shown on the church site on the Bromley Atlas of 1898. Money to erect the church was raised through subscription. The photographer who took this picture is not identified. (Courtesy of the Reisterstown Room.)

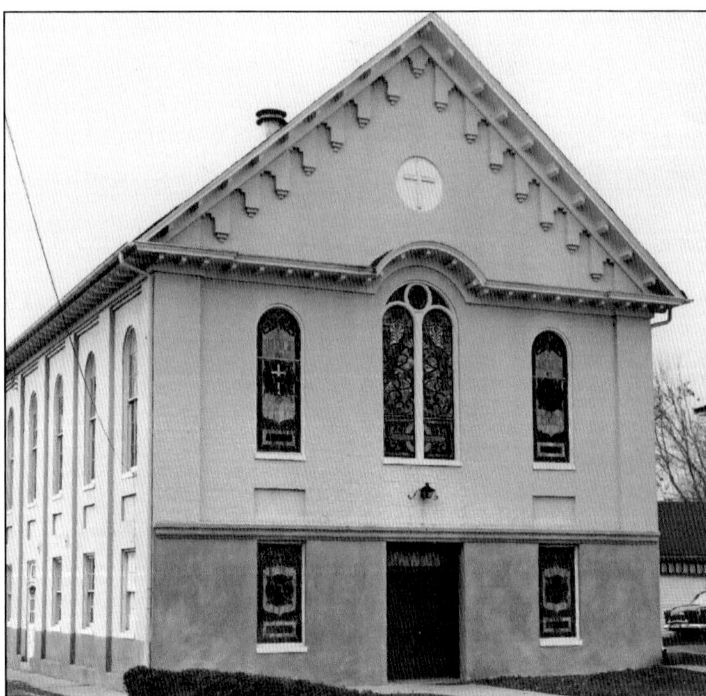

The Reisterstown United Methodist Church traces its beginnings to February 6, 1777. The original church building was called Asbury Chapel, a log cabin that was located on what is now a cemetery next to the Reisterstown Library. The Old Sanctuary (shown at right) was constructed in 1868 and was dedicated on January 1, 1870. It was renamed "Northside Chapel" in 2002. (Courtesy of the Reisterstown Room.)

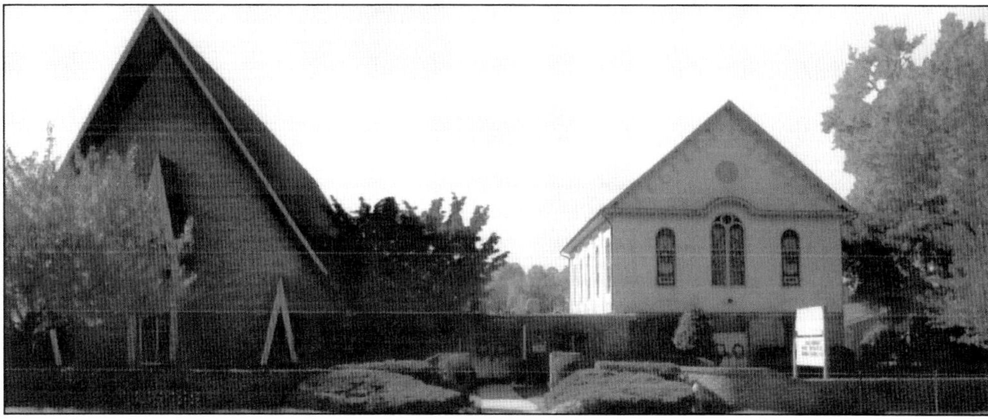

The Reisterstown United Methodist Church is located at 246 Main Street. This image shows the new and old sanctuaries. The new sanctuary, at left in the photograph, was dedicated on May 5, 1974. The original cornerstone was a brick sent to the congregation by fellow Methodists in England. Today it is on display in a glass case. (Courtesy of John and Susan Wright Jr.)

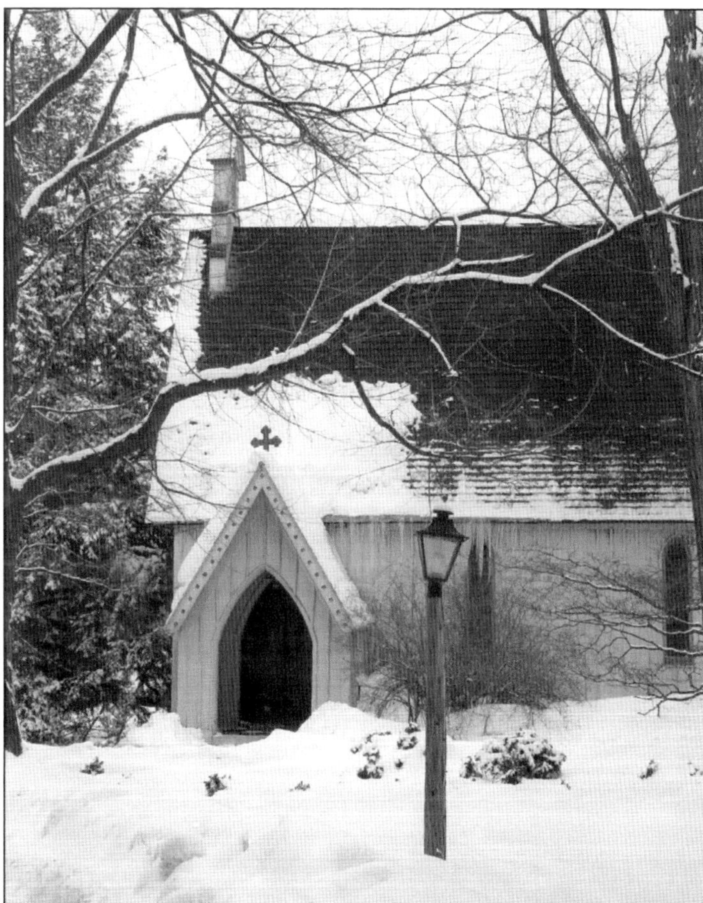

St. Michael's Chapel is a Gothic Revival–style chapel located on the grounds of Hannah More Academy. It was built in 1854 to serve as a house of worship for the community and students of Hannah More Academy. St. Michael's Chapel was an outgrowth of St. Thomas Parish in Garrison. (Courtesy of the Reisterstown Room.)

BIBLIOGRAPHY

Arnett, Earl, Robert J. Brugger, and Edward C. Papenfuse. *Maryland: A New Guide to the Old Line State*. 2nd ed. Baltimore, MD: The Johns Hopkins University Press, 1999.

Brooks, Neal A. *A History of Baltimore County*. Towson, MD: Friends of the Towson Library, Inc., 1979.

Davidson, Isobel. *Real Stories from Baltimore County History*. Baltimore, MD: Warwick and York, Inc., 1917. Print.

Dickson, Dr. Isaac N. *The Early Days of Reisterstown and Vicinity*. Reisterstown, Maryland: Kiwanis Club, 1947. Print.

Diggs, Louis S. *Holding On To Their Heritage*. Baltimore, MD: Uptown Press, 1996. Print.

Goodwin, Louise Bland. *Milestones in the history of Reisterstown, Maryland, 1758–1965*. Reisterstown, MD: L. B. Goodwin, 1966. Print.

Marks, Lillian Bayly. *Reister's Desire: The origin of Reisterstown Maryland, founded 1758, with a genealogical history of the Reister family and sketches of allied families*. Baltimore, MD: Garamond/ Pridemark Press, 1975. Print.

About the Organization

The Reisterstown Volunteer Fire Company can trace its beginnings to a mass meeting held in Landstreet Hall, located in Franklin High School on May 9, 1913. The meeting was presided over by a Professor Murphy, principal of the high school at the time. At this meeting it was decided to hold a picnic and supper to raise funds to start a volunteer fire company. The picnic and supper were a success, and the sum of $412.29 was raised. A subsequent public meeting was held on June 11, 1913, to announce the financial outcome of the picnic and also to organize a volunteer fire company and elect permanent officers. This meeting began by reminding people that the town had "been visited by three disastrous fires within a year, the first at A. H. Uhler destroying his barn and other outbuildings on May 11, 1912, putting the whole upper end of the town in jeopardy, one on March 22, 1913 destroying a fine residence belonging to Mr. Reister Russell and on May 4, 1913 which destroyed the double stable belonging to Messrs. Heise and Currie with other outbuildings." The latter fire at the double stable was brought under control by a bucket brigade carrying water from a well across Main Street. The town folks needed no further persuasion. Thirty-two men volunteered immediately. Two weeks later, on June 23, a second meeting was held, this time at Russell's Hall, whereupon another 22 men signed on as volunteers. These two groups of volunteers comprised the charter members of the Reisterstown Fire Company.

The Reisterstown Volunteer Fire Company has a long and storied history. Many of the volunteers come from families that have served for generations. Their dedication and sacrifice is exemplary, and they have earned much appreciation, not only for protecting our historic town from fires, but also for preserving our treasured history, much of which is included within these pages. Woven within this historic tapestry are the courage and dedication of members of the Reisterstown Volunteer Fire Company. Some images in this book are an attempt to capture their spirit.

About the Author

Local author Gayle Neville Blum has put together a collection of historical photographs on Reisterstown, a community she calls home. Blum has also authored Images of America: *Baltimore County*. She shares her love for the rich history of the area with her husband, Jim, and is privileged to pass its history on to her children, Jessica, Stella, James, Samuel, and Emerald.

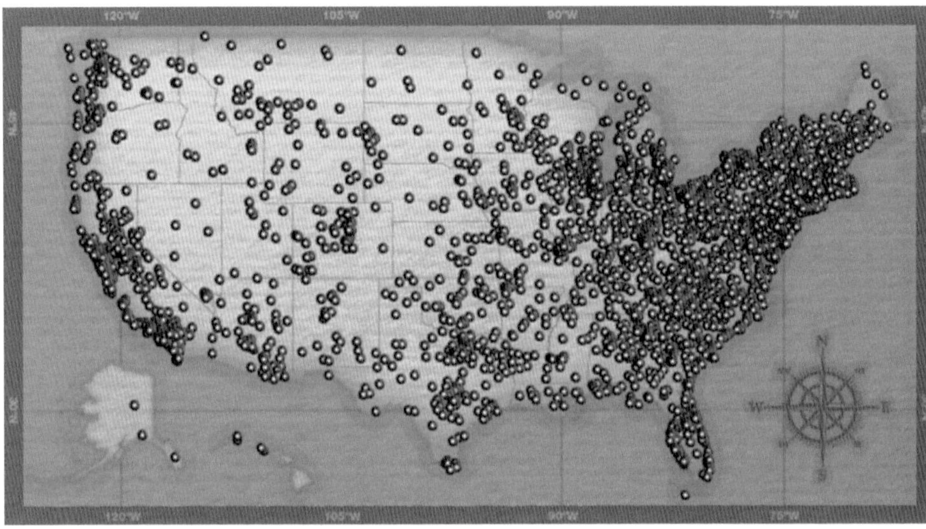